# Beyond Bo1

# New Perspectives on the North

eds. Ian Giles, Laura Chapot, Christian Cooijmans,
Ryan Foster and Barbara Tesio

Norvik Press
2016

Norvik Press Series C: Student Writing no. 3


A catalogue record for this book is available from the British Library.


ISBN: 978-1-909408-33-3


Norvik Press
Department of Scandinavian Studies
UCL
Gower Street
London WC1E 6BT
United kingdom
Website: www.norvikpress.com
E-mail address: norvik.press@ucl.ac.uk


Managing Editors: Elettra Carbone, Sarah Death, Janet Garton, C. Claire Thomson.


Cover design: Sarah Diver Lang and Elettra Carbone
Inside cover image: Sarah Diver Lang
Layout: Elettra Carbone

# Contents

# Acknowledgements

This volume was jointly edited by all members of the editorial team, with Ian Giles taking the lead in organising the project. Edinburgh artist Sarah Diver Lang developed the concept for our cover and created the handsome hand-drawn map on our title page. We are grateful to the contributors for their willingness to develop their research for this volume, for their cooperation throughout the process of editing the material, and for their (sometimes endless) patience.

We would like to thank the following for their generous support towards the costs of publishing this volume: the Anglo-Norse Society, London; the Anglo-Swedish Literary Foundation, London; Loganair,[1] Glasgow; and Åke Wibergs Stiftelse, Stockholm. We would also like to express our gratitude to the Árni Magnússon Institute for Icelandic Studies, Reykjavik; the Norwegian Maritime Museum, Oslo; Professor Arne Emil Christensen, Oslo; Shetland Museum and Archives, Lerwick; and Vertshuset Sinclair, Kvam for graciously permitting us to use their images.

The editors would like to thank the following individuals for their assistance in helping to launch this book on its voyage: Elettra Carbone; Alan Macniven; Gunilla Blom Thomsen; and Bjarne Thorup Thomsen. We would also like to extend our thanks to the Directors of Norvik Press. Finally, we would like to express our wholehearted gratitude for the help, guidance and encouragement offered to us by the late Helena Forsås-Scott in the early stages of this project.

**Endnotes**

1 Loganair provides a vital service to scholars of the Nordic region based in Orkney not only through its links to the Scottish mainland, but especially through its valuable lifeline from Kirkwall to Bergen.

# Introduction

I si tid gav den palestinske forfattaren Edward Saïd dei vestlege fordommane om Det fjerne austen namnet «orientalisme». Ordet boreal kjem av *Boreas*, som var det mytologiske greske namnet på nordavinden. På norsk omfattar det boreale nordlege strøk som ikkje ligg i Arktis, medan det på engelsk og spansk står for alt som er nordleg, kaldt og vinterleg. Ein hyperborear er rett og slett ein som held til i det høge nord. Kanskje «borealisme» kan vera namn på dei sørlege fordommane om folk som bur under nordlege himmelstrøk?

I alle fall verkar det som om desse fordommane lever i beste velgåande. (Fløgstad 2007: 13-14)

(At one time, the Palestinian writer Edward Saïd gave the name 'orientalism' to Western preconceived ideas about the Far East. The word 'boreal' comes from *Boreas*, which was the Greek mythological name for the north wind. In Norwegian, boreal covers northern areas outside the Arctic, while in English and Spanish it stands for everything that is northern, cold and wintry. A hyperborean is quite simply someone who inhabits the far north. Maybe 'borealism' could be a name for the Southern preconceived ideas about those who live at northern latitudes?

In any case, it seems as if these ideas are in the best of health.)[1]

Thus writes prominent Norwegian author Kjartan Fløgstad when introducing his 2007 volume of essays about Pyramiden, the Russian mining settlement on Svalbard. A few years later, Kristinn Schram adds:

In describing the cultural practices involved in exoticizing the inhabitants of the North, I use the term *Borealism*. Originating in the Latin *borealis* (the North), it is an appropriation of Edward Said's term *Orientalism* that refers to the ontological and epistemological distinction between East and West. His study, as do aspects of my own, reveals the assumptions and power relations involved in crosscultural relations. The image of one's ethnicity or regional background plays a significant role in the negotiation of power in transnational

> encounters. So making sense of images of the North (...) isin
> many ways a study of relations between the centres and margins
> of power. (2011: 310)

Although the term 'borealism' may not be familiar to all, it is most certainly a concept that many readers are likely to have engaged with in some form or another. For many years, a particular fascination with the boreal has been apparent in Britain – whether through romantic notions of Vikings during the nineteenth century, the permissive and liberated nature of society in the modern postwar era, or even the post-modern rediscovery of the north through works such as Peter Høeg's *Miss Smilla's Feeling For Snow*. This history, combined with the recent Nordic cultural wave – encompassing everything from popular television shows and fashion to foreign language theatre – illustrates the persistent popularity of the boreal in Britain and the rest of the Anglophone world. Yet, as both Fløgstad's and Schram's quotes suggest, cross-cultural relations can be fraught and complex. Cross-cultural exchanges can be enriching and empowering, but they can also lead to a certain cultural objectification and the propagation of preconceptions which are fuelled and sustained by uneven power dynamics between cultures. Fløgstad and Schram also both suggest 'borealism' as a concept which expresses the complexity of cultural formation and cross-cultural exchangesin relation to the north.

This volume therefore aims to engage with and move beyond borealism. The different contributions all play a role in deconstructing borealism: some bring to light new perspectives on various aspects of northern culture past and present, whilst others explore the complexity of cross-cultural relations not only between the north and its neighbours but also within northern cultures thereby destabilising imaginary boundaries between cultures and shedding new light on the narratives that construct the Nordic region. The appeal of the boreal may have originally drawn our diverse group of contributors to their field of research, whilst their respective disciplines are often expressly associated with the study of the Nordic world. However, the chapters in this volume move beyond parochial studies of the north, offering insights into shared human experiences and exchanges that are European, if not global in nature. Recent developments in the way the Nordics are studied beyond the region itself, as represented by this volume, offer an attractive and flexible framework for other disciplines within the humanities to replicate.

The Nordic Research Network (NRN) 2015 conference, the fourth event to be organised under the NRN banner since its inception in 2010, represented a successful forum for graduate and early career researchers working in the highly interdisciplinary area of Nordic research (Giles 2015). Across its two-day span in February 2015, fifty-three speakers delivered papers in parallel sessions at the University of Edinburgh. As might be expected, the range of presentations was tremendous, guaranteeing an exciting and dynamic overall experience at what was almost certainly the single largest gathering of Nordic scholars ever to take place in Britain, exceeding attendances at the British Association of Scandinavian Studies conferences held between the 1970s and 1990s.

The excellent work of Norvik Press over the years, and especially Broomé et al. (2014), served as our inspiration to put this resurgent Nordic spirit on the page. These chapters were selected on the basis that they represent, in our view, some of the best and most exciting work currently being undertaken by emerging scholars in the field. They are presented in a structure that seeks to draw thematic connections between what is a highly diverse assortment of chapters.

The book opens with Echoes of History, in which we aim to describe the historical reverberations of cross-cultural encounters. In his chapter, Stefan Drechsler examines the development of seals in Reynistaður that drew their inspiration from the old homeland of medieval Norway. Eleanor Parker, meanwhile, approaches the *Encomium Emmae Reginae* and the role played by it in Anglo-Danish history. In the final chapter of the section, Marc Chivers examines boat-building traditions in Shetland during the eighteenth and nineteenth centuries, long thought of as Viking in character, with intriguing conclusions.

The second section, Linguistic Liaisons, continues where the previous section leaves off by reflecting on the linguistic connections found between the Nordic region and the UK. Pavel Iosad offers a new approach to tonal stability in the North Germanic languages, arguing that they have undergone repeated tonogenesis, offering parallels to the West Germanic languages. Elyse Jamieson, meanwhile, investigates the Nordic origins of imperative commands in Shetland dialect, arguing that Scots-Norn language contact has allowed imperative verb raising to endure in Scotland's northernmost outpost.

The following section, Art and Society, examines the role of art in shaping and representing a developing society. The first chapter, by Jan D. Cox, reflects on the portrayal of the Battle of Kringen in Nordic art. Meanwhile, Kitty Corbet Milward approaches the issue of the role of women during the Norwegian industrial revolution – specifically in terms of women artists. The final chapter in this section is by Haftor Medbøe, who provides a fascinating account of the growth of jazz across Scandinavia over a period of almost a century until the present day.

Translating Scandinavia is a natural point of continuation from the previous section, given its approach to the issue of the representations of Scandinavian literature in the UK. Charlotte Berry has trawled the archives of publisher Chatto & Windus to provide the true story behind their translations of the late Swedish children's writer Maria Gripe into English. Ellen Kythor offers an in-depth examination of the agents involved in disseminating Danish literature in the UK over the past quarter of a century – ranging from translators to state funding bodies, and many others in between.

In the penultimate section, Crossing Cultures, we find insights into the effects of transnationalism and its impact on shaping identities, environment and modes of expression – whether old or new. The first chapter, by Silke Reeploeg, examines historical examples of cross-cultural, regional identities in Norway and Scotland, and seeks to distinguish coastal spaces as a specific subgenre of transnational studies. Pei-Sze Chow reflects on Max Kestner's 2009 film *Copenhagen Dreams*, with a particular focus on the depiction of the city's spatial identity and and the difficulties in establishing an Øresund identity.

The book concludes with Narratives of Identity, which endeavours to explore the crucial role of Nordic identities in a variety of contexts. Our first contributor, Shane McLeod, casts light on Norse burial practices in early Christian contexts. Karianne Hansen presents a thought-provoking account of the Norwegian experience in Auschwitz and the critical nature of a sense of belonging. The final chapter, by Cristina Sandu, examines the intersection of Estonian and Finnish identities through a reading of Sofi Oksanen's *Stalin's Cows*.

All of these contributions are innovative and thought-provoking, having much to offer academics at every level. We have found them most enjoyable and engaging to edit, and we hope that you enjoy reading them as much as we have, and that they help you to develop your own research interests. We sincerely encourage the trend for emerging scholars to be given the opportunity to publish at an early stage of their careers to continue, especially with support from publishers like Norvik Press, and as such, we expect another volume to be published soon.

*Ian Giles, Laura Chapot, Christian Cooijmans,*
*Ryan Foster, Barbara Tesio*
Edinburgh, summer 2016

## Endnotes

[1] Translation by Dr Guy Puzey, University of Edinburgh.

## References

Broomé, A., Chow, P.-S., Smalley, N., Taylor, L., Viitanen, E. (eds.) (2014). *Illuminating the North: Proceedings from the Nordic Research Network 2013*. London: Norvik Press.

Fløgstad, K. (2007). *Pyramiden: Portrett av ein forlaten utopi*. Oslo: Spartacus Forlag.

Giles, I. (2015). 'A Report From Nordic Research Network 2015 in

Edinburgh', *Scandicavica*, 54(2), pp.152-155.

Schram, K. (2011). 'Banking on Borealism: Eating, Smelling and Performing the North' in Isleifsson, S. and Chartier, D. (eds.), *Iceland and Images of the North*. Presses de l'Université du Québec. Available online on Project MUSE: https://muse.jhu.edu/book/21465 (Accessed: 17 June 2016).

# Biographies

## Editor Biographies

### Ian Giles
*University of Edinburgh*

Ian Giles is a PhD candidate at the University of Edinburgh researching the transmission of Scandinavian literature to the UK during the twentieth century. Other research interests include receptive multilingualism and the cinema of Ingmar Bergman. Ian is also a literary translator, and was shortlisted for the 2015 International Dagger by the Crime Writers' Association.

### Laura Chapot
*University of Edinburgh*

Laura Chapot is a PhD candidate in Comparative Literature at the University of Edinburgh. She investigates the discursive construction of the concept of 'decadence' in German and Scandinavian culture at the *fin de siècle*, using digital methods in combination with close readings across a large-scale corpus of mixed sources. She has also tutored in German language and literature, and was co-editor of *FORUM* – Edinburgh's Postgraduate Journal of Culture and the Arts – in 2013.

### Christian Cooijmans
*University of Edinburgh*

Chris is a PhD candidate in Scandinavian Studies at the University of Edinburgh, from which he also holds an MSc in Medieval History. A medievalist at heart, his current doctoral research focuses on the reach and repercussions of early Viking movements across the Carolingian realm. Besides all things Norse, Chris' academic interests include the digital humanities, as well as premodern historiography, palaeography, and manuscript studies.

## Ryan Foster
*University of Edinburgh*

Ryan Foster worked as a geography teacher, before going on to complete an MA in Lake District Studies from Lancaster University. His thesis investigated whether the place-name element –thwaite in the Lake District was evidence of a Viking landnám. He was awarded the Northern Scholars scholarship in 2013 to study for a PhD in Scandinavian Studies at the University of Edinburgh, where his research involves the study of Old Norse shieling names during the Viking Age.

## Barbara Tesio
*University of Edinburgh*

Barbara Tesio holds an MSc in Comparative Literature from the University of Edinburgh and is now completing her PhD in Scandinavian Studies at the same institution. Her research focuses on Karen Blixen's work, on the interaction between storytelling and popular culture and the subversive character of gothic literature. Barbara is also the co-ordinator of the Edinburgh based Flytte Poetry Project (www.flyttepoetryproject.co.uk) which explores the correlation between poetry, migration and creativity through performances and publications.

# Contributor Biographies

### Charlotte Berry
*Independent Scholar / Hereford Cathedral*

Charlotte Berry completed a part-time PhD at the University of Edinburgh in 2013 entitled 'Publishing, translation, archives: Nordic children's literature in the UK, 1950-2000'. She is a qualified and registered archivist in her day-job and specialises in medieval archives and material and print culture. She is currently planning future research into modern publishing and literary archives and into the history of children's literature publishing in the UK.

### Marc Chivers
*University of the Highlands and Islands*

Marc Chivers is a PhD student at UHI's Centre for Nordic Studies in Shetland. Marc's ethnographic inquiry, entitled, 'The Shetland Boat: History, Folklore & Construction' has examined the documented and material cultural evidence for the development and use of Shetland's vernacular boats. After completing his PhD, Marc would like to investigate Shetland's boat *noosts* (shelters) in order to determine their domestic and commercial use, and their connection to past and present communities.

### Pei-Sze Chow
*University College London*

Pei-Sze is based at University College London, where she was awarded her PhD in Scandinavian film and TV with a special focus on space and identity in the Øresund region. She is currently teaching on UCL's interdisciplinary Arts & Sciences programme while developing a postdoctoral project on screen culture in the peripheral regions of Denmark. She recently published a chapter on the transnational metropolis in *Bron/Broen* in the volume, *Global Cinematic Cities* (Wallflower Press, 2016).

### Kitty Corbet Milward
*University of Edinburgh*

Kitty Corbet Milward is a PhD student at the University of Edinburgh. Her research addresses the representation of Norwegian women's work with textiles in visual culture before 1905. Research placements have been completed with the National Gallery of Norway and the Norwegian Folk Museum. Prior to beginning her doctorate, Kitty was employed by the V&A, British Museum and Royal Academy of Arts. She sits on the UK Steering Committee for the National Museum of Women in the Arts.

### Jan D. Cox
*Independent Scholar*

Jan D. Cox completed a PhD at the University of Leeds in 2014 entitled 'The Impact of Nordic Art in Europe 1878-1889'. Publications in 2016 include 'Erik Werenskiold and James Guthrie: Parallel Pictures in Norway and Scotland in *Kunst og Kultur* (nr. 2/ 2016), an essay for the catalogue of Ribe Kunstmuseum, and a substantial online article 'The Swan and the Unicorn: The "Most Secret" Affair in Estense Ferrara' (academia.edu).

### Stefan Drechsler
*University of Aberdeen*

Stefan Drechsler is a PhD student at the Centre for Scandinavian Studies at the University of Aberdeen. He is currently writing his doctoral thesis about illuminated manuscripts from the Icelandic Augustinian monastery of Helgafell and has published articles in *Opuscula* and *Collegium Medievale* on the use of Christian and secular iconography, focussing on the illuminated fourteenth-century Icelandic manuscripts *Flateyjarbók* (GKS 1005 fol) and *Skarðsbók* (AM 350 fol).

## Karianne Hansen
*Independent Scholar*

Karianne Hansen is educated in History at the University of Bergen and earned her MSc in Contemporary History from the University of Edinburgh in 2015. The focus of her thesis is the experience of Jews deported from Norway to Auschwitz. Her research interests include the daily life and role of social interactions within the camp structure. She is currently carrying out research on non-Norwegian prisoners' experiences in Auschwitz.

## Pavel Iosad
*University of Edinburgh*

Pavel Iosad holds a PhD from the University of Tromsø and is a Lecturer in Theoretical Phonology at the University of Edinburgh. He works on numerous issues in theoretical and historical phonology (as well as theoretical historical phonology), with a focus on Celtic and North Germanic languages. He is currently engaged in a project on areal features in the phonology of the languages of north-western Europe.

## Elyse Jamieson
*University of Edinburgh*

Elyse Jamieson is a PhD student in Linguistics and English Language at the University of Edinburgh, currently working on the interactions in syntax between clause type, illocutionary force, and negation, with a focus on what happens in Scots. In general, Elyse is interested in understanding syntactic variation and change, working with data from regional dialects.

## Ellen Kythor
*University College London*

Ellen Kythor is working towards a PhD co-funded by the Danish Arts Foundation and University College London, investigating the market for translated Danish literature in the UK. As part of her studentship, she has established a translators' network in collaboration with Danish-English literary translators. Ellen has a BA in German and Scandinavian Studies and MA (Distinction) in Scandinavian Translation Studies, both from UCL.

### Shane McLeod
*University of Tasmania*

Shane McLeod completed a PhD at the University of Western Australia in 2011, with his doctoral dissertation published as *The Beginning of Scandinavian Settlement in England: The Viking 'Great Army' and Early Settlers, c. 865-900* (Brepols, 2014). He researches migration and acculturation during the Viking Age, particularly to and within Britain, and he is also working on the landscapes of Viking Age burials. Shane is currently a University Associate at the University of Tasmania.

### Haftor Medbøe
*Edinburgh Napier University*

Haftor Medbøe is Associate Professor of Music and Jazz Musician in Residence at Edinburgh Napier University where he lectures in composition and improvisation. His research interests lie predominantly in New Jazz Studies and Music Pedagogy. He is widely published and currently writing a monograph. As a musician and composer, Haftor has released several albums to critical acclaim, both with his eponymous group, and with other musical collaborators for Linn, Fabrikant and Losen Records.

### Eleanor Parker
*Independent Scholar*

Eleanor Parker received her doctorate in medieval literature from the University of Oxford, and subsequently held a Mellon Postdoctoral Fellowship at The Oxford Research Centre in the Humanities. Her research focuses on historical writing and romance in post-Conquest England, and she has published several articles on Anglo-Danish literary culture and the reign of Cnut. She is currently writing a book on the literature of the Vikings in England.

## Silke Reeploeg
*University of the Highlands and Islands*

Silke Reeploeg is a researcher and lecturer with University of the Highlands and Islands and based in the Shetland Islands. Her research interests are in the fields of Nordic and Northern cultural history and literature, and she has recently completed a PhD thesis in Nordic Studies. She is currently co-editing a book entitled *Seascapes and Dreamscapes: Northern Atlantic Islands and the Sea* due to be published by Cambridge Scholars Publishing in 2016/17.

## Cristina Sandu
*Independent Scholar*

Finnish-Romanian scholar Cristina Sandu recently graduated with an MSc in Comparative Literature from the University of Edinburgh. Her research focuses on, among other things, Finnish migrant literature. Cristina is currently writing her debut novel for Finnish publishing house, Otava. Her novel examines the Ceaușescu years in Romania and tells the story of an intellectual who manages to escape and start a new life in Finland.

# ECHOES OF HISTORY

# Reynistaðakirkja hin forna
## The Medieval Chapter Seal of the Benedictine Nunnery at Reynistaður

## Stefan Drechsler

Of all the ecclesiastical medieval Scandinavian seals, that of the Icelandic Benedictine nunnery of Reynistaður at Skagafjörður is certainly the most extraordinary, on account of the fact that the seal displays a unique depiction of a medieval Icelandic stave church (fig. 1). Typical for chapter seals, the depiction is encircled by the insignia of the ecclesiastical institution, written in a standard majuscule font: S[IGILLUM] • CAPITULI • REYNS • MONA. The motif of the seal is particularly interesting since no single ecclesiastical wooden building survived the Icelandic Reformation. On Scandinavian church seals, Romanesque stone churches are usually shown with two or four round towers at the sides and a large portal in the middle. In some instances, these churches are depicted as round buildings. In one instance, it has been suggested that they show the churches as they originally appeared (Bugge 1931: 92; see also *Biskupa sögur* III: Introduction). In the present paper, I propose a similar idea for the chapter seal from Reynistaður, which will in turn be compared with other church seals from the same time and area.

The nunnery of Reynistaður was established in 1295. It was not until 1299, however, that Jǫrundr Þorsteinsson († 1313), the bishop of the northern diocese at nearby Hólar, consecrated Hallbera Þorsteinsdóttir, a descendent of the influential Oddaverjar family, 'to Skagafjörður' (Storm 1888: 199). This most likely indicates that she was consecrated as the first abbess, possibly holding her office until her death in 1329 (Ármann Jakobsson and Ásdís Egilsdóttir 1993: 8). The nunnery was dedicated to the Holy Virgin and God at the same time (*DI* II: 300-

302). Already by 1299, Reynistaður had amassed a large amount of land: Bishop Jǫrundr not only established the convent but also gave it 23 lands (jarðir) and the half of a further four lands. This included the land of Reynistaður, the place where the nunnery once stood (DI II: 300-302). The next bishop at Hólar after Jǫrundr was the Norwegian Auðunn Þorbergsson rauði († 1322). He further strengthened the importance of Reynistaður, confirming Jǫrundr's decisions and officially giving 'God's will' to the convent in 1315 (DI II: 397-399). It is because of this, amongst other factors, that the nunnery accrued an immense number of lands and further goods in the fourteenth century (Árni Daníel Júlíusson 2014: 64-76; Sigríður Gunnarsdóttir 2009: 11).

In addition to the great wealth that the Benedictine nunnery accumulated, it has been suggested that Reynistaður became established as a centre for religious art and book production in the last third of the fourteenth century, even if no specific information is known about the workshop. Two máldagar (Church charters) from the same century, however, state that young boys and girls were sent to Reynistaður to receive their education (DI III: 752, DI IV: 642-644).

Several late-medieval embroideries have been assigned to the nunnery and specific motifs were probably shared between manuscript painters and embroiderers, since similar Christian iconographic models are found in the two works of art (Elsa E. Guðjónsson 1997: 89). Selma Jónsdóttir (1965: 138-144) has suggested that the nuns were responsible for the book painting of two Jónsbók manuscripts (AM 344 fol and AM 48 8vo), each written by the same scribe in the last quarter of the fourteenth century (Stefán Karlsson 1963: xxxvii), probably by the then treasurer of Reynistaður, Brýnjólfr Bjarnason, or someone related to him (Foote 1990: 57-58). The two manuscripts share a common iconography of a Calvary group that is also found in an embroidery from Hólar (Selma Jónsdóttir 1965: 126). On the basis of her comparison of the two Jónsbók manuscripts and several embroidered works, Selma (1965: 144) has claimed that various embroideries were made at Reynistaður for local clients related to Benedikt Brynjólfsson around the turn of the fifteenth century. Elsa E. Guðjónsson (1991: 21-22; 1997: 85-86) has added to this discussion. She claimed that Reynistaður, together with the second medieval Icelandic Benedictine nunnery at Kirkjubær in southern Iceland, must have been the main centre for embroidery production in Iceland between the late fourteenth and the middle of the sixteenth century. Elsa (1991: 43), however, has doubted Selma Jónsdóttir's attribution of these works to local clients, on the basis that no mention of the embroideries is made in the church annals from Reynistaður. According to a *máldagi* (Church charter) from 1408, however, the nunnery owned the greatest number of embroidered works in the whole of Iceland (*DI* III: 717-719; Elsa E. Guðjónsson 1991: 16).

The nunnery was likely well connected to a scriptorium known as Akrarskólinn, most active in the late fourteenth century (Lönnroth 1964: 71-72; Stefán Karlsson 1970: 131-132; Foote 1990: 39-53, 58; Ólafur Halldórsson 1963; Svanhildur Óskarsdóttir 2000: 53-57). The famous writing school is closely connected to a farm at Stóru-Akrar í Blönduhlíð that was run by the aforementioned Brynjólfr Bjarnason (Stefán Karlsson 1970). According to Foote (38-49), this group includes eleven manuscripts and fragments, among others the two mentioned *Jónsbók* codices as well as other manuscripts that mainly include legendary sagas and sagas of saints. Selma Jónsdóttir (1982: 105-124) has further suggested that the illuminations found in a manuscript related to the Akrar group, Helgastaðabók (Stock. Perg. 4to nr. 19) from 1375-1400 (Stefán Karlsson 1963: cvii-cviii), was executed by a related illuminator responsible for the two mentioned *Jónsbók* codices AM 344 fol, AM 48 8vo. Interestingly, on f. 012r, as well as on other folio leaves in Helgastaðabók, a Romanesque stone church architecture is depicted as part of a main initial. The form and style of this architecture, however, can hardly be a depiction of a real Icelandic church, since barely any medieval Icelandic churches were made of stone (Hörður Ágústsson 1982: 344).

Attached to the Akrar group are a further nine manuscripts, or fragments of manuscripts, all connected to the same scriptorium (Stefán Karlsson 1963; Svanhildur Óskarsdóttir 2000: 55-56). Most relevant to Reynistaður is Reynistaðarbók (AM 764 4to), a compilation of Christian encyclopaedic and pseudo-historical content that was written in 1376-

1386 (Ólafur Halldórsson 1977: 39). Svanhildur Óskarsdóttir (2000: 233-238) has suggested that Reynistaðarbók was directly written at Reynistaður by ten writers, possibly all nuns. It seems self-evident that Reynistaður, possibly in connection with Akrarskólinn, was a major cultural centre in Northern Iceland in the last quarter of the fourteenth century until the Plague in 1402-1404 meant that the workshop could no longer continue (Foote 1990: 60). It would be logical to assume that the cultural importance of Reynistaður is also mirrored in the chapter seal of the nunnery.

**Fig. 1**: Church seal of Reynistaður. 1459. Taken from Magnús Már Lárusson and Jónas Kristjáns-son (1965 I: 223). Copyright: Stofnun Árna Magnússonar á Íslandi, Reykjavík.

The seal of Reynistaður depicts a Northern Romanesque stave church (Fig. 1) in a West Norse-Icelandic form that is unknown in twelfth- and thirteenth-century Norwegian stave church architecture and early modern Icelandic churches. This raises the question as to what extent the depiction on the seal reflects a real stave church that once stood at the site of Reynistaður. To complicate things further, the seal itself is now lost and is only known from a copy drawing made by the manuscript collector Árni Magnússon (1663-1730) in a collection of seals in the early eighteenth century (AM 217 8vo; Kålund 1894: 453). The seal is found on f. 103r accompanied by a short section of information on the previous verso leaf. In his description of the provenance, Árni mentions that he found the seal attached to an agreement for a lease dated to the 11th September 1459 (*DI* V: 192-193). The letter was written by Abbess Barbara Finnsdóttir († 1461) from Reynistaður, who, according to the letter, sold half of Brúarland í Deildardal at Syðra vatn í Tungusveit to Ólafur bóndi Grímsson. The letter is extant today (AM Fasc. XIV, 14) and once included four seals, two of which are still attached. The first of these two seals is most likely one from the abbess, since it is attached to the lease agreement and a confirmation letter written by the same hand, possibly by Barbara herself. The seal of the abbess depicts a simplified version of a motif, Óláfr helgi enthroned, found on two contemporary ecclesiastical seals of archbishops from Niðaróss, used in the fifteenth century and earlier (Fjordholm et al. 2012: 59-70, 77-79). The seal of the abbess therefore follows a standard pattern known from Norway at least one hundred years earlier. The second seal, possibly from Ólafur Grímsson, depicts a chalice with a cloth. It is also a standard motif that is found in seals from two other secular Icelandic personalities at the time (Magnús Már Lárusson and Jónas Kristjánsson 1965 I: 253, 291).

The church seal of Reynistaður, therefore, cannot be dated earlier than 1459 with any certainty. In addition, the font used on the church seal follows a standard pattern that was used mainly in thirteenth century Europe (Norberg 1970: 209). In Iceland, however, the font is still found in Early Modern seals and therefore cannot be used to provide a secure dating. Hörður Ágústsson (1982: 584-585), however, has dated the seal according to the style of the stave church, coming to the conclusion that it must be as old as *c.* 1300, about the same time as Reynistaður was established. This may also be attested in its provenance; while the two seals of Abbess Barbara and Ólafur Grímsson follow traditional models, the church seal does not. Furthermore, no stave church is known as having been a model for a church seal, nor was it usual to use such a motif for a seal of a fifteenth-century Scandinavian monastic institution.

There are two other medieval ecclesiastical seals known from Iceland that depict churches: the chapter seals from the Benedictine monasteries of Þingeyrar and Munkaþverá. Þingeyrar is likewise located at Skagafjörður in North Iceland. Typical for monastic seals, the example from Þingeyrar depicts a single gable Romanesque-style architecture, with a large portal in the middle and pointed church towers at the sides (Fig. 2). On another occasion, I have argued for a stylistic connection between the seals from Þingeyrar and the seal from the Benedictine monastery at Niðarholm at the outskirts of Trondheim, dated to 1281 (Drechsler 2016: 225; Fjordholm et al. 2012: 111). Unlike the Þingeyrar seal, the rounded house in the middle of the Niðarholm seal is either a symbolic expression of either the octagon grave of St Olav at the nearby Trondheim dome, or a visual representation of the grave of Christ at Jerusalem. The seal from Niðarholm is thus solely symbolic. However, it appears likely that the two Benedictine houses shared at least a simplified model for their chapter seals.

Fig. 2: Church seal of Þingeyrar. 1489. Taken from Magnús Már Lárusson and Jónas Kristjánsson (1965 I: 165). Copyright: Stofnun Árna Magnússonar á Íslandi, Reykjavík.

The dating of the Þingeyrar seal remains problematic, since it is only extant as a copy from a document dated to 1489 (Magnús Már Lárusson and Jónas Kristjánsson 1965 1: 164-165). The model of that seal, however, was used on f. 069va in Flateyjarbók (GKS 1005 fol), a kings' saga compendium written and illuminated in 1387-1394 (Ólafur Halldórsson 1987: 60; Sverrir Tómasson 2007: 163-165). The seal from Þingeyrar, therefore, has a *terminus ante quem* of 1394. Similar to the seal from Reynistaður, the text reads: S[IGILLVM] : CAPITVLI : THINGEYRIS. Þingeyrar emerged in the thirteenth and fourteenth centuries as one of the most important monastic houses in medieval Iceland thanks to its saga literature writing and book production. Indeed, it has been suggested that Flateyjarbók was written at Þingeyrar (Sverrir Tómasson 2009: 19-20).

A Romanesque church is also depicted on the fourteenth-century seal from the Benedictine monastery of Munkaþverá (Fig. 3). Munkaþverá is situated at the south of Eyjafjörður, east of Hólar. The chapter seal from the monastery depicts a similar church to the one from Þingeyrar. On the Munkaþverá-seal, however, the church is shown from a different angle. The architecture is likewise depicted as a one-gabled Romanesque church with a large portal, a roof with clearly-visible tiles and four church towers at the four ends. Additionally, it depicts a comparable side-aisle to the example from Reynistaður. Unfortunately, the seal is slightly damaged. The remaining words, however, read similarly to the two previous examples: SIGILLVM : CAPITVLI : ... SIS. It is possible that the damaged part reads [MUNKEN]SIS, the name of the monastery. The seal from Munkaþverá can be securely dated to 1375, as it is attached to a land purchase document of Munkaþverá (AM Dipl. Isl. Fasc. III, 6; Stefán Karlsson 1963: 55-56). Originally, the document included nine seals. Five of them are lost, but the chapter seal of the monastery is situated at the second, and therefore correct, place, as the convent is named second. Like Þingeyrar and Reynistaður, it has been suggested that Munkaþverá was also a cultural centre in the fourteenth century in northern Iceland, producing manuscripts containing a wide range of medieval vernacular hagiographic literature. The book production at Munkaþverá is strongly linked to the scriptorium at Þingeyrar (Johansson 1997a and 1997b: 184-186; 2007, Louis-Jensen 1968: 10-18, Lönnroth (1964: 70-71).

**Fig. 3**: Church seal of Munkaþverá as it is fastened to AM Dipl. Isl. Fasc. III, 6. 1375. *Þjóðskjalasafn Íslands, Reykjavík. Photo and copyright: Stefan Drechsler.*

It is remarkable that the two chapter seals from Þingeyrar and Munkaþverá depict a similar architectural building, but from different angles. The similar roof titles and side-aisle depicted on the two seals make clear, however, that the copy of the chapter seal from Reynistaður made by Árni Magnússon in fact follows a pattern known from the Munkaþverá-seal from 1375. In consent with Hörður Ágústsson's (1982: 584-585) dating of the Reynistaður-seal, it could be suggested that the original seal was much older than the first known mention of it in 1459. Additionally, the similar style of the roof titles and side-aisle suggest that both were drawn on similar models. All three monastic houses were Benedictine and were in close contact during medieval times. This is exemplified by the North Icelandic Benedictine Writing School (*Norðlenski Benediktskólinn*) of Munkaþverá and Þingeyrar in the fourteenth century, famous for its hagiographic style of writing (Sverrir Tómasson 1985; 1992: 249-282, Sigurdsson 2011: 54-56). The first abbess of Reynistaður, Hallbera Þorsteinsdóttir, also illustrates the connection. Before Reynistaður, she was part of the convent at Munkaþverá (*Þorláks saga* 2002: 262). It would thus be logical to assume that the three church seals are related and were possibly made at the same place. Unfortunately, no information is known as to how and where such seals were made, nor were any original monastic stamps found at monastic sites that would indicate such a site of production. Another option would be that the discussed seals were ordered and originally made abroad. This has, however, no basis in fact, since no such church seals are known from the mainland and most of the medieval Benedictine chapter seals known from Scandinavia are only symbolic depictions of the respective churches. Due to the uncommon motifs used for the Icelandic church seals discussed, it seems more reasonable, therefore, to suggest that they were produced locally rather than abroad.

Apart from the already discussed Benedictine monastery at Niðarholm, the only related Benedictine house in medieval Scandinavia is Munkeliv in Bergen, Norway. The chapter seal of this monastery depicts a very symbolic stone architecture with St Michael at the portal, the patron of the convent (Trætteberg 1963: 566). This does not seem to be the case with the discussed Icelandic seals, in particular the one that originated from Reynistaður. To my knowledge, apart from Niðarholm and the Icelandic examples, the chapter seal of the Augustine monastery of Utstein at the isle of Klosterøy in Rogaland, Norway, is the only other medieval Scandinavian church seal that depicts the church of the convent. It is a Romanesque stone architecture with a single nave and a large rooftop. The seal is dated *c.* 1302 (Halvorsen et al. 2002: 60). Despite the difference of the stone architecture at Utstein, the roof of the church is shown with similarly styled tiles to those in the examples from Reynistaður and Munkaþverá. It is possible, therefore, that the church of Reynistaður indeed once resembled the church-depiction on the seal (Guðrún Harðardóttir 1995: 57-58).

It has been previously assumed that the seal depicts stave church architecture that strongly relates to the famous late twelfth century Borgund stave church from Lærdal in Sogn og Fjordane, Norway (fig. 4; Guðbjörg Kristjánsdóttir 2000: 192; Sigríður Gunnarsdóttir 2009: 13). The seal from Reynistaður indeed depicts a similar nave with ridge turrets in the form of dragon heads, typical for the common practice of adapting motifs from pre-Christian northern European art (Gräsland

2005). The stave church also features a middle rooftop with two further dragon heads at the sides, and a top stave. All three features are also found on two of the upper levels of the Borgund stave church.

**Fig. 4**: Borgund stave church in 1837. It was originally built in 1180. This picture is a sized version of a drawing made by Johann Christian Dahl. Copyright: Public Domain.

Yet another feature of the original church at Reynistaður might have mirrored Borgund, namely the original vaulted end of the choir, which was probably similar to the corresponding part of the choir at Borgund (Hörður Ágústsson 1977: 144-145). It is depicted on the church seal from Reynistaður as well. The *Skarðsárannáll* from 1640 in particular refers to the choir and the size of the 'large timber church'. The demolition of the last remains of the old church at Reynistaður in 1570 and 1640 has been described as follows:

> Stormviðri mikil affaranótt hins 4. Decembris hróflaðist víða um hús og hey [...]. Þá tók upp og braut allt í sundur það litla hvolfda trévirkishús fyrir Reynistaðarkirkju, sem verið hafði

sancta sanctorum þeirrar miklu trékirkju, sem forðum var á Reynistað, og Jón Jónsson lögmaður hafði látið ofan taka, þá nær fyrir 70 árum, er hann hélt Reynistaðarklaustur. (*Annálar* 1400-1800 I: 263).

(A great stormy weather raged around house and hay on the night of the fourth of December (1640). [...] There broke up, away and all asunder that little vaulted timber house before the church at Reynistað, which was the choir of the large timber church, which in the past stood at Reynistað and which the judge Jón Jónsson had taken down nearly seventy years ago when he lived at Reynistaðarklaustur.) Translation by the author.

Apart from these features, however, the Reynistaður stave church is unlike any other example of Norwegian stave churches. Rather, it relates to an early modern church architecture from Iceland known as Útbrotakirkja (Guðmundur Sigurðarson et al. 2006: 15), a 'church with side-aisles'. Útbrotakirkjur are wooden churches that resemble a Romanesque basilica with a nave, two side-aisles and, in the case of the major churches at Skálholt and Hólar, a transept before the added choir (Hörður Ágústsson 1982: 346).

Unlike many twelfth- and thirteenth-century Norwegian stave churches, the Icelandic Útbrotakirkjur from Reynistaður, Munkaþverá, and possibly also Þingeyrar, feature side-aisles. Lorentz Dietrichson (1892: 35) has suggested that medieval Icelandic churches mirror the thirteenth-century Norwegian 'Møretype' stave churches, which feature a single nave. This nave is supported by two rows of middle staves on the inside. Dietrichson's view has been supported by Hörður Ágústsson (1982: 346) who has suggested that medieval Icelandic Útbrotakirkjar would be related to the Norwegian 'Møretype' stave churches at Rødven, Grip, Mære, Kvernes, as well as to the oldest of all stave churches in Holtålen. Dietrichson's and Hörður's suggestions only hold true for a possibly similar arrangement of inner stave pillars that support the nave. The side-aisles of Útbrotakirkjur do not belong to the Norwegian stave church architecture. Håkon Christie (1996: 162), however, has suggested that the two major medieval churches in

Iceland at Hólar and Skálholt, built in 1310 and in the later fourteenth century respectively, follow the model of such 'Møretype' churches.

Hörður Ágústsson (1982: 346) argued that this type of church existed in medieval Iceland, and has also (2012: 66-72) discovered that a variety of smaller Útbrótakirkjur were built in the early modern period in Iceland. Similar to the various styles and dating of medieval Norwegian stave churches, Icelandic Útbrotakirkjur are of different age, size and style. Hörður (2012: 66) found examples of such churches from early modern Iceland. The earliest Útbrotakirkja, the Brynjólfskirkja at Skálholt, is dated to 1650 (Hörður Ágústsson 1990: 145-230). Exemplified by the former parish church at Laufás from 1631, such a parish church measured only 5.7 meters wide and 6 meters long, with the addition of a choir that was 4.5 meters long and 3.71 meters wide. Such an Útbrotakirkja would be in total 10.12 meters long and 5.27 meters high at the nave (Hörður Ágústsson 2012: 65). In his measurements, Hörður leaves out the width of the side-aisles, though one can assume that they would not exceed the width of about one meter each. Compared with the size of the nave and the side-aisles on the church seal of Reynistaður, it can be assumed that the original stave church was about that size.

The previously-discussed features of Borgund also suggest that twelfth- and thirteenth-century Norwegian architectural styles were adopted and then adapted to local standards. In the letter of Bishop Auðunn rauði, in which he officially gives 'God's will' to the convent of Reynistaður in 1315 (*DI* II: 397-399), he states that the nunnery owned half of the church place (*staðr*).[1] This would suggest that the *staðr* at Reynistaður kept its status as a parish church. The depicted church on the seal, therefore, might be such a parish church that also served the needs of a monastic church (Þór Hjaltalín et al. 2005: 133). According to a *máldagi* from 1408, at that time the church was in possession of ten chests and vestments (*DI* III: 717-719). It is possible that they were used by the nuns at Reynistaður (Anna Sigurðardóttir 1988: 113). A smaller parish church would have suited the size of a monastery church as well. Despite the 'large timber church' mentioned in the *Skarðsárannáll* from 1640, it is unlikely that the church at Reynistaður was considerably larger than a parish church made of turf, as Guðbjörg Kristjánsdóttir (2000: 192) has generally suggested for monastic houses in medieval Iceland.

Unfortunately, no remains of a medieval church at Reynistaður have been found so far. Furthermore, no archaeological excavation has been able to draw a conclusion as to the actual size and number of the buildings that were once part of the medieval nunnery.[2] The same holds true for most of the other medieval Icelandic monasteries and nunneries. However, since the nunnery at Reynistaður was in such high favour with the Bishops Jǫrundr and Auðunn rauði, it is feasible to argue that a stave church as described was also built at Reynistaður under the supervision of one of these two bishops. This is especially likely to have been the case with Auðunn rauði. It is recorded that he had the so-called Auðunarstofa in 1316–17 built at Hólar with imported wood from Norway. The Auðunarstofa was the Bishop's residence until 1320 when he left for Norway, not returning before he died some two years later. Hjörleifur Stefánsson (1997: 36) has suggested that Auðunn rauði must have had an influence on the architectural history at the diocese. Håkon Christie (1996: 162) has also mentioned that the diocese of Hólar owned woods in Norway that were used for building activities in the fourteenth century. In relation to the bishopric church built at Hólar in the same century, Christie concludes that Norwegian architects probably gave advice to the Icelanders in the construction of large buildings. His main argument is that the archbishop in Niðaróss had interest in having the dome churches built according to their Norwegian counterparts. It appears likely that Auðunn rauði as a former priest from Niðaróss would have a preference for a Norwegian-inspired stave church built at Reynistaður that could serve the Norwegian interests in a local, Norwegian-inspired (parish) church culture. Such a church might not only have triggered the importance of the place as a cultural centre in Skagafjörður, but might also have contributed to the importance of the suggested scriptorium and embroidery workshop at the same place some sixty years later, when it became active in the late 1370s.

# Endnotes

[1] In ecclesiastical-political terms, *staðr* (Old Norse for a place, or church) describes a medieval Icelandic parish church and the surrounding grounds that belong to that church. For the vital aspects of *staðr* and the related *staðamál* see Magnús Stefánsson (2000) and Benedikt Eyþórsson (2005) with further references.

[2] For a description of the modern church at Reynistaður see Þór Hjaltalín et al. (2005: 130-165). For a report on the current status of the archaeological excavations see Steinunn Kristjánsdóttir and Vala Gunnarsdóttir (2014) and Guðmundur Sigurðarson et al. (2006).

# References

A. Sigurðardóttir (1988). *Allt hafði annan róm áður í páfadóm. Nunnuklaustrin tvö á Íslandi og brot úr kristnisaögu.* Reykjavík: Kvennasögusafn Íslands.

*Annálar* 1400-1800 I = Hannes Þorsteinsson (ed.) (1922-1927). *Annálar 1400-1800. Annales Islandici posteriorum sæculorum* I. Reykjavík: Hið íslenzka bókmenntafélag.

Á. Jakobsson and Á. Egilsdóttir (1993). 'Abbadísin sem hvarf', in M. Eggertsdóttir et al. (eds.), *Þúsund og eitt orð sagt Sigurgeir Steingrímssyni fimmtugum, 2. október 1993.* Reykjavík: Menningarsjóður, pp. 6-8.

Á. D. Júlíusson (2014). *Jarðeignir kirkjunnar og tekjur af þeim 1000-1550.* Reykjavík: Center for Agrarian Historical Dynamics.

B. Eyþórsson (2005). 'History of the Icelandic Church 1000–1300. Status of Research', in H. Þorláksson (ed.): *Church Centres. Church Centres in Iceland from the 11th to the thirteenth Century and their Parallels in other Countries.* Reykholt: Snorrastofa, pp. 19-69.

*Biskupa sögur* III = Guðrún Ása Grímsdóttir (1998). *Biskupa sögur III.* Íslenzk fornrit XVII. Reykjavík: Hið íslenzka fornrítafélag.

Bugge, A. (1931). 'Nordens største rundkirke, Olavsklosteret i Tønsberg', Árbok 1931, pp. 87-97.

Christie, H. (1996). 'Kirkebygningene som kilde til norsk middelalderkistorie', in Rindal, M. (ed.), *Studier i kilder til vikingtid ok nordisk middelalder*. Oslo: Norges forskningsråd, pp. 155-169.

DI = Diplomatarium Islandicum (1857-1972). *Íslenskt fornbréfasafn 1-16*. Copenhagen: Hið íslenzka bókmenntafélag.

Dietrichson, L. (1892). *De norske stavkirker. Studier over deres system, oprindelse og historiske udvikling*. Kristiania: Cammermeyer.

Drechsler, S. (2016). 'Ikonographie und Text-Bild-Beziehungen der GKS 1005 fol Flateyjarbók', *Opuscula* XIV, pp. 215-300.

E. E. Guðjónsson (1991). *Reflar í íslenskum miðaldaheimildum fram til 1569*. Reykjavík: Self-published.

E. E. Guðjónsson (1997). 'Icelandic Church Pallia from the Middle Ages', in Lilja Á. and Kiran, K. (eds.), *Church and Art*. Reykjavík: National Museum of Iceland; Oslo: Norwegian Institute for Cultural Heritage Research, pp. 85-90.

Fjordheim, O. et al. (eds.) (2012). *Norske sigiller fra middelalderen. Bind 3. Geistlige segl fra Nidaros bispedømme*. Oslo: Riksarkivet.

Foote, P.(ed.) (1990). *A Saga of St. Peter the Apostle. Perg. 4to nr. 19 in the Royal Library, Stockholm*. Early Icelandic Manuscripts in Facsimile 19. Copenhagen: Rosenkilde and Bagger.

Gräsland, A.-S. (2005). 'The watchful dragon. Aspects of the Conversion of Scandinavia', in Mortensen, A. (ed.), *Viking and Norse in the North Atlantic*. Tórshavn: Annales Societatis Scientiarium Færoensis, pp. 412-421.

G. Kristjánsdóttir (2000). 'Sóknarkirkjur og búnaður þeirra', in G. F. Guðmundsson (ed.), *Íslenskt Samfélag og Rómakirkja*. Reykjavík: Alþingi, pp. 190-225.

G. Sigurðarson et al. (eds.) (2006). *Fornleifaskrá Reynistaðar. Byggðasafn Skagfirðinga – Rannsóknaskýrslur*. Sauðárkrókur: Byggðasafn Skagfirðinga. Available at: http://www.glaumbaer.is/

static/files/pdf/Rannsoknarskyrslur/bsk-2006-49-fornleifaskra-reynistadar.pdf (Accessed: 6 January 2016).

G. Harðardóttir (1995). 'Um íslenskar kirkjubyggingar á miðöldum', *Sagnir* 16, pp. 54-61.

Halvorsen, E. F. et al. (eds.) (2002). *Norske Diplom 1301-1310*. Corpus Codicum Norvegicorum Medii Aevi. Quarto Series Vol. X. Oslo: Selskapet til Utgivelse av Gamle Norske Håndskrifter.

H. Stefánsson (1997). 'Medieval Icelandic Churches', in Lilja Árnadóttir and Kiran, K. (eds.): *Church and Art*. Reykjavík: National Museum of Iceland; Oslo: Norwegian Institute for Cultural Heritage Research, pp. 35-41.

H. Ágústsson (1977). 'Fjórar fornar húsamyndir', *Árbók Hins íslenzka fornleifafélags* 74, pp. 135-159.

H. Ágústsson (1982). 'Island', in Ahrens, C. (ed.), *Frühe Holzkirchen im nördlichen Europa: zur Ausstellung d. Helms-Museums, Hamburg. Hamburg: Museum für Vor- und Frühgeschichte*. Hamburg: Helms-Museum, pp. 346, 577-590.

H. Ágústsson (1990). *Skálholt: Kirkjur*. Reykjavík: Hið íslenzka bókmenntafélag.

H. Ágústsson (2012). *Laufás við Eyjafjörð. Kirkjur og búnaður þeirra*. Reykjavík: Hið íslenzka bókmenntafélag.

Johansson, K. G. (1997a). 'Bergr Sokkason och Arngrímur Brandsson – översättare och författare i samma miljö', in Barnes, G. and Ross, M. Clunies (eds.), *Old Norse Myths, Literature and Society. Proceedings of the 11th International Saga Conference 2-7 Juli 2000*. Sydney: University of Sydney, pp. 181-197.

Johansson, K. G. (1997b). *Studier i Codex Wormianus: Skrifttradition och avskriftsverksamhet vid ett isländskt skriptorium under 1300-talet*. Gothenburg: Acta Universitatis Gothenburgensis.

Johansson, K. G. (2007). 'Texter i rörelse. Översättning, original textproduction och tradering på norra Island 1150-1400', in Johanterwage, Vera and Würth, Stefanie (eds.): Übersetzen im skandinavischen Mittelalter. Wien: Verlag Fassbaender, pp. 83-106.

Kålund, K. (ed.) (1894). *Katalog over Den Arnamagnæanske Håndskriftsamling utgivet af Kommissionen for Det Arnamagnæanske Legat.* Andet Bind. Copenhagen: Gyldendalske Boghandel.

Louis-Jensen, J. (ed.) (1968). *Hulda, Sagas of the Kings of Norway 1035-1177: Manuscript No. 66 Fol. in The Arnamagnæan Collection.* Early Icelandic manuscripts in facsimile 8. Copenhagen: Rosenkilde and Bagger.

Lönnroth, Lars (1964). *Tesen om de två kulturerna. Kritiska studier i den isländska sagaskrivningens sociala förutsättningar.* Scripta Islandica 15. Uppsala: Almqvist och Wiksell.

M. M. Lárusson and J. Kristjánsson (eds.) (1965). *Sigilla Islandica 1. AM 217 8vo.* Reykjavík: Stofnun Árna Magnússonar.

M. Stefánsson (2000). *Staðir and staðamál. Studier i islandske egenkirkelige og beneficialrettslige forhold i middelalderen.* Skrifter 4. Bergen: Historisk institutt Universitet i Bergen.

Norberg, R. (1970). 'Sigillomskrifter', *Kulturhistorisk leksikon for nordisk middelalder fra vikingetid til reformationstid* XV, pp. 209-210.

Ó. Halldórsson (1963). 'Úr sögu skinnbóka', *Skírnir* 137, pp. 83-105.

Ó. Halldórsson (1977). 'Eftirhreytur um rímur', *Gripla* 2, pp. 183-187.

Ó. Halldórsson (1987). 'Á afmæli Flateyjarbókar', *Tímarit Háskóla Íslands* 1/2, pp. 54-62.

S. Jónsdóttir (1965). 'Gömul krossfestningamynd', *Skírnir* 139, pp. 134-147.

S. Jónsdóttir (1982). 'Lýsingar Helgastaðarbókar', in S. Karlsson et al. (eds.), *Helgastaðabók, Nikulás saga Perg. 4to nr. 16 Konungsbókhlöðu*

*Stokkhólmi.* Manuskripta Islandica Medii Aevi II. Reykjavík: Lögberg bókaforlag, pp. 90-124.

S. Gunnarsdóttir (2009). *Nunnuklaustrið að Reynistað.* Reykjavík: Byggðasafns Skagfirðinga. Available at: http://rafhladan.is/bitstream/handle/10802/6869/XI%20Reynista%C3%B0arklaustur.pdf?sequence=1 (Accessed: 6 January 2016).

Sigurdsson, E. R. (2011). *The Church in Fourteenth-Century Iceland. Ecclesiastical Administration, Literacy, and the Formation of an Elite Clerical Identity.* PhD thesis. University of Leeds. Available at: http://academia.edu/1795158/The_Church_in_Fourteenth-Century_Iceland (Accessed: 6 January 2016).

S. Karlsson (ed.) (1963). *Islandske originaldiplomer indtil 1450. Tekst.* Editiones Arnamagnæanæ, Series A: 7. Copenhagen: Munksgaard.

S. Karlsson (1970). 'Ritun Reykjafjarðarbókar: Exkursus: Bókagerð bænda', *Opuscula* IV, pp. 120-140.

S. Kristjánsdóttir and V. Gunnarsdóttir (2014). *Kortlagning klaustra á Íslandi. Reynistaður.* Reykjavík: Háskóli Íslands. Available at: https://notendur.hi.is/~sjk/REY_2014.pdf (Accessed: 6 January 2016).

Storm, G. (ed.) (1888). *Islandske Annaler indtil 1578.* Kristiania: Det norske historiske kildeskriftfond.

S. Óskarsdóttir (2000). *Universal history in fourteenth-century Iceland: Studies in AM 764 4to.* PhD thesis. University College London. Available at: http://discovery.ucl.ac.uk/1382009/1/392044.pdf (Accessed: 6 January 2016).

S. Tómasson (1985). 'Norðlenski Benediktínaskólinn', in Louis-Jensen, Jonna et al. (eds.): *The Sixth International Saga Conference, Workshop Papers* II. Copenhagen: Det Arnamagnæanske Institut, pp. 1009-1020.

S. Tómasson (1992). 'Trúarbókmenntir í lausu máli á síðmiðöld', in

G. Nordal et al. (eds.), *Íslensk bókmenntasaga I*. Reykjavík: Mál og menning, pp. 265-418.

S. Tómasson (2007). Recension of: 'The Development of Flateyjarbók' by Rowe, Elizabeth Ashman. *Speculum*, pp. 1033-1034.

S. Tómasson (2009). 'Þingeyrar – stærsta íslenska menningarsetrið á miðöldum', *Húnvetningur* XXVII, pp. 7-23.

Trætteberg, H. (1963). 'Klostersegl', *Kulturhistorisk leksikon for nordisk middelalder fra vikingetid til reformationstid* VIII, pp. 548-569.

Þ. Hjaltalín et al. (eds.) (2005). *Kirkjur Íslands 5: Friðaðar kirkjur í Skagafjarðarprófastsdæmi*. Reykjavík: Þjóðminjasafn Íslands, pp. 130-165.

Þorláks saga = Ásdís Egilsdóttir (ed.) (2002). *Byskupa sögur* 2. Íslenzk fornrit 4. Reykjavík: Hið íslenzka bókmenntafélag.

# 'So very memorable a matter': Anglo-Danish History and the *Encomium Emmae Reginae*

## Eleanor Parker

The reign of Cnut as king of England between 1016 and 1035 saw a unique period of cultural and literary interaction between England and Scandinavia. As part of the Danish king's Scandinavian empire, England became the location of a multilingual court which fostered literary production of a range hardly paralleled in pre-conquest England. Cnut's involvement in the circulation of English texts played an important role in his self-presentation as a successor to the Anglo-Saxon kings (Treharne 2012: 17-43), while the poetry composed for the king in Old Norse provides evidence of a lively literary community of Norse-speakers at the English court in the early 11th century (Townend 2001).

Within ten years of Cnut's death, this court also saw the production of the *Encomium Emmae Reginae*, an account of the Danish conquest and of Cnut's reign written for, and in praise of, his wife Emma (Campbell 1998). Norman-born Emma, who had been the wife of the defeated English king Æthelred before she married Cnut in 1017, exemplifies more than any other figure the complex cultural situation of Cnut's reign, and the text composed in her praise reflects the multiple influences at play. The *Encomium* was written in 1041 or 1042 during the reign of Harthacnut, Emma's son by Cnut, who was king of England and Denmark for just two years before his sudden and early death. The author, though unidentified, was probably a monk of St Omer in Flanders (Campbell 1998: 36-37). He seems to have had little personal experience of England and must have relied heavily on what he was told by his informants, who presumably included Emma herself and others at the Anglo-Danish court (Tyler 2005a). The *Encomium* thus stands at the intersection of multiple narrative traditions, as a Latin history which quotes Virgil and Lucan but which was produced for, and with the assistance of, a mixed Scandinavian, English, and Norman audience (Tyler 2005a; Orchard 2001).

Although the *Encomium* tells the story of a successful conquest, it was written in response to a tense political situation. After Cnut's death in 1035, the throne was disputed between Harthacnut and Harold, Cnut's son by his first wife. For some years Emma was in a difficult position, and the succession crisis was not resolved even with Harold's death in 1040. Harthacnut was accepted as king, but in the following year Emma's son by Æthelred, Edward, returned to England after two decades of exile in Normandy to live at Harthacnut's court. Edward had a strong claim to the throne, and in 1041-2 there seems to have been an uneasy truce between Edward, his mother, and his half-brother. The *Encomium* is an attempt to defend Emma from her detractors and to bolster Harthacnut's claim to the English throne, and to this end it looks back to the Danish conquest of thirty years before as a foundational narrative for the Anglo-Danish dynasty now represented by Harthacnut. It tells how the Danes, led first by Cnut's father Svein and then by Cnut himself, conquered England in 1013-16; it then recounts the reign of Cnut and describes the turmoil which followed his death in 1035, including the murder of Emma's son Alfred and the accession of Harthacnut.

The *Encomium*'s narrative of all these events is drastically selective: it claims to tell the story of the Danish conquest and the establishment of a new Anglo-Danish dynasty, but its narrative involves many omissions and distortions of fact (John 1980). Most importantly, it does not mention that Emma had been married to Æthelred before she married Cnut, and it implies, by this omission, that Emma's sons by Æthelred were really the children of Cnut. The picture which emerges from the *Encomium* is of a new dynasty, its legitimacy guaranteed by Emma's marriage to Cnut. This dynasty includes both Harthacnut and his half-brother Edward as legitimate members, despite their different parentage. An informed audience – including Emma, Harthacnut, and Edward, and others who had been directly involved in the events described in the *Encomium* – would have been fully aware of the distortions of fact the author uses in order to produce this picture. His statement that Cnut wooed Emma after searching through many kingdoms for a suitable bride, his evasion about her previous marriage to Æthelred, and his implication that Cnut was the father of Emma's older sons could not have deceived a contemporary audience for a moment. But the *Encomium* is an avowedly polemical work, written to praise and defend Emma. If its distortions of truth are so transparent, how could it hope to be effective in achieving these intended aims? We must assume that for the text to accomplish its stated purpose, at least some members of its disparate audience must have understood something of its methods and its approach to the uses of fiction and history. This paper's analysis of the text's narrative strategies may, therefore, reveal something about the literary culture of the Anglo-Scandinavian court which the *Encomium* aimed to influence.

## History, Fiction, and Fable

Elizabeth Tyler, discussing the *Encomium* in the context of contemporary Latin historiography, has argued for the importance of paying attention to the text's self-conscious fictionality when it comes to the details of Emma's life:

> While many of his fictions have long been recognised as such by scholars, I do not think we have recognized how *openly* and *deliberately* fictional the *Encomium* is. And yet, the members of Harthacnut's court more than any other audience would have recognized the flagrant nature of many of these fictions... [T]hat audience would have asked what that fiction was doing, what meaning it created. (Tyler 2005b: 154, emphasis in original; cf. John 1980: 63-65)

Tyler argues that the *Encomium* is best understood within the context of a developing eleventh-century understanding of fictionality, and that its distortions of fact, which seem too obvious to deceive, were in

45

fact not meant to do so. The audience's complicity in accepting these fabrications as fiction rather than as lies is essential for understanding how the text works (Tyler 2005b: 151-2). The prologue of the *Encomium* draws attention to issues of fictionality by asserting the importance of adherence to the truth, but acknowledging that the truth of a statement may depend more on the way it is presented than on its inherent veracity:

> Hoc enim in historia proprium exigitur, ut nullo erroris diuerticulo a recto ueritatis tramite declinetur, quoniam, cum quis alicuius gesta scribens ueritati falsa quaedam seu errando, siue ut sepe fit ornatus gratia, interserit, profecto unius tantum comperta admixtione mendatii auditor facta uelut infecta ducit. Unde historicis magnopere cauendum esse censeo... Res enim ueritati, ueritas quoque fidem facit rei.

> (This quality, indeed, is required in history, that one should not deviate from the straight path of truth by any divergent straying, for when in writing the deeds of any man one inserts a fictitious element, either in error, or, as is often the case, for the sake of ornament, the hearer assuredly regards facts as fictions, when he has ascertained the introduction of so much as one lie. And so I consider that the historian should greatly beware... The fact itself, to be sure, wins belief for the veracious presentation, and the veracious presentation does the same for the fact.) (Campbell 1998: 4-5)

The author sets up a choice for the historian between saying too much (and straying from the path of truth) and saying too little (and omitting what he has been instructed to narrate), and declares himself to be choosing the first option, even if this involves introducing fictitious elements into the narrative:

> Malo itaque a quibusdam de loquacitate redargui, quam ueritatem maxime memorabilis rei per me omnibus occultari.

> (I prefer, accordingly, to be blamed by some for loquacity, than that the truth of so very memorable a story should be hidden

from all through me.) (Campbell 1998: 4-5)

The author's discussion of these issues shows him to be keenly alert to the advantages and dangers of using fables and fictional stories in the writing of history, and the Prologue reads more like a justification for introducing fictional elements than an assertion that he will not do so. From the beginning, then, the author self-consciously directs the reader's attention to moments in the text where the boundary between fiction and history is blurred, or deliberately crossed. The *Encomium*'s approach to these questions suggests that the audience at Harthacnut's court – Danes and English alike – were attuned to the use of such semi-historical narratives for political purposes, and indeed that they took an active role in telling them. The encomiast's source for his account of the conquest of 1013-16 must have been informants at the Anglo-Danish court, and this account contains episodes no less transparently fictional than the story of Emma's marriage. At several points in the narrative, the *Encomium* acknowledges the existence of alternative stories circulating about the events it is describing, suggesting that the text is self-consciously operating within a wider context of oral storytelling about the Danish conquest. This was a situation in which the key events and leading figures of the conquest were apparently still contested subjects of discussion, and the *Encomium* positions itself as a response to these alternative narratives not by refuting them, but by emphasising at such moments how permeable the boundary between history and fiction can be.

## Legends of the Conquest: The Battle of Assandun

The *Encomium*'s narrative of the Danish conquest begins with Svein's decision to invade England in 1013 and ends during the reign of his grandson, Harthacnut, which means that the text takes its shape not from the life of a single individual – not Emma herself, nor Cnut – but from the course of Danish rule in England. In this respect it has parallels with the skaldic poems composed for Cnut, which provide evidence that narratives of the conquest played an important role in the literary culture of the Anglo-Danish court (Townend 2001). From these poems it appears that stories of Scandinavian invasion, both of the immediate and the distant past, were welcomed by the royal patron and his followers. Several of the poems celebrate the events of the 1013-16 conquest of England, in which some of the audience for these poems would presumably have participated (Poole 1991: 86-115), while the *Knútsdrápur* compliment Cnut by comparing him to legendary Danish conquerors of the past (Frank 1994). The *Encomium*'s place within this culture of memorialisation and storytelling is reflected by its use of narratives which derive from Scandinavian literary tradition, particularly in its account of the Battle of Assandun, the final, climactic battle of Cnut's conquest, which was fought on 18 October 1016. The *Encomium*'s sense of the importance of Assandun is shared by the *Anglo-Saxon Chronicle* and by Óttarr's *Knútsdrápa*, which both memorialise the battle from their different perspectives (Townend 2011: 208-211). In the *Encomium* this battle occurs halfway through Book II, at the mid-point of the text as a whole, and the battle and its aftermath take up five chapters of action and dialogue; the events of a few weeks are narrated in not much less space than is devoted to the nearly twenty years of Cnut's reign. After describing the preparations for the battle, the encomiast says:

> Erat namque eis uexillum miri portenti, quod licet credam posse esse incredibile lectori, tamen, quia uerum est, uerae inseram lectioni. Enimuero dum esset simplissimo candidissimoque intextum serico, nulliusque figurae in eo inserta esset [i]mago, tempore belli semper in eo uidebatur coruus ac si intextus, in uictoria suorum quasi hians ore excutiensque alas instabilisque pedibus, et suis deuictis quietissimus totoque corpore demissus. Quod requirens Turchil, auctor primi prelii, 'Pugnemus', inquit, 'uiriliter, sotii, nihil enim nobis erit periculi: hoc denique testatur instabilis coruus presagientis uexilli.'

> (Now [the Danes] had a banner of wonderfully strange nature, which though I believe that it may be incredible to the reader, yet since it is true, I will introduce the matter into my true history. For while it was woven of the plainest and whitest silk, and the representation of no figure was inserted into it, in time of war a

raven was always seen as if embroidered on it, in the hour of its owners' victory opening its beak, flapping its wings, and restive on its feet, but very subdued and drooping with its whole body when they were defeated. Looking out for this, Thorkell, who had fought the first battle, said: 'Let us fight manfully, comrades, for no danger threatens us: for to this the restive raven of the prophetic banner bears witness.') (Campbell 1998: 24-25)

Inspired by this omen, the Danes rush on to victory, and win control of England. The description of this banner draws on a motif which appears in various contexts in Scandinavian literary tradition, but which is usually associated in English sources with the most famous Danish conquerors of England: Ívarr, Ubbe, and Hálfdan, the sons of Ragnarr Loðbrók, who ruled part of the north of England in the ninth century, and later became the focus of a wide array of legends in Scandinavian and English tradition (Smyth 1977; Parker 2014: 488-90). They are linked with raven banners several times in English sources, first in an entry in the *Anglo-Saxon Chronicle* for 878: this mentions a battle in which one of the sons of Ragnarr was killed and the Danes' banner, which they called 'ræfen', was captured (O'Brien O'Keeffe 2001: 62).[1] Although there is no indication of a legend attached to the banner in this earliest appearance, parallels to the description given in the *Encomium* can be found in later texts from Iceland, Scandinavia and England (Lukman 1958). In the twelfth-century *Annals of St Neots*, the *Chronicle*'s reference to the events of 878 is expanded with an explanation comparable to that in the *Encomium*: it says that the banner was woven by the sisters of Ívarr and Ubbe, and that the raven moved like a living bird if the army were to be victorious, but hung down motionless if they were to be defeated (Dumville and Lapidge 1985: 78).

A reference to Ívarr in one of the Old Norse poems written for Cnut suggests that legends about Ívarr and his brothers were known at the Anglo-Danish court in the 11th century: Sigvatr's *Knútsdrápa* praises Cnut by comparing him to Ívarr, implying that his victory over the sons of Æthelred parallels Ívarr's defeat of King Ælla (Whaley 2012: I.2, 658-659). In light of this, it seems likely that the encomiast learned of the banner he describes from a member of the Anglo-Danish court. If this banner was associated with Ívarr, linking it to the Danish victory at Assandun places Cnut's conquest within the context of a long history of Danish triumphs over English kings. The intention may have been to suggest that there is a historical precedent for Danish rule in England, and that with his conquest Cnut is following in the footsteps of great Danish kings of the past. The place of the raven banner in the nebulous area between history and legend is therefore part of its power: it associates the eleventh-century king with his larger-than-life predecessors of centuries before, mythologising his conquest and conferring some kind of mysterious supernatural favour upon it. Perhaps some among the encomiast's informants and audience really believed the Danes had a supernatural banner which predicted their victory at Assandun, but it seems more likely that such a story was accepted as a self-evident myth, which linked Cnut's conquest with earlier Danish invasions of England. In this context, the encomiast's observation that his readers may find the story of the raven banner difficult to believe, and his declaration that he will include it anyway – laying heavy emphasis on the language of belief and truth, *credam* and *incredibile, uerum* and *uerae... lectioni* – seems like a knowing aside rather than a manifestation of any real anxiety about credibility. If the audience can be relied upon *not* to believe it, its inclusion does not call into question the author's own assertions about his veracity. It would seem that the audience at Harthacnut's court could be expected to understand, in Tyler's words, 'that fiction, too, can be useful *and* truthful' (Tyler 2005b: 175).

## 'Truthful Report': Authorial Credibility in the Face of Controversy

The *Encomium*'s self-conscious emphasis on credibility and truth at the moment where a legend makes an appearance in this 'true narrative' is paralleled at other points in the text which deal with events or people which seem to have been particularly controversial. An early example occurs in Book I's glowing description of Cnut's father Svein. The *Encomium* is very much at odds with other English sources in its praise of Svein. Whereas in the *Encomium* he is presented as a wise Christian king, an innocent victim of his father's hatred, and an effective military leader much loved by his men, in later English sources Svein – who had spent decades raiding in England before being accepted as king in 1013 – is unsurprisingly viewed with hostility (Demidoff 1978-1979). The *Encomium*, although acknowledging that Svein knew he was unpopular with the English (Campbell 1998: 14-15), asserts that its positive view of Svein is true and incontrovertible: Book I opens by declaring Svein's virtues, 'ueridica comperi relatione' (as I have ascertained from truthful report) (Campbell 1998: 8-9), and later observes:

> At ne me credat aliquis hec falsa fingendo alicuius amoris gratia compilare: recte animaduertenti in subsequentibus patebit, utrum uera dixerim an minime.

> (And lest any man think that I am lying, and concocting what I say from regard for any person's favour, in what is to follow, it will be plain to any one paying due attention, whether I am telling the truth or not.) (Campbell 1998: 10-11)

The author is speaking here of Svein's capacity to inspire loyalty from his men, and it is quite possible that he is indeed relating what he had heard from his informants; he was certainly in a better position to know how Svein's followers felt about the king than any later English writer could be. But this emphasis on truth brings into the open the possibility that his words may *not* be believed, in an audacious rhetorical strategy which almost encourages the reader to challenge the truth of what is said.

Another controversial figure, perhaps the character in the *Encomium* who is most difficult to interpret, receives similar treatment from the author. Thorkell, one of Cnut's leading commanders, is a prominent figure in the narrative, and features in a heroic role at the Battle of Assandun, but his loyalty to Svein and Cnut is questioned on several occasions. The text puts forward a number of mutually inconsistent reports of his motives and behaviour, without attempting to reconcile them: when he remains in England after Cnut has returned to

Denmark, he is said to be seeking vengeance for his brother (Campbell 1998: 10-11), but it is also indicated that Cnut believed he had betrayed him (Campbell 1998: 16-17). The *Encomium* acknowledges both interpretations of his behaviour, yet asserts that the true reading of his conduct is entirely apparent (Campbell 1998: 16-17). Its reference to divergent interpretations suggests that Thorkell's behaviour was still being discussed and debated at the Anglo-Danish court. Although Thorkell himself was dead at the time of writing, there must have been many at court who remembered him. By stating that the true interpretation of Thorkell's behaviour is obvious, the *Encomium* in fact provides a reminder that it is *not,* and perhaps questions whether it would even be possible to arrive at an accurate understanding of this divisive issue.

The *Encomium*'s treatment of the immediate aftermath of the Danish conquest makes use of a similar strategy, in a deft move which allows the author to pass over the difficult consequences of the conquest in one illustrative story. The aftermath of Cnut's conquest was violent, as potential opponents were swiftly dispatched and any remaining members of the royal family were killed or exiled, but the *Encomium* passes over most of this. Its way of discussing what happened after the conquest is to describe a country ready for peace and a new beginning. There is to be a new dynasty, centred on Emma herself, whose marriage to Cnut in one stroke reconciles the Danes and the English.

This requires the *Encomium* to describe what happened to the previous dynasty, represented at this point by Edmund Ironside, Æthelred's son by his first wife. Edmund is cast in favourable terms as a worthy opponent for the Danes, though he is presented as the chief English commander rather than as a king with a rival claim to the kingdom. He is shown giving a rousing speech to his men at Assandun and bravely challenging Cnut to single combat, and he is finally defeated not because of his own weakness but because his chief adviser, Eadric, betrays him. After Cnut becomes king, the *Encomium* includes a short narrative which manages to reconcile praise for Cnut with a satisfying conclusion to Edmund's story: Eadric comes to seek a reward from Cnut for his betrayal of Edmund, but Cnut, recognising his disloyalty, has him killed, and thus, in a sense, avenges Edmund's death. The killing of Eadric was in fact only one among a number of political murders in the first years of Cnut's reign, but the *Encomium* recasts it as just punishment exacted on a traitor, a vivid little story with a memorable punchline. Eadric asks to be paid what he is owed for betraying Edmund and helping Cnut win the kingdom, but Cnut, punning on the ambiguous language of debt and repayment, orders one of his commanders 'Huic... quod debemus persoluito, uidelicet, ne nos decipiat, occidito' (Pay this man what we owe him; that is to say, kill him, lest he play us false) (Campbell 1998: 30-33). The author draws attention to this incident as a self-contained story by calling it an *exemplum*, a narrative intended to teach a lesson: in this case, he says, the moral is that soldiers should be loyal to the king. Eadric later developed a reputation as a notorious traitor, blamed for a wide variety of terrible crimes, and it is possible that the *Encomium*'s story records an early stage in this developing legend; it is not difficult to imagine such a memorable story being told at the Anglo-Danish court, embellished with the black humour of its grim wordplay. The *Encomium*, by classifying it as an *exemplum* and drawing a moral from it, signals that it is to be understood as a story, satisfying and useful within this narrative of the conquest, but not necessarily a factual record of exactly what happened to Eadric in 1017.[2]

## Conclusions

As one of the earliest works of Anglo-Scandinavian literature, the *Encomium* provides a unique perspective on the events of the Danish conquest: it is the closest insight available into the Danish conquerors' own interpretation and narrative of their conquest and its aftermath. To understand what this text can tell us about the conquest, however, requires an appreciation of its sophisticated use of fiction and legend, and the expectations it places on its audience to recognise and participate in its narrative strategies. Its self-conscious use of fictional elements should encourage one to ask why the stories it tells were found to be both useful and powerful for the author and his audience. It seems that these stories played an important role in helping the *Encomium* to navigate the dangerous waters of political tension and the consequences of conquest.

## Endnotes

[1] This is found in the B, C, D and E manuscripts of the Chronicle.

[2] The *Anglo-Saxon Chronicle* notes only that Eadric was killed in 1017, with no further details (see for instance O'Brien O'Keeffe 2001: 103).

## References

Campbell, A. (ed.) (1998). *Encomium Emmae Reginae*. Intr. Simon Keynes. Cambridge: Cambridge University Press.

Demidoff, L. (1978-9). 'The death of Sven Forkbeard – in reality and later tradition', *Medieval Scandinavia*, 11, pp. 30-47.

Dumville, D. and Lapidge, M. (eds.) (1985). *The Anglo-Saxon Chronicle, A Collaborative Edition 17: The Annals of St Neots*. Cambridge: D. S. Brewer.

Frank, R. (1994). 'King Cnut in the verse of his skalds', in Rumble, A. R. (ed.), *The Reign of Cnut: King of England, Denmark and Norway*. London: Leicester University Press, pp. 106-124.

John, E. (1980). 'The *Encomium Emmae Reginae*: A Riddle and a Solution', *Bulletin of the John Rylands University Library of Manchester*, 63, pp. 58-94.

Lukman, N. (1958). 'The Raven Banner and the Changing Ravens: A Viking Miracle from Carolingian Court Poetry to Saga and Arthurian Romance', *Classica et Medievalia*, 19, pp. 133-151.

O'Brien O'Keeffe, K. (ed.). (2001). *The Anglo-Saxon Chronicle: A Collaborative Edition 5: MS. C.* Cambridge: D. S. Brewer.

Orchard, A. (2001). 'The Literary Background to the *Encomium Emmae Reginae*', *Journal of Medieval Latin*, 11, pp. 157-184.

Parker, E. (2014). 'Siward the Dragon-Slayer: Mythmaking in Anglo-Scandinavian England', *Neophilologus*, 98, pp. 481-493.

Poole, R. G. (1991). *Viking Poems on War and Peace: A Study in Skaldic Narrative*. Toronto: University of Toronto Press.

Smyth, A. P. (1977). *Scandinavian Kings in the British Isles 850-880*. Oxford: Oxford University Press.

Townend, M. (2001). 'Contextualizing the *Knútsdrápur*: skaldic praise-poetry at the court of Cnut', *Anglo-Saxon England*, 30, pp. 145-179.

Townend, M. (2011). 'Cnut's Poets: An Old Norse Literary Community in Eleventh-Century England', in Tyler, E. M. (ed.), *Conceptualising Multilingualism in Medieval England, 800-1250*. Turnhout: Brepols, pp. 197-215.

Treharne, E. (2012). *Living Through Conquest: The Politics of Early English, 1020-1220*. Oxford: Oxford University Press.

Tyler, E. M. (2005a). 'Talking about history in eleventh-century England: the *Encomium Emmae Reginae* and the court of Harthacnut', *Early Medieval Europe*, 13, pp. 359-383.

Tyler, E. M. (2005b). 'Fictions of Family: The *Encomium Emmae Reginae* and Virgil's *Aeneid*', *Viator*, 36, pp. 149-179.

Whaley, D. (ed.) (2012). *Poetry from the Kings' Sagas. I. From Mythical Times to c.1035*. 2 vols. Turnhout: Brepols.

# A Similar but Different Boat Tradition: The Import of Boats from Norway to Shetland 1700 to 1872

## Marc Chivers

### Introduction

Shetland, having no forests of its own, had, until the latter half of the nineteenth century, a long history of importing timber and boats from western Norway. It is believed that this trade with Norway began when the Vikings first started to settle on Shetland, c.850 CE. West-Norwegian *færing* (a four-oared boat) and *seksæring* (a six-oared boat) types were imported from Bergen to Shetland, and this trade was, until the nineteenth century, framed within the much larger Norway-to-Scotland timber trade.

Boats from Norway were imported to Shetland in one of two ways: some were transported *set-up,* and, as this term suggests, were constructed in Norway and then shipped by way of being stowed and stacked, one inside another, upon the importing vessel's deck. The other method for transporting boats was called *unset-up*, whereby vessels were transported in component parts, and these 'kits' were commonly called *boats-in-boards*. These *boats-in-boards*, like the *set-up* boats, formed part of the importing ships' general timber cargo.

My analysis of this boat trade will determine when commercial boatbuilding began in Shetland, and, secondly, establish why Shetland's own distinct types of four and six-oared boats evolved. Shetland's boat types retained some characteristics that are still found in boats built in Os, near Bergen. These traditional Os-built boats are called *Oselvar* (estuary boat) and, remarkably, follow a building tradition that, as Christensen points out, retains features that date from the Viking Age (Christensen 2014: 93).

Because of Shetland's Norwegian heritage, there is a widely held belief that the nineteenth-century Shetland-built four and six-oared boats are of direct Viking descent (Stuart Bruce 1914: 290; Johnston 1932: 9; Halcrow 1950: 66; Sandison 1954: 8; Morrison 1973: 71, McGrail 1974, Henderson 1978: 52-55; Fenton 1978: 552). The association of Shetland's boats to the Norse era was fuelled by the intellectual nineteenth-century romantic vision of Shetland's Viking past (Rampini, 1884). This linking of Shetland's nineteenth-century boats to the Viking Age has blurred reality, which was one of an eighteenth- and nineteenth-century economic need to have suitable boats from which to fish.

Although some Oselvar traits exist within the nineteenth-century Shetland built boats, the vessels themselves are in fact unique to Shetland.

## Locating Shetland

Shetland is an archipelago of one hundred islands, representing the most northerly extremity of the British Isles. It lies on the $60^0$ north parallel, some hundred miles off the northern tip of the Scottish mainland, with Orkney in between. The closest Scottish ferry port to Shetland is Aberdeen, which is 211 miles south of Lerwick, Shetland's capital. Bergen is 225 miles east of Lerwick and Faroe lies 228 miles northwest of Shetland (Fig. 1).

## The History of the Boat Trade

The boat trade was part of a larger Scottish timber import, which developed after 1503, when the Scottish parliament declared that Scotland's woods were utterly destroyed as a result of building a navy

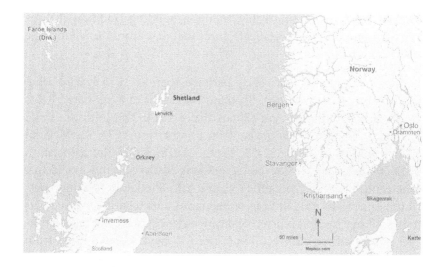

**Fig. 1**: Shetland's location.

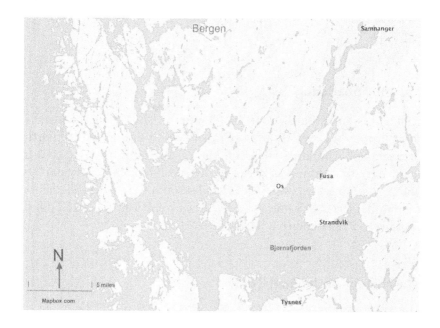

**Fig. 2**: Map illustrating the main boatbuilding areas that supplied boats to Shetland.

(Newland 2010: 46). Then, by the late-eighteenth century, England had depleted many of its own forests and had also become dependent upon Norwegian and Baltic timber imports (Hutchinson 2015: 6).

## The Boat Trade

The main places where boats for export were constructed were Os, Tysnes, Fusa, Strandvik and Samnanger (Fig. 2). By the end of the seventeenth century, Tysnes was the main supplier of boats to Shetland (Thowsen 1969: 150). Newland (2010: 46) identifies that, by the seventeenth century, timber was so important to Scotland that generous benefits were provided to Scottish merchants engaged in its trade. Then, in the eighteenth century, George II and his son-in-law, Frederick of Norway/Denmark, incentivised Scottish Episcopalians to settle and trade in Norway tax-free (Thomson 1991: 14). Scottish merchants living in Norway were therefore able to act as timber export agents for those living on the Scottish mainland, as well as Orkney and Shetland, thus making it easier to import boats from Norway. The British blockade of Norwegian ports between 1807 and 1814 stemmed the supply of timber and boats; Thowsen (1969: 156) has suggested that this may have been the origin of commercial boatbuilding in Shetland.

## Introducing Shetland's Traditional Boats

Before the advent of the internal combustion engine, people on Shetland, from a young age, would by necessity have been competent in handling boats under both sail and oar, and would have regarded travel by sea, in small open boats, as an everyday activity (interview with Wishart 2015).

Documented evidence of the boat trade begins in the 1500s, revealing a trading pattern that persisted into the eighteenth and nineteenth centuries. The eighteenth century saw a growth in Shetland's fishing industry for which bigger boats were needed (Goodlad 1971: 95). Thowsen (1969: 154) discusses the import of boats from Norway during

**Fig. 3**: *Oselvar færings* moored outside the Oselvarlaget in Os. Photo: Author.

the eighteenth and nineteenth centuries, consisting of two principal types: four-oared boats, (Fig. 3) and six-oared boats. Alongside these boat types, the primary sources describe the use of eight-oared boats, in Norwegian called *åttring*. These eight-oared boats were owned by the merchant lairds, a prominent example of their eighteenth century use being found within a letter written by Margaret Bruce to William John Nivane in 1742, which states: '... You'll receive from on board Lunas sloop twenty six short hundred ling and in the eight oaring six hundred and forty ditto hundreds; ...' (GD144/15/14).

Archival documents imply that these Norwegian boat imports were simply the same four, six, and eight-oared boats that were used in western Norway (D24/ 26th January 1762, GD144/12/12, GD144/59/12/2, SC 12/53/5:179). They were used in Shetland for fishing, travel, and for the flitting (transportation) of cargo and livestock. In Shetland, a four-oared boat is called a *fourareen*, sometimes pronounced and spelt *fowareen*, and often called a *fourern*. *Fourareens* ranged in size from approximately 16 to 20 feet long (9 to 12 feet of keel). The smaller-sized *fourareens* were known as *whillie boats*, and these were the family car of their day, being used for inshore fishing and transport. There were three principal six-oared types of boat. The biggest of these was called a *sixareen*, or a *sixern* (Fig. 4), and these boats ranged in size from about 24 to 30 feet long (17-22 feet of keel).

**Fig. 4**: The *sixareen* 'Industry' racing under squaresail at Walls. Photo: ©Shetland Archives.

*Sixareens* were used for deep sea fishing on the *haaf* (Old Norse: open ocean) and operated up to 50 miles offshore, setting up to seven miles of fishing line (Goodlad, 1971: 90). The larger sized *sixareens* had eight rowing positions, the eighth one (in the forward part of the boat) used when *andooing* (that is, keeping the boat on station by means of slowly rowing into the wind or tide depending on whichever was strongest). Other types of six-oared boat were named after the species of fish they caught, which was either haddock (Fig. 5) or cod. These boats were about 21-22 feet long with keel lengths of 13-15 feet.

The last six-oared types of boat are named after the parishes in which they were used. The *Ness yoal* (Fig. 6) is from the parish of Dunrossness and was developed to fish for saithe, which are prevalent along the edges of strong tidal rips. The *Ness yoal* was just over 23 feet long with a keel of 15 feet (Sandison 1954: 12). The *yoal* had to be fast and easily manoeuvrable when rowed. A similar type of boat was developed on Fair Isle (which lies 25 miles south of the southern tip of Shetland's Mainland) and called the *Fair Isle yoal*, which was usually about 22 feet long with a keel of 16 feet. The *Ness* and *Fair Isle yoals* are slightly different in design, and are regarded as separate boat types (March 1971: 49).

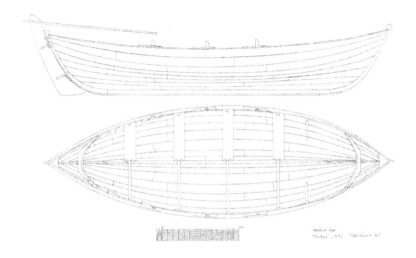

**Fig. 5**: The haddock boat 'Brothers' LK96. Built 1888 by Davie Leask, Lerwick. Drawing: ©Author.

**Fig. 6**: *Ness yoal* 'Kate' LK152 under sail, belonging to Brian Wishart & Leslie Moncrieff. Brian Wishart stern, John Polson, Billy Smith. Photo: ©Shetland Archives.

## The Eighteenth and Nineteenth Century Boat Trade

Evidence for expansion of fisheries is provided within the *First Statistical Account for Scotland* in 1791-1799. Here, the Reverend James Barclay states that, by 1740, the number of boats had increased to such an extent that the boats had to go further offshore to prevent their lines from tangling. It seems, in moving further offshore, they discovered a new fishing ground. This, in turn, increased their boat size allowing them to carry more fishing lines and hold more fish (Withrington and Sinclair (eds.) 1978: 465-466). Stuart Bruce (1914: 296) states that boats were imported from Norway *unset-up*, ready to be put together, each piece being properly numbered and marked. This statement by Stuart Bruce suggests that the boat imports were prefabricated and in 'kit-form', a view which is supported by Thowsen, who describes a 1714 manuscript in which the loading of boats onto Shetland ships is portrayed:

> These boats being loaded were delivered to the quay loosely clinked together with a few nails. Before being loaded, the planks were numbered and marked. Once loaded aboard the ship they were dismantled and once delivered to their destination reassembled according to the numbers and marks thus a small ship's hold can carry 70, 80, 100, even 120 boats (Thowsen 1969: 151).

Økland (2014) challenges this 1714 source, arguing against the notion of *unset-up* boats, instead suggesting that boats were mainly imported *set-up*. Økland reasons that building a boat, taking it apart, transporting it, and then rebuilding it makes no economic sense. Walter Duncan sr., who was a highly respected Shetland boat-builder, stated that setting-up the keel and stems was a time-consuming and difficult process, which, if not done correctly, would result in the boat having a twist built into the hull (Osler 1983: 55). Apart from cutting and shaping the keel, stems and the strakes, there was as much work involved in reconstructing a boat as there was in building it for the first time. Walter Duncan sr. stated that Shetland boat-builders would often pre-cut and shape keels, stems, and the lower strakes of common-sized boats. These would then be stored up in the rafters of the boatshed ready for later use (Osler 1983:53). The precise definition of what constituted a *boat-in-boards* is ambiguous. This is exemplified by the letter from Thomas Gifford to James Barclay in Bergen in 1731, listing items to be purchased, which conflicts with Thowsen's 1714 primary source evidence.

One 'long hundred' planks, a full inch thick and 16 ft long, cost £25, and a half a hundred 'sawen in two' £12 10s for the boat builders, much being supplied already cut to shape (March 1971: 34-37).

This request infers that the *kit-boats* may have been no more than timber, rough-cut to size and shape, which would have saved valuable cargo space and reduced construction time.

Archival documents provide evidence for the import of boats in both *unset-up* and *set-up* form. As such, if *boats-in-boards* were being imported as complete 'kits', it would be expected that these would be entered into the 1742 Shetland customs accounts. Timber cargo entries of ships returning from Norway appear in the customs accounts, although, boats *set-up* or *un-set-up* are not mentioned. Indeed, there is no mention of boat-related items until 1765, when a consignment of oars was imported. This is strange, and contrary to other documentary evidence, such as the entry written in Thomas Gifford's accounts by his Scottish Agent John Wallace, a resident of Bergen: 'Cash to Mr John Harrower for purchasing a cargo of boats [unclear] at the woods for our account as per your order of the 20th July last.' (GD144.10.11). In this document, the term 'at the woods', is used, which is a colloquial name for the region of Hordaland, where the timber trade was focused.

By 1765, the method by which timber cargos were entered into the customs accounts had changed, and for the first time the entry of 'crooked birch and fir wood for boats use' was made (SA.1.7.1). This suggests that *boats-in-boards* were being entered into the customs accounts in their component parts, rather than as whole items. This is later confirmed in a letter from James Hay, c. 1815. Within this correspondence, Hay provides details of how the *boats-in-boards* were to be entered into the customs accounts in order to avoid paying the correct duty: the boat strakes were entered as deals not exceeding 10 feet in length and 1½ inch thick. The keels and gunwales were entered as spars under 22 feet in length, not exceeding 4 inch in diameter (excluding the bark), and the stems and frames were entered as crooked-timber for boat use (D40/243/3/2). The blockade of Norwegian ports was lifted in 1814 and from this date *boats-in-boards* are recorded in the customs accounts. Why then were the Hay family still hiding their cargos of boats? The evidence points to smuggling, which during the eighteenth and nineteenth centuries was rife in Shetland. Smith points out that the lairds were heavily involved in this activity from 1770, and the most prodigious smuggler at this time was James Hay (Smith 1986:149).

From 1817 boat-builder boards are listed within the customs accounts, confirming that commercial boatbuilding had begun in Shetland. This ties in with correspondence from James Hay to the Commissioners of Customs in 1818, whereby he defends himself against an allegation of fraudulently undervaluing a cargo of boats to the Lerwick Customs Officer. Within a draft letter to the Commissioners, Hay writes:

> … Having for many years been deeply interested in the fisheries of this country we were under the necessity of procuring from different places every material for its prosecution & particularly fishing boats from Norway as until within late years it was deemed impracticable to manufacture a fishing boat in Shetland, where necessity the mother of invention (during) the late war to 1814 w$^h$ rendered it almost impossible to procure them from Norway) stimulated the Shetland carpenters to attempt making boats at home, wherein they have so well succeeded & materials by wrecks & otherwise have become so plenty as rendered importation almost unnecessary… (Acc.3250/85/4).

This letter states that boatbuilding in Shetland had been regarded as impractical, which suggests that the boat trade with Norway was a pragmatic business decision based upon price and convenience. The last sentence of this letter is important, as it illustrates that by 1818 boatbuilding in Shetland was well established. So much so, that according to James Hay there would soon be no need to import

Norwegian boats.

A letter from John Mouat of Garth to the Board of Customs in Edinburgh in 1822 provides evidence of the continued commercial importance placed upon the import of *boats-in-boards* from Norway. Within this letter, Mouat states that: '... these boats being light and tender are liable to injury when repeatedly handled and turned over before they are rebuilt' (GA/1822). Mouat's statement contradicts the earlier suggestion that *unset-up* boats consisted of pre-cut and shaped component parts. Thowsen describes the Tysnes County Prefect's report of 1836-1840, within which:

> ... it is reported that the boat builders in Tysnes construct some larger boats: "... under the name Jæltebaade (i.e. Shetlands-boats), in the manner that all the boats materials (keel, frames, planking etc.) are made ready for clinking, the different parts are numbered and transported to Bergen ... (Thowsen 1969: 155).

The fact that the term *Jæltebaade* is used infers that boat builders in Tysnes were building boats to a Shetland specification. This trade was still active in 1860 when the County Prefect reported that 30 *Jæltebaade* were imported each year to Shetland (Thowsen 1969: 156). This account suggests that the *boats-in-boards* were not pre-built and then taken apart prior to shipment, but were in fact, pre-cut and shaped boat components made ready for assembly and fastening. It has been presumed, that the *boats-in-boards* were simple 'self-assembly kits'. This, it seems, is not true, as this 1860 Hay and Company correspondence illustrates:

> ... Most of the fishermen find the
> boats built [unclear] here so much cheaper that
> they are not willing to go to the expense of
> the Norway boats -- which you are perhaps aware
> require a good deal of material and workmanship
> after we get them to fit them for sea...
> (D31/1/36).

This letter states that the boats are expensive and require a lot of material and skilled labour before they are ready to be used.

The commercial trade in boats from Norway finally ends on the 26th November 1872 when Hay and Company reply to their Agents in Bergen, stating that:

> … No boats can be sold here now except those built by our own workmen, and we have to import square timber from the east coast of Norway, for the special purpose of boat-building… (D31/1/58:261).

Thus ended this long established boat import trade with Norway. It is clear that by 1872 the timber trade itself had come to an end in Hordaland, and that Hay and Company were now importing timber from eastern Norway.

## Shetland Boats Are Similar but Different to Those of Western Norway

Originally the boats imported to Shetland were the same as the four, six and eight-oared-boats used in western Norway. This raises the question of whether Shetland's own boat types are direct descendants of those of the Viking Age. There are no surviving written documents from Shetland's Norse past, and it seems some people, including Charles Rampini, who was Sheriff-substitute of Caithness, Orkney and Shetland, saw virtue in this, writing in 1884: 'During all that long period Shetland had literally no history … Yet we have one consolation. Happy is the people that has no history' (Rampini 1884: 31). This was the period when Shetland's modern Up-Helly-Aa annual winter fire festival, with the burning of a 'Viking galley' was invented. This is also, I believe, a period in which Shetlanders began to assert the Viking provenance of Shetland's own open boats.

The notion that Shetland's boat types can trace their ancestry back to the Viking Age is very romantic. And whilst Shetland boats do, at first glance, resemble Viking boats, sharing similarities with their west Norwegian neighbours, they have, as I have shown, evolved out of a more complex eighteenth and nineteenth-century Shetland boatbuilding tradition (Fig. 7).

Nineth-century *Gokstad færing*. Viking Ships museum, Oslo.

Nineteenth-century *Oselvar færing*. Bergen museum.

The Gardie boat (*fourareen*) built by R. Nicholson, Haroldswick, Unst. Unst Boat Haven museum.

**Fig. 7**: A comparison between boat types. Photos: Author.

Munro (2011: 13) points out that in Norway, as in the United Kingdom, there are differences in boat types and construction methods from one region to another. The Bjørnafjorden area, and Os in particular, has a very conservative approach to boat building (Christensen 2014: 93). A few of the similarities and differences between Shetland's own boat types and those of the *Oselvar* type are illustrated in Fig.13. These differences serve to demonstrate how Shetland boat builders have developed their own methods of construction in Shetland, introducing a tradition of boat building that dates back to the end of the eighteenth century.

Some of Shetland's boat builders did retain some features of the west Norwegian boat building tradition into the late nineteenth century. An example of this was the practice of incorporating mouldings on the bottom edge of each of the strakes on both the outside and the inside of the boat; these mouldings are called *sneck[1]* or *strek høvel* in Shetland (Norwegian: strake plane). An *Oselvar* boatbuilder, Hallgeir Forstrønen Bjørnevik (2015) has stated that this moulding, although now considered decorative, actually has a function; it enables the boat strakes to flex slightly at the point where they are joined. Hallgeir points out that:

> ... the whole boat benefits from this flexing ... because the boat will be more soft to work in when out fishing. In a stiff boat your body will start hurting sooner than in a more flexible boat. This was important for the fishermen, and the first thing they did with a new boat was to shake it to see how flexible it was. Fishermen said it was better to take in some water than have a stiff boat. (Bjørnevik, interview, 2016).

This moulding pattern dates from 1000 CE (Fig. 8.4) and can be found in a few twentieth-century boats, but only on the sheer strake, which in Shetland is called the *reebing*.

Christensen (interview, 2014) observed that Shetland's boats, having narrower and more numerous strakes, resemble boats from eastern Norway. This is possible due to Shetland's timber imports, which became centred there in the nineteenth century. Christensen (1968: 12) discussed the Viking boatbuilding legacy, which he claimed still existed on the west coast of Norway and on the Baltic coasts of Finland and Sweden. These regions retained much of the boatbuilding traditions, including the hull-form that was present in the Viking Age. Meanwhile, western Sweden, eastern Norway, and Denmark have boat types further removed from those of that period.

Originally, when Shetland imported boats from western Norway, these imports probably retained boatbuilding characteristics handed down from the Viking Age. However, although Shetland's boats may resemble those of the Viking Age, they are in fact born from an eighteenth-century Shetland boatbuilding tradition. It must be remembered that, during the eighteenth and nineteenth centuries, as Shetland's fishing practices changed, the size of boats imported increased, and the hull form of these boats became broader and deeper (Thowsen 1969: 172). The four and six-oared west-Norwegian boats, which were originally imported to Shetland and of possible Viking lineage, became built according to a Shetland specification, and evolved into the four and six-oared Shetland boats discussed within this paper.

## Conclusion

Analysis of eighteenth and nineteenth-century documents reveals that commercial boatbuilding in Shetland was established by 1814. Ambiguity in the documentary evidence means it is not possible to determine whether the *boats-in-boards* were pre-constructed (dismantled for transportation), or if they simply represented timber which had been rough-cut to size and shape. Analysis of archival documents reveals that *boats-in-boards*, prior to 1814, were not correctly entered into Shetland's customs accounts in order to reduce their value, and so reduce the import duty payable upon them. New evidence reveals that *boats-in-boards* were not simple reassembly 'kits', and that the building of boats from boards required more skill, materials, and time to construct than has previously been acknowledged.

The analysis of the history of the boat trade between Shetland and Norway has added a critical perspective to the widely asserted view that Shetland's traditional boats can trace their ancestry directly to those of the Viking Age. To conclude, Shetland's boat building traditions have clearly been influenced by boat imports from Norway. However, over a period of 200 years, a boatbuilding tradition has emerged that is unique to Shetland and its location straddling the Nordic and North Atlantic world.

**Figs. 8**: A few of the similarities and differences in construction methods between the boats from western Norway and Shetland. Photos: Author

The completed *hals* ready for fitting.

Planing the *hals* using a bollow plane.

Axing the *hals* (garboard hood end) creating the desired curve and twist.

**Fig. 8.1**: Oselvar boatbuilder Hallgeir Forstrønen Bjørnevik making a *hals* for an *Oselvar* boat.

Note: wide, axe carved, curved garboard strake on an *Oselvar* boat.

Note: the narrow steamed garboard on this Shetland *fourareen*. 'Spindrift' Built by Lowrie Smith. Bressay, c.1937.

**Fig. 8.2**: Comparison between the garboard strake of an *Oselvar* and a *fourareen*

71

*Keipe*, (oarlock) nineteenth century Oselvar boat.

*Kabe*, (oarlock) haddock boat 'The Brothers' LK 96 Built 1888, Lerwick, Shetland.

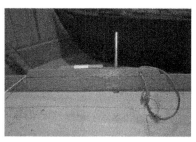

*Kabe* on the *halv yoal*, '*phar-lap*', built c.1890 by Geordie Eunson, Punds, Eastshore. Shetland Museum.

*Kabe*, *fourareen*, built by Davie Bruce, Whalsay, c.1959.

**Fig. 8.3**: West Norwegian and Shetland arrangements for rowing. All use the same system: in Norway called Keipar and in Shetland called the kabe. Shetland has a greater variation on this system.

Viking Age moulding drawn by Emeritus Professor Arne Emil Christensen, Oslo.

*Gokstad færing*, c. AD 900. Viking Ship Museum, Oslo.

Moulding drawn by Emeritus Professor Arne Emil Christensen, Oslo.

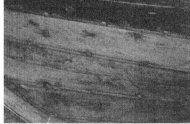

Hardanger *åttring*. Norwegian Maritime Museum, Oslo.

*Fourareen*, built by John Laurenson, Nesting. c.1880. Owned by Tommy Isbister, Trondra.

*Oselvar*, built by Stig Henneman, Oselvarverkstaden, Os, 2014.

**Fig. 8.4**: Comparison between decorative hull mouldings AD 900-2014.

## Endnotes

[1] Standard size fir or pine boards (Smith 1984: 331).

[2] Lower Scots: *a cut, incision* (Jakobsen, 1928: 851).

## References

Christensen, A. E. (2009). *Trebåten*. Kulturhistorisk vegbok. Tema. Available at: http://www.grind.no/pdf/kvh-21-tema.pdf (Accessed: 5 October 2015).

Christensen, A. E. (1968). *Boats of the North: A History of Boatbuilding in Norway*. Oslo: Det Norske Samlaget.

Fenton, A. (1978). *The Northern Isles: Orkney and Shetland*. Phantassie: Tuckwell Press.

Goodlad, C. A. (1971). *Shetland Fishing Saga*. Lerwick: Shetland Times Ltd.

Halcrow, A. (1950). *The Sail Fishermen of Shetland and Their Norse and Dutch Forerunners*. Lerwick: T. & J. Manson.

Henderson, T. (1978). 'Shetland Boats and their Origins', in Baldwin, J. R. (ed.), *Scandinavian Shetland. An Ongoing Tradition?* Edinburgh: Scottish Society for Northern Studies, pp. 49-55.

Hutchinson, R. (2015). *The Norwegian and Baltic Timber Trade to Britain 1780-1835 and Its Interconnections*. Available at: https://www.academia.edu/6709494/The_Norwegian_and_Baltic_Timber_trade_to_Britain_1780-1835_and_its_interconnections (Accessed: 10 Feb 2015).

Jakobsen, J. (1928) *An Etymological Dictionary of the Norn Language in Shetland*. London: David Nutt (A.G. Berry).

Johnston, A. (1932) 'The Shetland Sixern', *The Model Yachtsman and Marine Model Magazine*, April, pp. 9-12.

March, E. (1971). *Inshore Craft of Great* Britain *in the Days of Sail and Oar*, Volume One. Newton Abbot: David & Charles.

McGrail, S. (1974). *The Building and Trials of the Replica of an Ancient Boat: The Gokstad Faering. Part 1. Building the Replica.* Maritime Monographs and Reports. No. 11. Greenwich: National Maritime Museum.

Morrison, I. (1973). *The North Sea Earls. The Shetland / Viking Archaeological Expedition.* London: Gentry Books.

Munro, A. (2011). *More Similarity Than Difference? Physical and Cultural Connections in the Open Boats of the Northern Isles.* MLitt thesis. University of the Highlands & Islands. [Centre for Nordic Studies, Shetland].

Newland, K. (2010). *The Acquisition and Use of Norwegian Timber in Seventeenth Century Scotland, with Reference to the Principal Building Works of James Baine, his Majesty's Master Wright.* PhD thesis. Univerisity of Dundee. Available at: http://discovery.dundee.ac.uk/portal/files/3408813/Newland_phd_2010.pdf (Accessed: 14 March 2014).

Osler, A. (1983). *The Shetland Boat: South Mainland and Fair Isle. Maritime Monographs and Reports No. 58.* Greenwich: Trustees of the National Maritime Museum.

Rampini, C. (1884). *Shetland and the Shetlanders. Two Lectures delivered before the Philosophical Institution, Edinburgh on the 5th and 8th February 1884.* Kirkwall: William Peace & Son.

Sandison, C. (1954). *The Sixareen and Her Racing Descendants.* Lerwick: T. & J. Manson.

Smith, H, D. (1984) *Shetland Life and Trade 1550-1914.* Edinburgh: John Donald Publishers Ltd.

Smith, R. J. (1986). *Shetland in the World Economy: A Sociological History of the eighteenth & nineteenth centuries.* PhD thesis.

University of Edinburgh. [Shetland Archive].

Smith, B. (1990). *'Shetland, Scandinavia, Scotland, 1300-1700: The Changing Nature of Contact'*, in Simpson, G. G. (ed.), *The Mackie Monographs I Scotland and Scandinavia 800-1800*. Edinburgh: John Donald Publishers Ltd, pp. 25-37.

Stuart Bruce, R. (1914). 'The Sixern of Shetland', *The Mariner's Mirror*, 4 (9), pp. 289-300.

Thowsen, A. (1969). 'The Norwegian Export of Boats to Shetland, and Its Influence Upon Shetland Boat Building and Usage', in Peterson, L. and Thowsen, A. (eds.), *Norwegian Yearbook of Maritime History*. Bergen: Sjøfartshistrisk Årbok, pp. 145-208.

Thomson, A. (1991). *The Scottish Timber Trade, 1680-1800*. Unpublished PhD thesis, University of St. Andrews.

Withrington D. J. and Grant, I. R. and Sinclair, J. (Sir) (eds). (1978). *The Statistical Account of Scotland 1791-1799 Volume XIX Orkney and Shetland*. Ilkley: E. P Publishing Limited.

Økland, K, M. (2014). *Boat Trade across the North Sea*. St. Magnus Conference, Lerwick. Available at: https://www.youtube.com/results?search_query=St.+Magnus+Conference%2C+Lerwick. (Accessed: 6 October 2015).

## Archive Sources

### National Library of Scotland, Special Collections.

ACC.3250/85/4 Papers of the Hay family.

### Shetland Archives

D24/Box27

D31/1/36. Hay & Company correspondence with Alexander Grieg.

D31/1/58:261. Hay & Company correspondence with Alexander Grieg.

D40/243/3/2. James Hay Instructions.

GD144/10/11. Bruce of Symbister collection of papers.

GD144/12/12. Bruce of Symbister collection of papers.

GD144/15/14. Bruce of Symbister collection of papers.

GD144/59/12/2. Bruce of Symbister collection of papers.

SA/1/7/1. Shetland's Quarterly Custom reports, 1742-1772.

SC12/53/5 folio 68r. Missive letter by Alexander Wallace and Son to Thomas Bolt, seventeenth July 1779.

**Gardie House (Private Collection)**

GA/1822. Letter from John Mouat of Garth to the Board of Customs Edinburgh, 1822.


## Interview Sources

Christensen, A. E. (2014). *Hjeltebåt questions, please can you help?* [email] to Chivers, M. [8 January, 2014].

Bjørnevik, H. F. (2015). Interviewed by Marc Chivers, Båthallen, Hordaland Museet, Norge. 10 March.

Bjørnevik, H. F. (2016). Chapter for the Oselvar Master to comment on! [email] to Chivers, M. [20 January, 2016].

Wishart, B. (2015). Interviewed by Marc Chivers. Sandwick, Shetland. 11 September.

# LINGUISTIC LIAISONS

# Tonal Stability and Tonogenesis in North Germanic

## Pavel Iosad

The origin of North Germanic tonal accents is a question with a long history and a range of available answers. Although the basic facts are not in dispute, the accents' historical development remains controversial. In this paper, I aim to contribute an argument in favour of the view that tonal accent arose in post-Viking Age North Germanic in connection with changes in syllable count (Oftedal 1952; Elstad 1980; Bye 2004, 2011; Hognestad 2012). I will argue that the genesis of 'accent 1' and 'accent 2' as a grammaticalization of syllable count need not be seen as an isolated, unique phenomenon in the history of the North Germanic languages: instead, it is a recurring event, as demonstrated by the genesis of new 'tonal accent' oppositions triggered by apocope in at least three further separate instances in Central Scandinavia, Zealand, and East Slesvig. I will also adduce further typological parallels from West Germanic and from Goidelic Celtic.

The organization of this paper is as follows. In section 1, I will review the data and the competing accounts of the origins of tone accents. In section 2, I will consider tonogenesis in Central Scandinavian varieties and in Zealand Danish, and argue that these events, as well as the 'common Scandinavian' type of accent contrast, can be accounted for via the phenomenon of tonal stability. In section 3, I will briefly review two similar cases from West Germanic and Goidelic Celtic that support a link between tonal stability and tonal accent genesis. Section 4 provides a short conclusion.

## Tonal Accent in North Germanic

By 'tonal accent' I refer to the distinction between two major classes of words expressed by laryngeal activity in the stressed syllable (and, in many varieties, also the following one): normally pitch movement but also glottal closure. Thus, in most varieties of Norwegian the lexical items *bønder* 'farmers' and *bønner* 'beans' are identical on the segmental level (both [bønːər] or the like) but differ in pitch contours, although the precise nature of that difference varies significantly across dialects. Traditionally, words such as *bønner* are said to bear 'accent 1' (*acute* in the Swedish tradition), and words such as *bønder* are said to have 'accent 2' (or *grave*).

### Typology of Tonal Accent

Geographically, the accent distinction is distributed as follows:

- In most Norwegian and Swedish varieties, the distinction is expressed by different pitch contours associated with stressed syllables (the difference can, however, persevere into a following unstressed syllable);

- In many varieties of Danish, including Standard Danish, the distinction is realized using a phonetically complex phenomenon known as *stød*, whose main component involves glottal occlusion, although it can also be accompanied by changes in pitch and intensity (Fischer-Jørgensen 1989);

- In some varieties, pitch and glottal occlusion (or at least creaky voice) coexist: for instance, in many Danish dialects on Funen stød and rising pitch stand in complementary distribution (Andersen 1958; Ejskjær 1990);

- Finally, some varieties lack the tonal accent system altogether: these include Finland and Tornedal Swedish, Norwegian varieties in Finnmark and North Troms, Faroese, and Icelandic. In some cases the lack of tonal accent is normally attributed to language contact (with Finnish in Finland and with the Sámi languages in Northern Norway); in others it is supposed that the contrast

81

never arose, as in Icelandic (see, however, Haukur Þorgeirsson 2013 for arguments that it may have been present historically).

In terms of phonetic realization, there are several approaches to the typology: possible criteria include pitch levels, the shape of the pitch curve, and the timing of tonal peaks and troughs relative to the stressed syllable.

- In terms of pitch level, it is common, especially in the Norwegian tradition, to distinguish between 'low tone' and 'high tone' varieties, with the distinguishing feature being the tone found on the stressed syllable in accent 1 words. In Norway, 'high tone' dialects are found in the south-west and in the north, whilst 'low tone' dialects are found in Eastern Norway and in Trøndelag. Most Swedish varieties with a tone accent contrast are 'high tone', with the exception of west-central (Götaland) varieties abutting the East Norwegian area;

- In terms of curve shape, the important distinction is that between the shapes of accent 2 curves, with a difference between 'single-peak' accent 2 (western and northern Norway, southern Sweden, Gotland, and Dalarna) and 'double-peak' accent 2 (southern, eastern, and central Norway, and most of central and northern Sweden, including Central Standard Swedish). Generally, in single-peak systems the distinction between accent 1 and accent 2 lies in the timing, with accent 2 peaks timed later than accent 1;

- Finally, Gårding (1977) offers a typology that combines the single vs. double-peak accent contrast with a distinction between early and late-timed peaks: in her system, types 1A and 1B are both single-peak systems, but in 1B peaks are placed later than in cognate 1A dialects; and 'low-tone dialects' are essentially 2B dialects, where the peak in accent 1 is shifted so far rightwards as to leave the stressed syllable entirely, leaving it with a low tone.

Thus, the typology of North Germanic tonal accents submits to treatments that emphasize different aspects of their phonetic properties. The same difference in emphasis can also be observed in various approaches to the history of the tonal accent distinction.

## The History of Tonal Accents

In the literature, we find three broad approaches to the history of tonal accents in North Germanic languages: I shall call them the 'double-peak' approach, the 'peak delay' approach, and the 'stød-first' approach. In this paper, I endorse the 'peak delay' account, and concentrate on a critique of the 'double-peak' one; I do not address the 'stød-first' argument that stød historically preceded tonal accents (e.g. Liberman 1984; Lahiri & Wetterlin 2015) for reasons of space and focus.

The 'double-peak' scenario builds on two observations. First, as already noticed by Kock (1885; see also d'Alquen & Brown 1992), in the modern languages accent 2 is normally found in words that were at least trisyllabic in Proto-North-Germanic, and had undergone syncope in the 1st millennium CE. In the modern languages, such words tend to be disyllabic. Accent 1, on the other hand, is found in words that had not undergone syncope because they were too short in the relevant era, and which tend to be monosyllabic in the modern languages. Hence, Swedish *dom* 'judgement' has accent 1, because it goes back to Proto-North-Germanic *$dŏmaz$, with a single stressed syllable and no syncope. An accent 2 word like *döma* 'to judge', on the other hand, represents Proto-North-Germanic *$dŏmijăn$, with two stressed syllables. Both stresses would be retained even following syncope, so that the word would assume the form *$dŏmà$, with a stress clash (two adjacent stressed syllables). It is this clash that would have been reinterpeted as a double-peaked accent 2: hence, under this approach (Riad 1998, 2003, 2005), the double-peaked variety of accent 2 (as in Stockholm Swedish) is considered to be the most archaic. A second observation adduced in favour of this scenario is the so-called 'combinatorial accent 2', a phenomenon whereby all compounds, irrespective of the accentual properties of their components, receive accent 2 (Riad 1998, 2014). The existence of this phenomenon again underlines the connection between accent 2 and the presence of more than one ictus in a word. Hence, the 'double-peak' scenario privileges the shape of the tonal curve.

The 'peak delay' scenario takes as its starting point a different observation, namely that the distribution of accent 1 and accent 2 is largely predictable from the number of syllables in the word at the Old Scandinavian stage. In this scenario, accent 1 on *dom* 'judgement' is attributable to the fact that it goes back to an Old Scandinavian monosyllabic form, like Old Icelandic *dómr*, whereas the accent 2 on *döma* is due to the disyllabic shape of a form like Old Icelandic *dæma*. In this scenario, the rise of a distinctive tonal accent is connected not with the late Proto-North-Germanic syncope but with later disruptions in syllable count. Specifically, proponents of this theory (e.g. Oftedal 1952; Elstad 1980; Bye 2004; Hognestad 2012) argue that these later disruptions did not change the tonal pattern of the word, and hence the distribution of the tonal patterns became unpredictable from syllable count. Particular attention is drawn to the incorporation of the definite article into the nominal form, so that *bit it* 'the bit', still with the 'monosyllabic' tone pattern on *bit*, becomes unpredictably distinct from *bitit* '(has) bitten'. Another factor is the epenthesis of vowels in word-final clusters of rising sonority, hence *føtr* 'feet' corresponding to Modern Swedish *fötter* with accent 1 (contrast *nyckel* 'key' with accent 2, cf. Old Icelandic *lykill*). Thus, the proponents of this theory do not privilege the exact shape of the tonal curve but focus on its domain. In fact, early proponents (Oftedal 1952; Öhman 1967; Elstad 1980) tended to remain fairly agnostic on the precise phonetic difference between mono- and disyllabic words that would later morph into a tonal accent distinction.

In recent years, this approach has been given a more precise phonetic grounding by authors such as Bye (2004; 2011), Lorentz (2008), and Hognestad (2012). They have argued that disyllabic words would be associated with a different pitch pattern compared to disyllabic words thanks to *peak delay*, a phenomenon well known from intonational phonology (e.g. Ladd 2008). In languages with peak delay, longer domains are associated with a later placement of the tonal peak; hence, disyllabic words would have associated their peaks further to the right compared to monosyllabic words. Under this scenario, the historically original system is Gårding's (1977) 1A, with a single-peak accent 2 and the peak placed in the stressed syllables in both classes, with only timing the difference between the two accents. This system is found in peripheral areas such as southern Sweden and Western and Northern Norway.

## Tonal Stability and Typology

Tomas Riad's œuvre presents the most sustained argument for the 'double-peak' theory and against the 'peak delay' approach. In Riad (2005) he summarizes a number of objections to the 'peak delay' approach. In this short paper I cannot hope to deal with them all, so I will focus on a single one (but see Bye 2011; Hognestad 2012 for more discussion). Specifically, I address Riad's typological objection. Under the peak delay approach, syllable count before cliticization of the definite article and epenthesis appears to be such an important element of the sound system that it is signalled (by tone) even after syllable counts have been disrupted. Riad (2005: 4) asks:

> Det har visserligen demonstrerats att tajmningen av en given intonation kan variera beroende på ordlängd [...], men man undrar varför denna typ av tonala kontraster inte uppstår oftare ur stavelseantalsskillnader.

> (It has indeed been demonstrated that the timing of a given intonation may vary depending on word length [...], but one wonders why this type of tonal contrasts does not arise from syllable count distinctions more often)[1]

Lahiri & Wetterlin (2015) express a similar reservation about the typological unusualness of a syllable-count origin for tonal accents, and argue that their stød-first approach is typologically superior, since the genesis of tones from glottalization or loss of glottal consonants is very well attested cross-linguistically (Kingston 2011). In the remainder of this paper I show that the preservation of syllable counts, via tonal stability, is a recurring event in the history of the North Germanic languages, and also has certain parallels outside this subgroup.

| Stage | Form | Tone placement | Form | Tone placement |
|---|---|---|---|---|
| Before peak delay | [akr] 'field' | Early | [lykill] 'key' | Early, predictable |
| Peak delay in longer forms | | Early | | Late, predictable |
| Phonologiza-tion | [$^H$akr] | Early | [ly$^H$kill] | Late, predictable |
| Epenthesis and phonemi-cization | [$^H$aker] <br><br> *[a$^H$ker] | Early | [ly$^H$kill] | Late, unpredict-able |

**Table 1:** The Genesis of Tonal Accent

## Tonal Stability in North Germanic

The basic mechanism for the genesis of tonal accent contrasts from syllable counts is *tonal stability*, i.e. the persistence of tonal specifications in the face of changes in the segmental make-up. This phenomenon is well known in the theoretical literature (e.g. Goldsmith 1976), and presents a major piece of evidence supporting the autosegmental approach to tone. The genesis of tonal accent in North Germanic varieties, particularly in Swedish and Norwegian, is explained under the 'peak delay' scenario as the persistence of the *alignment* of tonal specifications (specifically the high tone peak) following segmental changes.

Here, peak delay (i.e. a later placement of the tonal peak) arises first as an automatic consequence of the presence of a second syllable. At some point, the difference between earlier and later placement of the peak enters the phonological grammar.[2] Crucially, changes in the conditioning environment do not lead to changes in tonal associations. In other words, the grammar does not deterministically enforce a later peak placement in disyllables: otherwise we would expect the newly disyllabic [aker] to have 'accent 2' (late tonal placement). That this does not happen (Modern Swedish *åker* has accent 1) is due to tonal stability.

In theoretical phonological terms, this phenomenon is the typological *explanandum* for the 'peak delay' theory of tonal accent genesis. In the remainder of this paper, I argue that tonal stability is attested in North Germanic and further afield beyond the genesis of the accent 1 vs. accent 2 contrast, and hence that the 'peak delay' account is not typologically suspect.

## Central Scandinavian 'Circumflex Accent'

Probably the best-known case of tonal accents reflecting earlier syllable counts is found in the case of the so-called 'circumflex accent', a tonal accent distinction in monosyllables following apocope. In most Norwegian and Swedish varieties, monosyllables do not show a tone accent contrast (cf. Vanvik 1956). However, in a large area of Central Scandinavia such contrasts do exist, and they reproduce old syllable counts. Apocope in some form is found in Norway from Nordmøre through Trøndelag and parts of Helgeland to Salten and Lofoten; in the Swedish-speaking area it is characteristic of most dialects from Härjedalen and Jämtland north- and eastwards, including Swedish-speaking Finland.

In many areas apocope does not neutralize the distinction between monosyllables and disyllables. For instance, in the variety of the Skogn area around Levanger in Nord-Trøndelag (Dalen 1985), tonal distinctions are found in both mono- and disyllabic words: *kast* 'a throw' (accent 1) vs. *kâst* 'to throw' (circumflex accent), and *kaste* 'the throw' (accent 1) vs. *kaste* 'throw (present)' (accent 2). For other descriptions of dialects with circumflex accent, see Dahlstedt (1962); Apalset (1978); Elstad (1979); Almberg (2001); Lorentz (2008); Kristoffersen (1992, 2011); Kelly (2015).

The circumflex accent normally reflects historical accent 2 in disyllables.[3] In fact, many synchronic analyses assume that accent 2 on polysyllables and 'circumflex' on apocopated disyllables reflect the same underlying tonal melody, even if the surface curves are not identical; see Lorentz (2008) for Salten and Dalen (1985) for Skogn. Other synchronic analyses are available; see, for instance, Kristoffersen (2011). Historically, however, 'circumflex accent' clearly exemplifies pitch distinctions persisting after changes in the segmental make-up that have consequences for syllable structure. From a theoretical phonological perspective, it demonstrates a clear example of tonal stability: the tonal specification and its association remain intact despite segmental changes. The 'circumflex' situation is also similar to that hypothesized under the 'peak delay' scenario in that at least at the initial stage of the phonemicization of the 'new' tonal accent ('circumflex' or 'accent 1') the tonal contours themselves remain intact, and the surface differences are only in how they are distributed within the domain.

## Zealand Danish

Another of similar phonologization of timing of a tonal contour is provided by the dialects of the Danish islands, in particular that of Zealand (for overviews, see Ejskjær 1990, 2005). As described by Ejskjær (1967) and Larsen (1976) for eastern Zealand, forms corresponding to disyllables with final schwa in the standard language are frequently – in fact predominantly – realized without that final schwa.[4] However, forms such as [hʌb̥] '(a) hop' and [hʌb̥] 'to hop' (Standard *hop*, *hoppe*) are not identical: instead, as Larsen (1976) documents, they show different pitch contours. Apocopated words show a 'later and smoother' rise in pitch ('jævnere og senere rejsning') compared to original monosyllables.

Once again, a 'tonal accent' – the use of pitch to distinguish between two types of stressed syllables – has been born thanks to the perseverance of tonal melody despite the change in segmental structure. Crucially, this phenomenon is probably historically independent from the Central Scandinavian 'circumflex' accent: in Zealand Danish, the cognate of the accent 1 / accent 2 distinction is the stød / non-stød contrast. The relatively recent date of the tonogenesis in apocopated words is also suggested by the fact that the tonal contours involved are still identical, and by the still not entirely obligatory status of apocope. Hence, Zealand Danish presents a second, independent case of 'tonal stability'.

**East Slesvig and Other Cases of 'Circumflex Accent'**

Within the Danish-speaking area, Zealand Danish is unique in combining stød with a newer tonal contrast. It is, however, not unique in failing to neutralize the distinction between monosyllables and apocopated words. A particularly clear case where this contrast is preserved is found in East Slesvig (including the island of Als), and on the island of Rømø off the west Slesvig coast. Ejskjær (1990), citing Bjerrum (1949), describes them as lacking stød (hence with no reflex of the accent 1 / accent 2 distinction) but distinguishing between monosyllables ([¹reŋ] *ring* 'ring') and apocopated disyllables ([²reŋ] *ringe* 'small'). Here, tonal accents apparently contrast *only* in monosyllables, unlike the Central Scandinavian situation (but like Zealand Danish), and hence again the distinction is likely to be historically independent.

A similar situation is found in dialects of islands off the south coast of Funen such as Ærø, where 'accent 1' is found in old monosyllables and some, but not all, apocopated disyllables, whereas the other apocopated disyllables show 'accent 2'. There is again no common Danish stød (corresponding to the Swedish and Norwegian accents) in these varieties.

The use of tone to preserve syllable count distinctions after apocope is attested in other varieties (see Haugen 1976: §11.3.10(4) for a list). One example is Öland Swedish (Selmer 1930), although the system there is again different: e.g., the circumflex accent can correspond to accent 1 in contrasts like *tak* 'roof' vs. *tâk* 'the roof' (Standard Swedish ¹*taket*).

To conclude, the genesis of the accent 1 / accent 2 opposition in North Germanic under the 'peak delay' hypothesis presupposes a scenario where tonal stability enables contrasts in syllable count to be preserved using pitch differences. Far from being a unique and typologically unusual event, this kind of phonologization is amply and uncontroversially attested in the later history of the North Germanic languages; moreover, the several later events are likely to be independent from each other, lending further plausibility to the scenario. In the next section I briefly consider two further typological parallels.

## Tonal Stability Outside North Germanic

Similar scenarios for the genesis of 'tonal accents' can be found in West Germanic and in Goidelic Celtic, both relying at least partly on tonal stability for their genesis.

In West Germanic, tonal accents are found in Low and Middle Franconian dialects in Limburg and around the Middle Rhine. Unlike Norwegian and Swedish 'tonal accents' (but like the 'circumflex accents' and stød), they are also contrastive in monosyllables. Although there is no agreement on the precise reconstruction of their history (de Vaan 1999; Gussenhoven 2000; Köhnlein 2013, 2015; Boersma forthcoming), it is clear that at least at some stage in their development the tonal contrasts, in some varieties, survived segmental changes that potentially disrupt syllable structure, notably apocope. Hence, we find that forms with apocopated schwa can be tonally distinct from morphologically related monosyllables: Geleen Limburgian [kniin] 'rabbit' vs. [kniin] 'rabbits'. All reconstructions assume that this lack of neutralization between mono- and disyllables is due to the fact that a contrast in tonal placement had been established before apocope. This offers a strong parallel to North Germanic cases of tonogenesis out of syllable counts; the 'circumflex accents' of Section 2 are particularly similar.

An even closer parallel to the phonemicization of tone due to epenthesis, as required under the 'peak delay' scenario, is found in Goidelic Celtic. In Scottish Gaelic, two sound changes that potentially neutralize syllable count distinctions have failed to do so, with the contrast expressed tonally (see in particular Ternes 2006). The first is the deletion of intervocalic voiced fricatives: in Lewis Gaelic [ʎɔːr] *leabhar* 'book' (Old Irish *lebor*) shows the same kind of pitch pattern as [aː] *adha* 'liver', which is a historical disyllable (Old Irish *óa*, Middle Irish *áe*) and contrasts with [aː] *àth* 'ford' (Old Irish *áth*); see Oftedal (1956); Brown (2009); Iosad (2015). Even more relevant is the interaction between tone and epenthesis. In Gaelic, words like [palʲak] *balg* 'belly' (Old Irish *bolg*) contrast in pitch patterns with old disyllables such as *ballag* 'skull'. Specifically, as Brown (2009) shows, in the latter the low pitch accent targets the first vowel but in the former it targets the second one. This is the clearest case of tonal associations persisting despite epenthesis, in parallel to the emergence of the contrast sketched in Table 1: epenthesis in *balg* does not lead to neutralization with a disyllable like *ballag*.[5]

## Conclusion

In this article I have aimed to show that the genesis of tonal accents from metrical structure (in particular syllable counts), which is required under the 'peak delay' scenario for North Germanic, is not typologically as rare as some critics have suggested: it has repeatedly, and probably independently, occurred both within North Germanic and also in other European languages (see Kehrein 2008 for additional, albeit more remote, parallels). Whatever the merits of other objections to the 'peak delay' scenario advanced in work such as that by Riad (2005), this particular argument can, I suggest, be rejected.

The underlying mechanism that facilitates the persistence of syllable count contrasts is *tonal stability*: a basic consequence of autosegmental phonology and its separation between tonal specification and segmental representation. The same insight underlies some recent synchronic analyses of European 'tonal accent' systems that emphasize differences in the mapping between tones and segments rather than differences in tonal melodies (e.g. Kristoffersen 2006; Hermans 2009; Morén-Duolljá 2013; Kehrein forthcoming; Köhnlein 2016).

Finally, it must be noted that 'European' tonal accent systems, characterized by the persistence of tonal mappings and alignments over changes in segmental structure (Ladd 2004) appear to be cross-linguistically rare. Thus, the 'peak delay' scenario is relatively well supported typologically *within* the European linguistic area, but we should not perhaps expect to find ample parallels elsewhere. The question of what it is about European languages that facilitates the genesis of this type of tonal accent is a promising avenue for future research.

# Endnotes

[1] All translations author's own unless otherwise specified.

[2] It is immaterial here how exactly this difference is represented; see Morén-Duolljá (2013); Köhnlein (2013) for some discussion. For more on the concept of phonologization as envisaged here, see Iosad & Honeybone (2015).

[3] However, the circumflex accent is often found in syncopated definite singular forms of sonorant-final nouns like *mannen* 'the man', *sønnen* 'the son', where we historically expect accent 1; see in particular Christiansen (1947).

[4] This phenomenon is found in Standard Danish: Basbøll (2005) refers to it as 'schwa assimilation'. According to Basbøll, however, in the standard language it is both variable and neutralizing: *masse* 'mass' can be pronounced with or without the schwa, but when it is absent, *masse* is not distinct from *Mads* 'personal name'.

[5] The difference between North Germanic and Gaelic is that in the former the tones stay put despite the changed context, while in latter the low tone keeps the association and hence apparently 'moves rightwards' (although it is still associated to the same vowel with the same timing as before epenthesis). Boersma (forthcoming) offers a very similar scenario for the initial phonologization of the tonal contrast in Franconian.

# References

Almberg, J. (2001). 'The circumflex tone in a Norwegian dialect', in van Dommelen, W. and Fretheim, T. (eds.), *Nordic Prosody: Proceedings of the VIIIth conference, Trondheim 2000*. Frankfurt: Peter Lang, pp. 19-28.

d'Alquen, K. and Brown, R. (1992) 'The origin of Scandinavian accents I and II', in Rauch, I., Carr, G. F., and Kyes, R. L. (eds.), *On Germanic Linguistics: Issues and Methods*. Berlin; New York: Walter de Gruyter, pp. 61-80.

Andersen, P. (1958). *Fonemsystemet i østfynsk. På grundlag af dialekten i Revninge sogn*. København: J. H. Schultz forlag.

Apalset, A. (1978). 'Apokope og circumfleks i Leksvikmålet', in Hoff, I.

(ed.), *På leit etter ord: Heidersskrift til Inger Frøyset*. Oslo, Bergen, Tromsø: Universitetsforlaget, pp. 11-26.

Basbøll, H. (2005). *The Phonology of Danish*. Oxford: Oxford University Press.

Bjerrum, M. (1949). *Felstedmaalets tonale accenter*. Århus: Universitetsforlaget.

Boersma, P. (forthcoming). 'The history of the Franconian tone contrast', in Kehrein, W., Köhnlein, B., Boersma, P., and van Oostendorp, M. (eds.) *Segmental Structure and Tone*. Berlin: Mouton.

Brown, M. (2009). *An Investigation into Prosodic Patterns in the Ness Dialect of Scottish Gaelic*. MA (Hons) dissertation, University of Edinburgh.

Bye, P. (2004). 'Evolutionary typology and Scandinavian pitch accent'. MS., University of Tromsø.

Bye, P. (2011). 'Mapping innovations in North Germanic using GIS', *Oslo Studies in Language*, 3(2), pp. 5-29.

Christiansen, H. (1947). 'Stavingskontraksjon og tonelag', in Stang, C. S., Krag, E., and Gallis, A. (eds.), *Festskrift til professor Olaf Broch på hans 80-årsdag*. Oslo: Det Norske Videnskapsakademi, pp. 49-55.

Dahlstedt, K.-H. (1962). *Det svenska vilhelminamålet: Språkgeografiska studier över ett norrländkst nybyggarmål och dess granndialekter. Del 2: Kvantitet. Apokope*. Uppsala: Almqvist & Wiksell.

Dalen, A. (1985) *Skognamålet: Ein fonologisk analyse*. Oslo: Novus.

Ejskjær, I. (1967). *Kortvokalstødet i sjællandsk*. København: Akademisk forlag.

Ejskjær, I. (1990). 'Stød and pitch accents in the Danish dialects', *Acta Linguistica Hafniensia*, 22(1), pp. 49-75.

Ejskjær, I. (2005). 'Dialects and regional varieties in the 20th century.

III: Denmark', in Bandle, O., Braunmüller, K., Jahr, E. H., Karker, A., Naumann, H.-P., Telemann, U., Elmevik, L., and Widmark, G. (eds.), *The Nordic Languages*. Berlin: Walter de Gruyter, pp. 1721-1741.

Elstad, K. (1979). 'Det nordnorske circumflekstonemet', in Gårding, E., Bruce, G., and Bannert, R. (eds.) *Nordic prosody*. Lund: Gleerup, pp. 165-174.

Elstad, K. (1980). 'Some remarks on Scandinavian tonogenesis', *Nordlyd*, 3, pp. 62-77.

Fischer-Jørgensen, E. (1989). 'Phonetic analysis of the stød in Standard Danish', *Phonetica*, 46(1), pp. 1-59.

Goldsmith, J. A. (1976). *Autosegmental phonology*. PhD thesis. Massachusetts Institute of Technology.

Gussenhoven, C. (2000). 'On the origin and development of the Central Franconian tone contrast', in Lahiri, A. (ed.) *Analogy, leveling, markedness*. Berlin, New York: Mouton de Gruyter, pp. 213-260.

Gårding, E. (1977). *The Scandinavian word accents*. Lund: G. W. K. Gleerup.

Haugen, E. (1976). *The Scandinavian languages: An introduction to their history*. London: Faber; Faber.

Haukur Þorgeirsson (2013). *Hljóðkerfi og bragkerfi: Stoðhljóð, tónkvæði og önnur úrlausnarefni í íslenskri bragsögu ásamt útgáfu á Rímum af Ormari Fraðmarssyni*. PhD thesis. University of Iceland.

Hermans, B. (2009). 'The phonological structure of the Limburg tonal accents', in Nasukawa, K. and Backley, P. (eds) *Strength relations in phonology*. Berlin: Mouton de Gruyter, pp. 317-372.

Hognestad, J. K. (2012). *Tonelagsvariasjon i norsk*. PhD thesis. University of Agder.

Iosad, P. (2015). '"Pitch accent" and prosodic structure in Scottish

Gaelic: Reassessing the role of contact', in Hilpert, M., Duke, J., Mertzlufft, C., Östman, J.-O., and Rießler, M. (eds) *New trends in Nordic and general linguistics*. Berlin: Mouton de Gruyter, pp. 28-54.

Iosad, P. and Honeybone, P. (2015). 'The emergence of laryngeal contrast in Old English and Brythonic: The long path to contrast'. MS., University of Edinburgh.

Kehrein, W. (2008). 'The birth of tonal accents: How many paths? And how many Romes?' Presentation at the Tone Workshop, Marburg.

Kehrein, W. (forthcoming). 'There's no tone in Cologne: Against tone-segment interactions in Franconian', in Kehrein, W., Köhnlein, B., Boersma, P., and Oostendorp, M. van (eds.), *Segmental Structure and Tone*. Berlin: Mouton.

Kelly, N. E. (2015). *An Experimental Approach to the Production and Perception of Norwegian Tonal Accent*. PhD thesis. University of Texas, Austin.

Kingston, J. (2011). 'Tonogenesis', in Oostendorp, M. van, Ewen, C. J., Hume, E., and Rice, K. (eds.), *The Blackwell Companion to Phonology*. Oxford: Blackwell Publishing, pp. 2304-2333.

Kock, A. (1885). *Språkhistoriska undersökningar om svensk akcent*. Lund: J. W. Gleerup.

Köhnlein, B. (2013). 'Optimizing the relation between tone and prominence: Evidence from Franconian, Scandinavian, and Serbo-Croatian tone accent systems', *Lingua*, 131, pp. 1-28.

Köhnlein, B. (2015). 'A tonal semi-reversal in Franconian dialects: Rule A vs. Rule B', *NOWELE*, 68, pp. 81-112.

Köhnlein, B. (2016). 'Contrastive foot structure in Franconian tone-accent dialects', *Phonology*, 31, pp. 87-123.

Kristoffersen, G. (1992). 'Cirkumflekstonelaget i norske dialekter, med særlig vekt på nordnorsk', *Maal og Minne*, 1992(1), pp. 37-61.

Kristoffersen, G. (2006). 'Markedness in Urban East Norwegian tonal accent', *Nordic Journal of Linguistics*, 29(1), pp. 95-135.

Kristoffersen, G. (2011). 'Cirkumflekstonelaget i Oppdal', *Norsk lingvistisk tidsskrift*, 29(2), pp. 221-262.

Ladd, D. R. (2004). 'Alignment allophony and European "pitch accent" systems'. Presentation at the Tone and Intonation in Europe conference, Santorini.

Ladd, D. R. (2008). *Intonational Phonology*. Cambridge: Cambridge University Press.

Lahiri, A. and Wetterlin, A. (2015). 'The diachronic development of *stød* and tone accent in North Germanic', in Haug, D. T. T. (ed.), *Historical Linguistics 2013: Selected Papers from the 21st International Conference on Historical Linguistics, Oslo, 5-9 august 2013*. Amsterdam: John Benjamins, pp. 53-67.

Larsen, J. (1976). 'Det sjællandske »tostavelsesord«', in Hald, K., Lisse, C., and Sørensen, J. K. (eds.), *Studier i dansk dialektologi og sproghistorie tilegnede Poul Andersen*. København: Akademisk forlag, pp. 193-206.

Liberman, A. (1984). *Germanic Accentology*. Minneapolis: University of Minnesota Press.

Lorentz, O. (2008). 'Tonelagsbasis i norsk', *Maal og Minne*, 2008(1), pp. 50-68.

Morén-Duolljá, B. (2013) 'The prosody of Swedish underived nouns: No lexical tones required', *Nordlyd*, 40(1).

Oftedal, M. (1952). 'On the origin of the Scandinavian tone distinction', *Norsk tidsskrift for sprogvidenskap*, 16, pp. 201-225.

Oftedal, M. (1956). *The Gaelic of Leurbost, Isle of Lewis*. Oslo: W. Aschehoug & Co.

Öhman, S. (1967). 'Word and sentence intonation: A quantitative model', in *Transmission Laboratory Quarterly Progress and Status Report (STL-QPSR)*. Stockholm: Department of Speech Transmission, Royal Institute of Technology, pp. 20-54.

Riad, T. (1998). 'The origin of Scandinavian tone accent', *Diachronica*, 15(1), pp. 63-98.

Riad, T. (2003). 'Diachrony of the Scandinavian accent typology', in Fikkert, P. and Jacobs, H. (eds.), *Development in Prosodic Systems*. Berlin: Mouton de Gruyter (Studies in generative grammar, 58), pp. 91-144.

Riad, T. (2005). 'Historien om tonaccenten', *Studier i svensk språkhistoria*, 8, pp. 1-27.

Riad, T. (2014). *The Phonology of Swedish*. Oxford: Oxford University Press.

Selmer, E. W. (1930). *Apokope und Zirkumflex I: Eine theoretische Experimentalstudie auf Grund der ölandischen Akzentverhältnisse*. Oslo: Jacob Dybwad.

Ternes, E. (2006). 3rd revised edition. *The Phonemic Analysis of Scottish Gaelic, Based on the Dialect of Applecross, Ross-shire*. Dublin: Dublin Institute for Advanced Studies.

de Vaan, M. (1999). 'Towards an explanation of the Franconian tone accents', *Amsterdamer Beiträge zur älteren Germanistik*, 51, pp. 22-44.

Vanvik, A. (1956). 'Norske tonelag', *Maal og Minne*, pp. 92-102.

# Imperative Commands in Shetland Dialect: Nordic origins?

## Elyse Jamieson

### Introduction

The dialect spoken in the Shetland Islands today is a variety of Scots reported to be heavily influenced by the islands' Nordic history. One feature of the dialect, which may have origins in this history, is the presence of 'verb raising' in imperative commands with overt subjects (OSIs) (e.g. Jonas 2002, Melchers 2010).

1. <u>*Tak*</u>   <u>*du*</u>   *dy*   *time.*

   Take   you   your   time.

   'You **take** your time.' (Jamieson 1998:10)

Verb raising in OSIs is characterised by the verb appearing before the subject, as seen in example 1. This contrasts with present-day Standard English, where the subject precedes the verb (see gloss of example 1).

At first glance, example 1 may seem like an instance of a conservative variety that has retained the imperative word order found in older varieties of English and Scots (example 2).

2. *Lord,*  ***help***  þou *me.*

   Lord,  help  you me .

   'Lord, help me.' (PPCME (Kroch and Taylor 2000, CMEARLPS, 83.6343 c.1350, my translation)

However, it is also extremely similar to OSIs in present-day Scandinavian languages (example 3).

3. *Komdu!*
   Come-you!
   'You come!' (Icelandic, cf. Nordström 2010:234)

Following the data presented in Jamieson (2015), this paper will consider verb raising in OSIs in Shetland dialect in terms of the two input varieties to the dialect – Scots, and Norn, the West Norse language spoken in Shetland until around the eighteenth century – in order to address the origins of the feature. By investigating the relationship between the syntax of imperatives and the syntax of questions and negative declaratives, I will conclude that although verb raising in OSIs was a feature of older varieties of English and Scots, it was contact between Scots and Norn that enabled Shetland dialect to retain verb raising to the present day.

However, I will then look at the ongoing loss of acceptability of these constructions in the dialect: a phenomenon sped up by increased contact with other varieties of Scots and English, shifting Shetland dialect further from its Nordic roots.

## Shetland Dialect: History And Contact Patterns

The Shetland Islands are the most northerly part of the United Kingdom, over 200 miles from Aberdeen, on the mainland of Scotland, and only twenty miles further from Bergen, on the west coast of Norway.

Although the Shetland Islands are part of the UK today, this was not always the case. The islands were settled by a Scandinavian population around 800CE, and remained under Norwegian rule until 1469. During the centuries of Scandinavian settlement, a West Norse language known as 'Norn' was spoken in Shetland. Norn was part of the 'West Norse dialect continuum', a family of languages spanning from the west of Norway through Shetland and Orkney, the Faroe Islands, Iceland and Greenland (McColl Millar 2008: 240). Unfortunately, little evidence of

Norn remains today: see Barnes (1998) for a comprehensive overview.

When Scotland was gifted the Shetland Islands in 1469, Scots became the official language, and by 1600 as much as one third of the islands' population consisted of migrants from mainland Scotland (Knooihuizen 2009: 484). Despite this linguistic pressure, use of Norn continued. There is much debate about when Norn finally died out. General consensus holds that it continued to be used in some capacity until the early eighteenth century (e.g. Barnes 2010, Knooihuizen 2005). However, there are examples of Norn and reports of older speakers in rural areas who 'spoke Norn' until the middle of the nineteenth century (see Wiggen 2002, Rendboe 1984). There was thus considerable language contact between Norn and Scots over a period of at least 250-300 years.

McColl Millar (2008) presents the most detailed study of this contact to date, demonstrating how present-day Shetland dialect was formed in the early nineteenth century as part of a 'koinéisation' process. By this process – over generations – speakers establish a mutually intelligible variety in a situation where there is language contact. Features common to both varieties are likely to be retained, while features salient in only one of the dialects (especially the less prestigious variety) are likely to be lost (Trudgill 1986). So, although the dialect spoken in the isles today is very much a variety of Scots, with a typically 'Northern' Scots vowel system (McColl Millar 2007) and a number of broad Scots lexical items, the dialect also contains a number of particularly 'divergent' features. Language contact is often cited as the cause of these.

One such variant is the *be*-perfect, where dialect speakers produce perfective sentences with *be* rather than standard English *have*. Potential Norn contact sources for this feature are explored in Pavlenko (1997). Phonologically, TH-stopping is one of Shetland dialect's marked features, with speakers producing /d/ and /t/ in place of word-initial /ð/ and /θ/ respectively (see Knooihuizen 2009 for more information on the dialect's phonetics and phonology). These features are unlikely to be Scots in origin. However, whether they descend from Norn or are entirely independent developments is up for discussion.

Other features of the dialect have more opaque origins. For example, Shetland dialect maintains a distinction between second person informal/singular pronoun *du* and formal/plural pronoun *you*. This matches the distinction found in older forms of Scots and standard English, where *thou* was used for a singular addressee, and *you* was the plural and polite form. This distinction was lost by the early eighteenth century in Standard English (Lass 2000: 153), although reported as productive until at least the end of the nineteenth century in Paisley Scots (Beal 1997: 346). This could thus be an instance where Shetland dialect has retained the conservative Scots feature.

However, the West Norse languages also exhibit a singular/plural distinction in second person pronouns, e.g. Icelandic nominative singular *þú* and plural *þið*. This was also the case in Norn (Barnes 1998). Both input varieties thus had the second person pronominal distinction, and it is therefore difficult to posit a singular source for the feature in Shetland dialect. An analysis incorporating influence from both input varieties seems preferable, in line with the assumptions about language contact and new-dialect formation made in McColl Millar (2008).

Having established a general overview of the development of features in Shetland dialect, we turn to the feature in question: OSIs.

## Overt-Subject Imperative Verb Raising in Present-Day Shetland Dialect

Verb raising in OSIs is extremely common in Shetland dialect literature

4. ***Tell you** me dis,*  *is da sun haet*  *or caald?*
 Tell you me this,  is the sun hot  or cold?
 'You **tell** me this: is the sun hot or cold'
 (Williamson 1990:10)

5. ***Smile du.***
 'You **smile**.' (Hakki 1998:12)

101

6. **_Come du_, _Jess._**
'You **come**, Jess.' (Thompson 1995:15)

As part of my thesis (Jamieson 2015), I set out to establish the acceptability of this type of construction – and its Standard English counterpart with subject-verb word order – for present-day dialect speakers. Using an adapted version of the 'interview method' (Thoms 2014, Barbiers and Bennis 2007, Cornips and Poletto 2005), 24 speakers were asked to rate a variety of examples on a scale from 1 ('totally

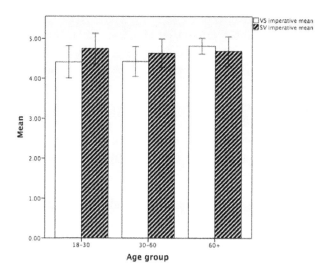

**Fig. 1**: Mean acceptability ratings for verb raised (VS) overt-subject imperatives ('go you') and Standard English subject-verb order (SV) imperatives ('you go'), by age group

ridiculous, never used in Shetland dialect') to 5 ('perfectly acceptable, I say it myself, I hear it around the community'). Mean acceptability ratings are presented in Figure 1.

Running a repeated measures ANOVA test showed that, overall, both word orders are equally acceptable for speakers. However, it also showed that this was dependent on the age of the speaker. While both word orders were shown to be equally acceptable in the 30-60 and 60+ groups, speakers aged 18-30 gave a significantly higher rating to the standard English order than the traditional dialect order. Furthermore, the mean acceptability rating for the verb raised imperatives given by the 18-30 group was significantly lower than that given by the 60+ group, providing further evidence of declining in acceptability across the generations. (For detailed statistics, see Jamieson 2015.)

The remainder of this paper will address two main questions. Firstly, why has verb raising in OSIs persisted in Shetland dialect, despite loss in other varieties of Scots and English? Can this be explained by language contact patterns? Secondly, why is the acceptability of the construction reducing in the present day?

Regarding the first question, it will be necessary to understand verb raising in OSIs in relation to other constructions in the dialect which could also, until recently, undergo verb raising – namely, questions and negative declaratives. This in turn will make connections to the morphology of the dialect. Both of these factors build a syntactic analysis which links the continued presence of verb raising in the dialect to the contact that took place between Scots and Norn. We will return to the second question in the final section of this chapter.

## Verb Raising and Contact in Shetland Dialect

As I have shown, verb raising in OSIs is acceptable at least for older speakers of present-day Shetland dialect. However, verb raising, with the verb appearing in a higher position in the clause, was until recently accepted in other constructions in Shetland dialect: negative declaratives (example 7) and questions (examples 8 and 9). We can identify that verb raising has occurred in example 7 as the verb is above the negative marker (*no*); in examples 8 and 9, the location of verb above the subject signifies verb raising.

> 7. *I **ken**no*      *what tae*      *gie*      *da kye.*
>    I know-not      what to      give      the cows.
>    'I don't know what to give the cows.' (Laurenson 1991: 36)

8. *Ever **saa***     *<u>you</u> da*     *laek?*
   Ever saw     you the     like?
   'Did you ever see the like?' (Johnson 1996:6)

9. *So whit*     ***<u>tinks</u> <u>du</u>,***     *sweet Mairi?*
   So what     think you,     sweet Mairi?
   'What do you think, sweet Mairi?' (Tulloch 1993: 37)

We will call the type of construction in example 7 'V-to-I' and that in examples 8 and 9 'V-to-C'. These labels describe the position of the verb in the clause – for more information see Jamieson (2015).

Both V-to-I (example 10) and V-to-C are acceptable in present-day Icelandic. In example 10, V-to-I is visible because the verb (*keypti*) is above the negative marker (*ekki*).

10. *... að*    *hann*    ***keypti***    *ekki*    *bókina*
    *... that*    *he*    *bought*    *not*    *the-book*
    '... that he did not buy the book'
    (Icelandic, cf. Bobaljik 2002: 130)

Both were also acceptable in Faroese, but following the recent loss of V-to-I (Heycock et al. 2012), Faroese now patterns with the mainland Scandinavian languages in permitting only V-to-C as part of a general verb second (V2) word order – where the verb is placed second in any main clause.

Neither V-to-I nor V-to-C are acceptable in present-day Standard English – however, V-to-C was the word order in questions until the Early Modern English period (c. 1450). This was almost entirely replaced by the *do*-support we see in the present day by 1700 (Kroch 1989:16). V-to-I was also available to speakers during the late Middle English and Early Modern English periods, but it was rapidly heading towards loss during that time (see Kroch 1989).

These losses were, in part, the result of contact. The northern dialects of English during this time were stable V2 varieties, influenced by the Scandinavian population who had settled there (Kroch and

Taylor 1997). However, in the southern dialects of English, loss of morphological case distinctions meant that a strict subject-verb-object (SVO) order was a better fit to the language than V2[1] and thus SVO soon took over. Contact between northern V2 and southern SVO can be seen to be the cause of the overall loss of verb raising in English (Kroch and Taylor 1997, Yang 2000).

How did this contact affect Scots, and thus Shetland dialect? Jonas (2002: 263) demonstrates that the Early Scots introduced to Shetland in the fifteenth century had lost general V2, but retained verb raising in V-to-I, V-to-C and OSI contexts: it was a variety in the midst of the contact-induced re-analysis process. On the mainland, contact continued with the prestigious SVO of the south; on the other hand, Early Scots in Shetland came in contact with Norn.

The scarce evidence of Norn that we have, combined with general knowledge of the West Norse dialect continuum, suggests that Norn was a V2 language with V-to-I – like present-day Icelandic (Jonas 2002: 262). Therefore, the language Early Scots came into contact with

| | V2 | V-to-C | V-to-I | OSI verb raising |
|---|---|---|---|---|
| Early Scots | X | ✓ | ✓ | ✓ |
| Norn | ✓ | ✓ | ✓ | ✓ |
| **Present-day Shetland dialect** | **X** | ? – possibly still used by older speakers (Jamieson 2015) | **X** – but attested until late 20th century (Jonas 2002) | ✓/? |
| Present-day English | X | X | X | X |

**Table 1**: Verb raising in Early Scots, Norn, present-day Shetland dialect and present-day English

in Shetland was very different to the SVO that influenced the loss of V-to-C and V-to-I in English and mainland Scots. In fact, in terms of word order, Early Scots was rather more similar to Norn than it was to the southern English of the time.

Having outlined the relevant features of the historical contact process,

I will now posit a syntactic analysis for the one-time retention of V-to-I and V-to-C in Shetland dialect. I will then provide an explanation for the ongoing acceptability of verb raising in imperatives, before moving on to consider the reduction in acceptability in the final section.

## A Syntactic Explanation

### V-to-I

As we have noted, Icelandic is the only present-day Scandinavian language that retains V-to-I. This is frequently analysed as being due to 'rich morphological agreement' (Bobaljik and Thráinsson 1998). In effect, the 'Rich Agreement Hypothesis' (RAH) (e.g. Rohrbacher 1999) states that because Icelandic has a certain number of morphological verb endings corresponding to different combinations of [speaker], [participant] and [plural] features of the subjects (Koeneman and Zeijlstra 2014), it is able to produce this type of construction. Rich agreement also permits constructions known as 'transitive expletives', where an expletive subject (*there*) appears alongside the subject and object of a transitive verb (example 11).

> 11. *Það   hefur   einhver köttur   étið     mýsnar*
>      there  has     some    cat      eaten    mice-the
>      'Some cat has eaten the mice.' (Icelandic, cf. Bobaljik and Thráinsson 1998: 56)

Under the RAH, languages without rich agreement should not exhibit V-to-I or transitive expletive constructions. This hypothesis is borne out for the mainland Scandinavian languages.

Turning back to Shetland, Jonas (2002) discusses V-to-I in Shetland dialect, and concludes that it does not meet the RAH criteria. Instead, she suggests that the availability of verb raising in constructions like questions and imperatives permits some residual V-to-I in the dialect.

However, there are reasons to reject this analysis. Firstly, as we have discussed, the mainland Scandinavian languages robustly retain verb raising in questions and imperatives, with no evidence of V-to-I. If V-to-I were a likely residual effect of such verb raising, we would expect it in these varieties too.

Secondly, Shetland dialect can be argued to have the requisite 'richness' of morphological agreement for the RAH (Table 2). The extra 'richness' which is not afforded to standard English comes from second person singular *du*, and the Northern Subject Rule (NSR), in which non-pronominal third person plural subjects take *–s* verb endings (*the birds sings*) rather than the standard –Ø ending (Ihalainen 1994).

| 1st sg. | *I get* | –Ø | [+ speaker] | [+ participant] | [– plural] |
|---|---|---|---|---|---|
| 1st pl. | *we get* | –Ø | [+ speaker] | [+ participant] | [+ plural] |
| 2nd sg. | *du gets* | –s | [– speaker] | [+ participant] | [– plural] |
| 2nd pl. | *you get* | –Ø | [– speaker] | [+ participant] | [+ plural] |
| 3rd sg. | *he/she/it gets* | –s | [– speaker] | [– participant] | [– plural] |
| 3rd pl. | *they get* <br> *pl. NP get(s)* | –Ø / –s | [– speaker] | [– participant] | [+ plural] |

**Table 2**: Agreement morphology in Shetland dialect

This means that in order to account for the morphological agreement system in Shetland dialect, all three relevant features must be invoked:

| | |
|---|---|
| *Subject is **singular**, and not the **speaker**:* | –s |
| *Subject is singular, and not a **participant** in the exchange:* | –Ø / –s |
| *Elsewhere:* | –Ø |

It is important to note that the NSR is part of many other varieties of present-day English and Scots (Pietsch 2005); this alone is not enough to satisfy the RAH, only requiring [participant] and [plural] features. Similarly, the second person singular/plural distinction alone would not be enough, requiring only [speaker] and [plural] features. It is the combination of both which constitutes rich agreement.

This argument is strengthened by the presence of transitive expletive constructions in Shetland dialect (example 12).

12. *Dey ir*      *a lok o*      *fok*      *eaten da cakes.*
     There are      a lot of      folk      eaten the cakes.
     'A lot of people have eaten the cakes.'

It seems, therefore, like Shetland dialect meets the criteria for an RAH analysis of V-to-I verb raising – as Norn did, and as present-day Icelandic does. However, it is worth noting that although there are links to be made here, rich agreement morphology was also a part of older Scots varieties (Bernstein and Zanuttini 2012). I am not arguing, therefore, that rich agreement in Shetland dialect is 'Nordic'. Rather, the suggestion is that Scots' contact with Norn during the new-dialect formation process meant the features required for rich agreement were in the majority and were thus strongly represented in the development of the variety established from the language contact. This led to continued acceptability of V-to-I in Shetland dialect, while it was lost in other varieties of Scots and English that also lost rich agreement morphology.

## V-to-C and OSI verb raising

Moving on to consider verb raising in questions and imperatives, these phenomena are explained straightforwardly in Scandinavian varieties by their V2 word order. However, V2 was lost in Scots many centuries ago – before Scots became the official language in Shetland. Why, therefore, has verb raising in questions and imperatives continued to be available in Shetland dialect for so long?

To explain this, we need to look at clause structure. In order for a verb to appear as it does in V-to-I constructions (e.g. example 7), the verb must first be able to move out of the position in which is it originally generated. To illustrate, in example 7, main verb *know* appears before the negative marker – having 'raised' out of its base generated position. In the English gloss, the verb has remained in-situ.

In order for a verb to be able to 'raise', there must be some independent feature of the morphology that necessitates it (Roberts and Roussou 2003). I posit that the rich agreement morphology that permitted V-to-I was what was required to 'free' the verb from its base generated position in Shetland dialect – and thus make it technically available for *any* movement to a higher position in the clause.

However, varieties established through new-dialect formation tend to adopt majority features. Therefore, as verb raising was part of both input varieties in questions and imperatives, this was where raising was retained – with general SVO word order prevailing elsewhere.

## Loss of Verb Raising

Given the above syntactic analysis, why are we seeing a reduction in the acceptability of verb raising in imperatives (Fig. 1)?

Once again, contact is crucial to this explanation – but this time, the contact is between present-day Shetland dialect and other varieties of Scots and English. Dialect levelling, where the most salient features of a dialect are lost (Trudgill 1986), is happening rapidly in Shetland – a place that was, even until the 1990s, extremely isolated. It appears that in as little as a generation, speakers have largely shifted from being 'bidialectal' in Shetland dialect and a form of Scottish Standard English (SSE) to being purely speakers of an SSE variety (Smith and Durham 2011, 2012, Sundkvist 2011) – a consequence of improved technological and transportation links in the last twenty-five years.

As part of this levelling process, the morphological agreement which provided the trigger for V-to-I, and, by proxy, verb raising in questions and imperatives, is weakening. The singular second person pronoun *du* is being reanalysed: *du* now indicates 'Shetlandness' (Thomson 2014), a social rather than a grammatical distinction. In Melchers (1985), high school students reported using *du* with teachers (previously referred to only with formal *you*), as long as they were Shetlanders, while an older speaker reported in Jamieson (2015) bemoans the fact that younger speakers are 'mixing up' these features, and using *du* in the 'wrong' situations. Importantly for the analysis above, Durham (2013: 126) reports that in her data there were 'occasional instances of *du* used without the expected morphological inflection' – e.g. without the verbal –s ending.[2]

Re-analysis of the second person singular pronoun, moving away from a grammatical distinction towards a social one, reduces the 'richness' of agreement morphology as defined by Koeneman and Zeijlstra (2014). Loss of verb raising is thus predicted as a result.

Indeed, there is reduced acceptability of verb raising in the dialect. Jonas (2002) reports V-to-I as 'residual', while in Jamieson (2014) V-to-I was rated as near 'unacceptable' by dialect speakers. V-to-C in questions was rated significantly lower than SVO questions by all age groups in Jamieson (2015). This suggests these constructions are nearing complete loss.

Imperative word order is levelling too (Fig. 1) – moving away from verb raising, towards SVO. This can be explained by a combination of factors. Firstly, the loss of the grammatical trigger for the base verb movement, as discussed above; secondly, contact with other varieties of Scots and English. While the loss of the syntactic trigger can be seen to be the underlying cause of the change, the speed at which this change is taking place in the present day is almost certainly influenced by language contact. The more dialect speakers come into contact with SVO OSIs, the more they 'accommodate' towards this standard, and produce more SVO in place of verb raising. The effect of this accommodation is reflected in the word orders acquired by younger speakers – hence the reduction in acceptability.

## Conclusions

The continued acceptability of verb raising in imperatives in present-day Shetland dialect can be seen to be a result of contact between Scots and Norn during the dialect's formation. Certainly, we cannot argue this is a 'Nordic' feature of the dialect. However, the fact that verb raising in negative declaratives, questions and imperatives was part of both varieties during the new-dialect formation process meant these were more likely to be retained in the resulting dialect. In particular, the existence of the morphological trigger permitting V-to-I enabled verb raising to the higher clause positions exhibited by verbs in questions and imperatives, as it provided necessary evidence for the base movement. This allowed Shetland dialect to establish verb raising in the constructions which permitted it in both of the input varieties to the dialect, despite a general SVO word order.

However, reduction in acceptability of verb raising is ongoing. In fact, imperatives are the last of the three construction types to move towards 'unacceptable' judgment ratings from speakers. This is further evidence of the shift towards SSE in Shetland, reported by Smith and Durham (2011, 2012) and Sundkvist (2011).

Just as it was during the formation of the dialect, language contact is central to the changes taking place now. Firstly, contact has led to the re-analysis of second person singular pronoun *du*, reducing the richness of morphological agreement in the dialect. This has weakened the trigger for movement out of the verb phrase. While I posited that the loss of the morphological trigger is the underlying reason for loss of verb raising in the three constructions, I also suggested that the reason this is happening now – at such a rapid pace – is due to increased contact between Shetland dialect and other varieties of Scots and English.

I therefore conclude that while verb raising in Shetland dialect can be seen to be a result of contact between Scots and Norn, its loss is further evidence of Shetland dialect moving away from its Nordic history, towards an SSE future.

## Endnotes

[1] When languages do not distinguish roles (e.g. subject, object) by case marking (e.g. accusative, dative), they are more likely to have strict word order in order to make the roles clear (Sapir 1921).

[2] Though the re-analysis of the second person pronoun distinction is enough to affect the 'richness' of the dialect's agreement, it is worth nothing that Durham (2013) also reports weakening of the NSR among younger speakers.

## References

Barbiers, S. and Bennis, H. (2007). 'The Syntactic Atlas of the Dutch Dialects: A discussion of choices in the SAND project', *Nordlyd*, 34, pp. 53-72.

Barnes, M. (1998). *The Norn Language of Orkney and Shetland*. Lerwick: The Shetland Times.

Barnes, M. (2010). 'The Study of Norn' in McColl Millar, R. (ed.), *Northern Lights, Northern Words. Selected Papers from the FRLSU Conference, Kirkwall 2009*. Aberdeen: Forum for Research on the Languages of Scotland and Ireland, pp. 26-47.

Beal, J. (1997). 'Syntax and Morphology' in Jones, C. (ed.), *The Edinburgh History of the Scots Language*. Edinburgh: Edinburgh University Press, pp. 335-377.

Bernstein, J. and Zanuttini, R. (2012). 'A diachronic shift in the expression of person' in Galves, C., Cyrino, S., Lopes, R., Sandalo, F. and Avelar, J. (eds.), *Parameter Theory and Linguistic Change*. Oxford: Oxford University Press, pp. 157-175.

Bobaljik, J. (2002). 'Realizing Germanic inflection: Why morphology does not drive syntax', *Journal of Comparative Germanic Linguistics*, 6, pp. 129-167.

Bobaljik, J. and Thráinsson, H. (1998). 'Two heads aren't always better than one', *Syntax*, 1, pp. 37-71.

Cornips, L. and Poletto, C. (2005). 'On standardizing syntactic elicitation techniques', *Lingua*, 115(7), pp. 939-957.

Durham, M. (2013). 'Was/were alternation in Shetland English', *World Englishes*, 32(1), pp. 108-128.

Ihalainen, O. (1994). 'The dialects of England since 1776' in Burchfield, R. (ed.), *The Cambridge History of the English Language, Vol. 5: English in Britain and Overseas: Origin and Development*. Cambridge: Cambridge University Press, pp. 197-270.

Hakki (1998). 'King of the Dogs', *The New Shetlander*, Hairst 1998, p. 12.

Heycock, C., Sorace, A., Hansen, Z., Vikner, S. and Wilson, F. (2012). 'Detecting the late stage of syntactic change: the loss of V-to-T in Faroese', *Language,* 88(3), pp. 558-600.

Jamieson, E. (2014). *Aspects of verb raising in the Shetland dialect of Scots: acceptability and use.* Undergraduate dissertation. University of Edinburgh.

Jamieson, E. (2015). *An investigation of verb raising in the Shetland dialect of Scots.* MSc by Research. University of Edinburgh.

Jamieson, R. A. (1998). 'The last black hoose', *The New Shetlander,* Voar 1998, p. 10.

Johnson, L. (1996). 'Unsaesonal', *The New Shetlander,* Voar 1996, p. 6.

Jonas, D. (2002). 'Residual V-to-I' in Lightfoot, D. (ed.), *Syntactic Effects of Morphological Change* Oxford: Oxford University Press, pp. 251-270.

Knooihuizen, R. (2005). 'The Norn-to-Scots language shift: another look at socio-historical evidence', *Northern Studies,* 39, pp. 105-117.

Knooihuizen, R. (2009). 'Shetland Scots as a new dialect: phonetic and phonological considerations', *English Language and Linguistics,* 13(3), pp. 483-501.

Koeneman, O. and Zeijlstra, H. (2014). 'The Rich Agreement Hypothesis rehabilitated', *Linguistic Inquiry,* 45(4), pp. 571-615.

Kroch, A. (1989). 'Reflexes of grammar in patterns of language change', *Language Change,* 1, pp. 199-244.

Kroch, A. and Taylor, A. (1997). 'Verb movement in Old and Middle English: Dialect variation and language contact' in van Kemenade, A. and Vincent, N. *Parameters of Morphosyntactic Change.* Cambridge: Cambridge University Press, pp. 297-325.

Kroch, A. and Taylor, A. (2000). Penn-Helsinki Parsed Corpus of Middle English, 2nd edition http://www.ling.upenn.edu/hist-corpora/PPCME2-RELEASE-3/index.html (1.2 million words).

Lass, R. (2000). 'Phonology and Morphology' in Lass, R. (ed.), *The Cambridge*

*History of the English Language vol. III: 1476-1776.* Cambridge: Cambridge University Press, pp. 56-186.

Laurenson, T. (1991). 'Nearly Voar', *The New Shetlander*, Voar 1991, p. 36.

McColl Millar, R. (2007). *Northern and Insular Scots.* Edinburgh: Edinburgh University Press.

McColl Millar, R. (2008). 'The origins and development of Shetland dialect in light of dialect contact theories', *English World-Wide*, 29(3), pp. 237-267.

Melchers, G. (1985). '"Knappin", "Proper English", "Modified Scottish": Some language attitudes in the Shetland Islands' in Görlach, M. (ed.), *Focus on: Scotland.* Amsterdam: John Benjamins, pp. 87-100.

Melchers, G. (2010). 'Shetland dialect in a typology of World Englishes', *Scottish Language*, 29, pp. 37-52.

Nordström, J. (2010). *Modality and Subordinators.* Amsterdam: John Benjamins.

Pavlenko, A. (1997). 'The origin of the *be*-perfect with transitives in the Shetland dialect', *Scottish Language*, 16, pp. 88-96.

Pietsch, L. (2005). '"Some do and some doesn't": Verbal concord variation in the north of the British Isles' in Kortmann, B., Herrmann, T., Pietsch, L. and Wagner, S. (eds.), *A Comparative Grammar of English Dialects: Agreement, Gender and Relative Clauses.* Berlin: Mouton de Gruyter, pp. 125-209.

Rendboe, L. (1984). 'How "worn out" or "corrupted" was Shetland Norn in its final stage?', *NOWELE*, 3, pp. 53-88.

Roberts, I. and Roussou, A. (2003). *Syntactic Change: A Minimalist Approach to Grammaticalization.* Cambridge: Cambridge University Press.

Rohrbacher, B. (1999). *Morphology-Driven Syntax: A Theory of V-to-I Raising and Pro-Drop.* Amsterdam/Philadelphia: John Benjamins.

Sapir, E. (1921). *Language, an introduction to the study of speech.* New York: Harcourt, Brace and Co.

Smith, J. and Durham, M. (2011). 'A tipping point in dialect obsolescence? Change across the generations in Lerwick, Shetland', *Journal of Sociolinguistics,* 15(2), pp. 197-225.

Smith, J. and Durham, M. (2012). 'Bidialectalism or dialect death? Explaining generational change in the Shetland Islands, Scotland', *American Speech,* 87(1), pp. 57-88.

Sundkvist, P. (2011). 'The Shetland Islands: globalisation and the changing status of standard English', *English Today,* 27(4), pp. 19-25.

Thompson, L. (1995). 'Merran Goes Back', *The New Shetlander,* Hairst 1995, p. 15.

Thoms, G. (2014). 'Report for "Refining the questionnaire method of judgment data collection: a Buckie pilot study" pilot project', Ms., University of Edinburgh.

Thomson, A. (2014). 'Insular languages, global ideologies: The ideologies of a ~~British, Scottish,~~ Northern Island community', *Scottish Language,* 31-32, pp. 128-160.

Trudgill, P. (1986). *Dialects in Contact.* Oxford: Blackwell.

Tulloch, D. (1993). 'Mairi', *The New Shetlander,* Voar 1993, p. 37.

Wiggen, G. (2002). *Norns død, især skolens rolle.* Oslo: Det Norske Videnskaps-Akademi.

Williamson, A. (1990). 'Da Huntin Lumbister', *The New Shetlander,* Voar 1990, p. 10.

Yang, C. (2000). 'Internal and external forces in language change', *Language Variation and Change,* 12, pp. 231-250.

# ART AND SOCIETY

# The Battle of Kringen (1612) and Its Impact on Norway's Culture and History

## Jan D. Cox

The Battle of Kringen has a recognised place in Nordic culture as indicated by representations of the event in the fields of art, poetry, theatre, music and dance. One of the most famous depictions is of the landing of Scottish mercenaries on the Norwegian coast a week before the battle, painted in 1876 by Norway's leading Romantic artist, Adolph Tidemand. Previously, in 1848, Tidemand had collaborated with youthful landscape painter Hans Gude to produce that most iconic representation of nineteenth century Norway *Brudeferd i Hardanger* (Bridal Party in Hardanger, Nasjonalmuseet, Oslo). This famous picture showed colourful characters painted by Tidemand crammed into a large, overloaded rowing boat, while Gude contributed an atmospheric landscape, at the rear of which the eye is drawn to an historic stave church above the jetty. The whole image was a Romantic construct and an illustration of Norway's history, scenery and people; to this day it is representative of the growing sense of Norwegian nationhood in the mid-nineteenth century. Ironically, Tidemand based himself in Düsseldorf for the majority of his career, making periodic study visits to his homeland. Twenty-eight years after *Bridal Party*, an ailing Tidemand again collaborated with a landscape painter – Morten Müller, a former pupil of both himself and Gude – to produce a Romanticised historical painting of the Scottish mercenaries entitled *Sinclairs landing i Romsdal* (Sinclair's Landing in Romsdal, Fig. 2), completed in April 1876 just four months before Tidemand's death (Dietrichson 1878: 122). The landing and subsequent battle were episodes in the Kalmar War between Denmark-Norway and Sweden. The war had begun in early 1611, and the death of Charles IX of Sweden in October of that year meant that the Swedish crown – and the war – was inherited by his sixteen-year-old son Gustavus Adolphus, later christened 'The Lion of the North'.

In a letter of November 1611, Gustavus declared to the Scottish soldier and diplomat Sir James Spens that Sweden was 'in need of foreign soldiers [...] wherewith to check the attacks of the enemy' (Michell 1886: 20) and Spens engaged Colonel Andrew Ramsay to organise a Scottish contingent. Like Spens, Ramsay had strong links with James I of England, in that his brother Sir John Ramsay was a favourite of the monarch, and had reputedly saved the King's life in 1600 when the monarch was still James VI of Scotland. Andrew Ramsay went to Scotland and began recruiting troops for the mission. Ramsay was not choosy as to whom he 'enlisted', later proclamations declaring that his men had 'violently pressed and taken many honest men's sons, and [...] carried them to their ships against their will' and that '"honest men's bairns and servants" were held on board as "slaves and captives"' (Michell 1886: 40-41). Additionally, prisoners in Scottish jails were promised their freedom if they were prepared to fight at Sweden's behest.

This must all be viewed against the fact that James I was married to a Danish wife and was the brother-in-law of the Danish King, Christian IV. James took immediate steps to distance himself from the Scottish expedition, but 'good numbers of [the troops] were already embarked before His Majesty heard the news', and the King then declared that he 'doth utterly disavow any acts of theirs (Michell 1886: 36-37). However, there is also the possibility that James turned a blind eye to the activities of his close compatriots, until forced to act when Denmark complained (Cowan 2015). Andrew Ramsay, in turn, had appointed three leaders of the expedition, each commanding around one hundred men. In overall command was another of his brothers, Lt. Col. Alexander Ramsay, who set sail in one vessel from Dundee. Captain George Hay and Captain George Sinclair sailed in another with their men from Wick.

The Scots landed at Romsdal in Norway on 19/20th August 1612, lightly-armed and expecting little resistance from the Norwegians. But it seems likely that the Norwegian populace had been antagonised by the death of their kinsmen earlier in the war (Cowan 2015). After a week's swift march, during which the Norwegians had kept a close eye on them, the Scots had to traverse a narrow pathway at Kringen (Fig. 1) – barely room for a carriole to pass along – with a steep slope on one side and a river on the other (Michell 1886: 60). On 26th August, when the 300 Scots were in formation as a thin, sinuous column, and fully exposed on the path, they were ambushed at both front and back, and at the same time carefully-prepared logs and rocks were rolled onto them from the slopes above.

**Fig. 1**: The narrow pathway at Kringen on which the Scots were attacked on 26 August 1612 is indicated by the arrow (www.otta2000.com)

Captain George Sinclair was one of the first to be killed. Some Scots tried to escape by jumping into the river. Some drowned, and those who made it across were killed as they reached the far bank. Around 170 Scots were killed and 134 taken prisoner. The Norwegian army of around 400 suffered six dead and about twelve injured. The surviving Scots were locked in a barn while the Norwegians drank in celebration. The following morning, the Norwegians decided that they could not spare men at harvest time to guard and accompany the Scots, or find the resources to feed them, so all bar eighteen were massacred. Spared and sent to Denmark were the surviving senior officers: Alexander Ramsay, Henry Bruce, James Moneypenny and James Scott. The remainder of the Scots either agreed to work in the local area or take service in the Danish army (Michell 1886: 53).

In the years that followed, a legend arose that told how brave Norwegian farmers had overcome a far greater force of Scottish soldiers in the battle, triumphing by virtue of their cleverness and cunning. This legend involved a number of strands: when the Scots landed, a crafty local farmer named Peder Klognaes persuaded the Scots that the water was too shallow for their ships, so they initially had to walk an extra fourteen miles, which gave the local people additional warning; the wily Norwegians did not engage the Scots straight away – one man at the rear of the Norwegian forces rode his horse facing backwards in order to make the Scots think that he was coming towards them; the Scots raped and pillaged their way across the country, a justification for the later massacre; a Norwegian girl called Pillar-Guri (or Prillar-Guri) stood as look-out on a highpoint – when the Scots reached a certain spot she blew her ram's horn or lure in order both to distract the Scots and alert the Norwegians; finally, that the 'leader' of the expedition, George Sinclair, was killed by the very first shot, a specially-chosen silver bullet.

An early account of the legendary version was provided by the poet Edvard Storm, himself born in Vågå in the heart of the Gudbrandsdalen valley where the Norwegian forces originated. In 1781 he wrote *Sinklars Visa* (The Ballad of Sinclair); there are nineteen verses in the original Norwegian, and eighteen in the translation that appears in Michell. Storm's verse numbers are appended below:

1. Herr Zinklar drog over salten Hav,
Til Norrig hans Cours monne stande;
Blant Guldbrands Klipper han fant sin Grav,
der vanked så blodig en Pande.

7. Ham fulgte fiorten hundrede Mand
Som alle havde ondt i Sinde.
8. De skiendte og brændte hvor de drog frem,
Al Folket monne de krænke.

12. De Bønder av Vaage, Lessøe og Lom,
Med skarpe Øxer paa Nakke
I Bredebøigd til sammen kom,
Med Skotten vilde de snakke.

15. Det første Skud Hr. Zinklar gialdt,
Han brøled og opgav sin Aande;
Hver Skotte raabte, da Obersten faldt:
Gud frie os af denne Vaande!

18. Ei nogen levende Siel kom hjem,
Som kunde sin Landsmand fortælle,
Hvor farligt det er at besøge dem
Der boe blandt Norriges Fielde. (Storm 1781)

(Herr Sinclair sailed across the sea,
And steered his course to Norway's Strand;
Mid Gudbrand's rocks his grave found he,
There were broken crowns in Sinclair's hand.

And with him fourteen hundred men,
On mischief all that band were bent,
they spared nor young or aged then,
But slew and burnt as on they went.

Peasants of Vaage, Lesje and Lom,

with axes sharp on shoulders set,
To parley with the Scots are come,
and now at Bredebygd are met.

The first shot pierced Herr Sinclair's breast,
He groaned, and forth his spirit gave,
And as he fell, each Scot cried out:
"O God, in this our peril save".

And not a soul of that array,
To Scotland e'er returned to tell
His countrymen of that dark day
And how the sad event befell.) (Michell 1886: 71-74)

Storm's ballad romanticised the event and altered the facts to exaggerate the extent of the Norwegian achievement. It was Sinclair, the leader of the expedition, who was killed by the first Norwegian shot, commanding 1400 – not 300 – men. The Scots were merciless in their pillage of the countryside through which they passed; another verse describes 'the child they killed at mother's breast'. And in the Norwegian language, it is the *bønder*, the landowning peasant-farmers, who achieved this great victory against Scottish soldiers. Finally, in an idealised conclusion, no Scot returns home to tell of their great defeat.

In reality, four surviving Scottish officers did return to their homeland. A memo from James I to Robert Anstruther declared 'As for the prisoners unto us you may say, finding them likewise no otherwise in fault than as abused by [Andrew] Ramsey (sic.). Wee have sent them home to their countrye', adding that for his crimes Ramsay had been 'banished [...] out of all oure dominions; w[hi]ch next unto death, is the highest punishment wee could inflict' (Trowbridge 2015).

Let us analyse Storm's words. Firstly, it suited both sides to proclaim Sinclair as the leader of the expedition. The Norwegians could claim that they killed the Scots commander with their first shot, and the surviving Scottish officers – Ramsay, Bruce, Scott, and Moneypenny – were able to downplay their role when questioned by the murderous

Norwegians and place the blame squarely on the shoulders of the deceased Sinclair. Secondly, the bravery of the Norwegians in obtaining victory was emphasised by a near five-fold increase in the size of the Scots detachment, all of whom were declared to be violent and merciless toward the local population. There is little evidence for this, or indeed time. The Scots were covering about twenty miles a day, as their main priority was to get across Norway and into Sweden as swiftly as possible.

Not only was it the *bønder* who achieved this victory – land-owning farmers who were perceived to be the backbone of the Norwegian nation – but they came from Vågå, Lesja and Lom (modern spellings), villages in the 140-mile long Gudbrandsdalen valley. Because of its inland location, Gudbrandsdalen was seen as a culturally pure part of Norway, untainted by foreign influences; Vågå and Lom were the site of two of Norway's last remaining stave churches, 'tangible signs of Norway's medieval past, its culture and its long history' (Cox 2014: 50).[2] Tidemand – in whose picture *Bridal Party in Hardanger* the stave church was a pure invention – made a study-visit to Gudbrandsdalen, including Lom, in 1843 (Dietrichson 1878: 124), followed in 1846 by his *Bridal Party* co-painter Hans Gude, travelling with fellow-artists August Cappelen and Johan Fredrik Eckersberg. During this same period, the renowned collectors of Norwegian folk-tales Peter Christen Asbjørnsen and Jørgen Moe – Norway's counterparts to the Brothers Grimm – published their collection of traditional stories that they had gathered from rural Norway. Although Asbjørnsen was born in Christiania (Oslo), his father's family came from Otta, the town closest to the site of the Battle of Kringen.

Erik Werenskiold had visited Tidemand in Düsseldorf in 1874, and the senior painter had advised him to continue his studies in Munich, at that time a growing and thriving centre for European art students; Werenskiold duly arrived in the Bavarian capital in December 1875. Later, while on a home visit to Norway in 1878, Asbjørnsen and Moe asked him to illustrate a new edition of their folk-tales. Werenskiold set out for Gudbrandsdalen in order to find settings and characters that reminded him of their stories, and provide inspiration for his subsequent drawings. He was successful in his mission, incorporating the local landowners and peasants in his sketches: 'I have never come across anything that seems more Norwegian to me than Vågå' (Østby 1977: 268). Werenskiold incorporated the door of Vågå stave church into a preliminary drawing he made of a rural burial service entitled *En Bondebegravelse* (1878, Rustic Funeral)[1], and then replaced it with the door of Lom stave church in a more detailed version *En Fattig Begravelse i en Norsk Fjældbygd* (1878, A Poor Burial in a Norwegian Mountain Hamlet), which was published in the magazine *Ude og Hjemme* in Copenhagen in June 1879 (Cox 2014: 43-45). It is notable that Werenskiold removed the stave church entirely from his painted version of 1883-1885 entitled *En Bondebegravelse* (*Peasant Burial*: Nasjonalmuseet, Oslo), because he wished his painting to depict Norway's people as forward-looking modern Europeans, and not as looking back to an historic past.

In the wake of Storm's fanciful ballad, in 1828 the youthful poet and playwright Henrik Wergeland wrote the tragedy *Sinklars Død* (*The Death of Sinclair*). Later in the century, after his early demise, Wergeland became an iconic figure for the Norwegian nationalist movement. Then, in 1833, Andreas Faye referred to the Battle of Kringen in his *Norske Sagn* (*Norwegian Sagas*), mentioning the story of Pillar-Guri, whom he calls Prellegunhild, and that of the man who rode his horse facing backwards (Neverdal 2014). It was Faye's book of sagas which later provided the inspiration for Asbjørnsen and Moe's initial collections of folk stories. Faye was followed by Hans Krag, who was parish priest in Vågå from 1830 to 1842, and during his tenure wrote:

> Furthermore they let a Girl, with the Name Guri, commonly called Pillarguri, who could blow a Stut or Horn well, take up position on a Mountain Peak, Selsjordskampen, on the west Side of Laagen, from where she could clearly see the surrounding landscape and the advancing enemy. When the main body of the Enemy had arrived at a place near the Farmers' agreed Position, she should sound the Horn to attract the Enemy's Attention to where she was, which was in the opposite direction

to that of the Farmers' army, and give an early warning signal to the Farmers, who from their Ambush position could not see the Enemy, about how far they had come. (Krag 1838) In 1860, in preparation for the 250th anniversary of the battle, a large stone monument in the shape of a gravestone was erected at Vik stating 'Here lies Scots Captain Georg Sinklair buried after he was felled at Kringelen 26 August 1612'.

**Fig. 2**: Adolph Tidemand & Morton Müller, *Sinclair's Landing i Romsdal*, 1876, oil on canvas, 178 x 290cm. Nasjonalmuseet, Oslo (public domain).

That the battle continued to occupy the minds of Norwegians is confirmed by Tidemand and Müller's aforementioned picture of 1876, *Sinclairs Landing i Romsdal*[3] (Fig. 2), which purports to show the initial landing of the Scots, in five ships rather than the actual two. In the picture, a man is about to be clubbed over the head by a Scotsman, his daughter is weeping with her head in her hands while her mother implores the Scots to spare her husband. Meanwhile, another Scot is carrying off the family's goods and chattels. In front of them a priest wrestles with a young girl with blonde pigtails, perhaps another daughter of the same family. In the foreground, George Sinclair stands triumphant, his sword aloft, and next to him a piper provides a musical accompaniment to the pillage. Müller's landscape illustrates the majesty of Norway's fjords and mountains, and every Norwegian viewer of the picture would have known that revenge on Sinclair and his 'evil band' was only a few days ahead.

The reason behind this plethora of stories and images is clear.[4] The Scots were on their way to support Sweden, the country which had been granted sovereignty over Norway following the defeat of Denmark in the Napoleonic wars earlier in the nineteenth century. The battle at Kringen was a defeat for Sweden's allies, the Scots, and provided a story that helped inspire the burgeoning independence movement in Norway, which led eventually to separation from Sweden in 1905. Moreover, Kringen was a specifically Norwegian military victory, something that had been in very short supply since the days of the Viking sagas. A recent placard in English at the Norwegian Museum of Cultural History in Oslo went so far as to claim that 'The fate of the Scottish expedition helped boost Norwegian self-esteem and national pride. It formed the basis of the romantic idea of the strong and heroic Norwegian peasant-farmer throughout the eighteenth and nineteenth century' (as observed by the author in the Norwegian Museum of Cultural History, Oslo, September 2011).

In 1897, the Norwegian artist Georg Nilsen Strømdal painted a picture of *Slaget i Kringom* (Battle of Kringen, Fig. 3), which illustrated the remnants of the front of the Scottish column which had been assailed by logs and rocks. Several be-kilted Scots lie dead or dying, a final dispatch being conducted by Norwegian farmers armed with long staves. One of the stricken figures in the foreground wears a distinctive helmet and breastplate that corresponds with that worn by Sinclair in Tidemand and Müller's picture. Today, Strømdal's painting is part of a permanent exhibition at Sinclair's Inn (*Vertshuset Sinclair*), a modern café and motel that advertises the presence of 'George Sinclair's grave (1612) just to the south of the inn'; the exhibition also includes an image of Tidemand and Müller's picture (Vertshuset Sinclair 2015).

**Fig. 3**: Georg Nilsen Strømdal, *Battle of Kringen*, 1897, Oil on canvas. Scottish March Collection, Kvam. By kind permission of Vertshuset Sinclair.

After independence was achieved in 1905, Norway was swift to utilise the 300-year anniversary of the battle in 1912. Norway's new King Haakon VII came to Kringen to unveil a specially-commissioned monument to Pillar-Guri and drew an estimated crowd of 8000 to the remote area. Haakon VII, originally Prince Carl of Denmark, had chosen his name to promote the concept of an historical continuation from the Norwegian King Haakon VI, who had ruled the country over 500 years previously. The monument was topped by an image of Pillar-Guri blowing her lure or horn, and below were carved the words 'Memorial of the Battle of Kringom 26 August 1612'. In a speech to the King and assembled dignitaries, Colonel Henrik Angell, who in that same year wrote a commemorative book about the battle, declared:

> Your Majesty, men and women of Norway! It was 300 years ago today. A tone from the lure was heard from the Pillarguri peak. Then a landslide started up there on Høgkringenaasen. It was only a young girl who blew the lure. It was only a small force of farmers who charged down a hill. But that lure had tones, just like the old battle lure, when it rallied to battle and the farmerhorde advanced as they had always done, with sharp axes in strong hands. It resounded from mountain to mountain, and the echo from village to village and throughout the land of Norway. It has been a long time now since we heard the Norwegian battle lure and seen Norwegian farmers go forward into manly fight; but we had waited a long time for the tones to call us. It was the longing of the Norwegian people. It was therefore something greater which was set in motion by the tone of the lure on the 26th August 1612, than the small avalanche created by the farmers. It was the rebirth of the Norwegian people. (Angell 1912)

It is obvious that very strong claims are once again being made for the importance of the battle and its links to Norway's historical past, and that in 1912 it clearly provided a rallying-call to the newly-reborn Norwegian nation.

In 1998, The Deutsches Historisches Museum in Berlin hosted an exhibition entitled *Myths of Nations: A European Panorama*. Norway's contribution covered five episodes of Norwegian history from Leif Erikson's discovery of America to the founding of the Norwegian National Assembly at Eidsvoll in 1814.[5] The museum chose Strømdal's picture of *The Battle of Kringen* as a suitable overarching image (Deutsches Historisches Museum 1998). After dismissing the battle as 'an episode of little consequence in the Kalmar War' they went on to explain that:

The memory of this victory – and thus of their contribution to the Danish triumph over the Swedes – enhanced the Norwegians' national pride in the nineteenth century. An important part of this tradition is the idealisation of the Norwegian peasants, their courage, their cleverness in fighting and above all their love of freedom. Hand in hand with this image was the glorification of the Norwegian mountains as the home of an intensely freedom-loving, proud and daring people. So the pictures of the event are as much a monument to the mountainous landscape as they are to the battle itself, as depicted for example by Adolph Tidemand and Morten Müller. (Deutsches Historisches Museum 1998)

The ballad known as *Sinklars Visa* is still popular today, not just in Norway where it is a traditional folk standard, but also in the Faroe Islands, where local people have a chain dance that they perform as they sing the ballad unaccompanied (see Anon. 2013, *Hr. Sinclar*). As a present-day Faroese student explains '[Faroese scholars] referred to the ballads as a way to convey and remember historical events, since there wasn't any writing in Faroese. On a side note, my grandfather used to sing this when he pottered around the house!' (Online interview with Annika Christensen, University of Leeds, 11 February 2015). In 2008, the Faroese folk-metal band Tyr recorded a version of *Sinklars Visa* on their album *Land*, with lyrics credited to Edvard Storm, and its subsequent popularity has meant that they have performed it regularly ever since at their live concerts.

In 2012, the 400th anniversary of the battle occurred. *The Scotsman* newspaper ran a story headlined 'Scots invasion of Norway that ended in a "war crime"', and accurately explained that it is 'an event which has become a potent symbol of nationalism in Norway yet has been all but airbrushed from Scottish history' (Garavelli 2012). An organising committee consisting of expat Scots and dignitaries from the Kringen area got together to publicise 'Kringen 2012' as an opportunity to cement the historic links between the two nations, and to emphasise a spirit of peaceful co-operation and understanding. The Scottish delegation that travelled to Norway was led by the twentieth Earl of Caithness, the current head of the Sinclair family. It is interesting that the myth of the pre-eminence of Sinclair rather than Ramsay has been maintained, in line with cultural significance rather than historic fact.

The Battle of Kringen had little military significance when placed alongside the numerous other conflicts in which Scottish mercenaries took part in the seventeenth century. The Scots had no reason to remember an ignominious military defeat which included the death of three hundred Scotsmen. However, for the Norwegians it became symbolic of a growing nationalism and demand for independence in the nineteenth century, and reflected the Norwegian peoples' self-perceived traits of bravery and cunning, personified in the shape of the land-owning farmers, the *bønder*. The battle provided an easily-understood message for the use of poets, painters and playwrights, and its importance has been exaggerated and mythologised until it has become a cultural icon rather than a signifier for the reality of massacre and war. Tidemand, Müller and Strømdal would argue that the job of a painter is not just to record but to evoke a response in the viewer, hence the appropriate collective noun 'a misbelief of artists'.

## Endnotes

[1] The title is as per Østby (1977). *En Bondebegravelse* is more commonly translated as 'Peasant Burial' when referring to Werenskiold's 1883-1885 oil painting of the same title.

[2] See also Cox 2014: 50-62 for a fuller discussion of the Norwegian *bønder* and stave churches.

[3] The picture was commissioned in 1874 by Hans Rasmus Astrup (1831-1898), whose son Ebbe Carsten Morten Astrup (1876-1955) married Cecilie Fearnley (1878-1902), the grand-daughter of the artist Thomas Fearnley (1802-1842).The picture passed to the Norwegian National Gallery in 1908 upon the death of Hans Astrup's widow, Augusta Elisabeth Astrup. Hans Astrup's uncle, Nils Astrup (1778-1835), was the great-grandfather of the painter Nikolai Astrup (1880-1928).

[4] At the time of his death, Tidemand had embarked on another related picture, an uncompleted work depicting Christian IV, who had led Denmark-Norway in the Kalmar War against Sweden (Dietrichson 1878: 122-123).

[5] This latter event is captured in the famous Nationalist painting *Riksforsamlingen*

*på Eidsvoll 1814*, painted in 1885 by Oscar Wergeland (1844-1910). Wergeland was a friend of Erik Werenskiold in Munich, and a relative of Henrik Wergeland (1808-1845) who had written *Sinklars Død* in 1828. Henrik was closely associated with the campaign for Norway to have 17th May as its national day, and Henrik's father Nicolai Wergeland (1780-1848) was present at Eidsvoll in 1814, as depicted in his great-nephew Oscar's painting.

## References

Angell, H. 1912. 'Unveiling of the Kringen Monument', *Aftenposten*, 27 August, quoted by Neverdal, G., trans. Henderson, N. (2014: 2011), 'What Significance did this event have for Norwegian History?' Available at: http://www.kringen1612.no/Hvilken_betydning_fikk_slaget_i_Kringen_i%20Norges_historieENG.htm#Aftenposten_-_august_1912 (Accessed 16 October 2015). Anon. (2013). *Hr. Sinclar (Sinklars vísa)*. Available at: https://www.youtube.com/watch?v=qXmc1P2vLq4 (Accessed: 30 October 2015).

Cowan, P. (2015 [2012]) *Scottish Military Disasters – Book Extract.* Available at: http://scottishmilitarydisasters.com/index.php/titles-sp-26803/26-smd/46-extract (Accessed: 24 October 2015).

Cox, J. D. (2014). *The Impact of Nordic Art in Europe 1878-1889*. PhD thesis. University of Leeds.

Deutsches Historisches Museum (1998). *Myths of Nations – A European Panorama: Norway*. Available at: http://www.dhm.de/archiv/ausstellungen/mythen/english/norweg.html (Accessed: 27 October 2015).

Derry, T.K. (1973). *A History of Modern Norway 1814-1972*. Oxford: Clarendon Press.

Dietrichson, L. (1878). *Adolph Tidemand, hans Liv og hans Vaerker*. Christiania: Chr. Tønsbergs Forlag.

Garavelli, D. (2012). 'Scots invasion of Norway that ended in a "war crime"', *The Scotsman*, 25 August. Available at: http://www.

scotsman.com/lifestyle/scots-invasion-of-norway-that-ended-in-a-war-crime-1-2488018#axzz3qiSODPVn (Accessed: 27 October 2015).

Fjågesund, P. and Symes, R. (2003). *The Northern Utopia: British Perceptions of Norway in the Nineteenth Century*. Amsterdam and New York: Editions Rodopi.

Krag, H. P. S. 1838. *Sagn, samlede i Gudbrandsdalen om slaget ved Kringlen den 26de august 1612, og udgivne i forbindelse med hvad historien beretter om denne tildragelse.* Quoted by Neverdal, G., trans. Henderson, N. (2014: 2011), 'The Battle at Kringen. 26th. August 1612', Available at http://www.kringen1612.no/Slaget_i_Kringom_1612ENG.htm (Accessed: 16 October 2015).

Laird, I. (2012). *Norway: The Battle of Kringen, 26th August 1612.* Available at: http://www.laird.org.uk/Norway/Kringen.htm#About this Page (Accessed: 25 October 2015).

Michell, T. (1886). *History of the Scottish Expedition to Norway in 1612*. Edinburgh: T. Nelson.

Neverdal, G. trans. Henderson, N. (2014 [2011]) 'The Scottish March of 1612' and the Battle of Kringen. Available at: http://www.kringen1612.no/indexENG.htm#Some_sources (Accessed: 16 October 2015).

Storm, E. (1781). *Zinklars Vise.* Available at: https://no.wikisource.org/wiki/Zinklars_vise (Accessed: 3 December 2015)

Trowbridge, B. (2015). *The Battle of Kringen, 1612: uncovering an obscure Norwegian conflict.* Available at: http://blog.nationalarchives.gov.uk/blog/the-battle-of-kringen-26th-august-1612-what-the-records-at-the-national-archives-have-to-say-about-this-obscure-norwegian-battle/ (Accessed: 27 October 2015).

University Of St. Andrews – Institute Of Scottish Historical Research (2015). *The Scotland, Scandinavia and Northern European Biographical Database.* Available at: http://www.st-andrews.ac.uk/

history/ssne/index.php (Accessed: 14 October 2015).

Vertshuset Sinclair (2015). *The Scottish Expedition 1612.* Available at: http://www.vertshuset-sinclair.no/the-scottish-expedition.html (Accessed: 1 November 2015).

Østby, L. (1977). *Erik Werenskiold.* Oslo: Dreyer.

# 'I'm Glad My Life's Work Has Not Been in Vain':[1] Weaving Women in Kristiania during the *fin-de-siècle*

## Kitty Corbet Milward

Harriet Backer's painting *En Vevstue* (1884, A Weaving House) intrudes on a woman engaged in the act of creation: a figure is shown in profile, working at an upright loom, her slippers removed and the door firmly shut, thus allowing concentrated activity in a closed, cluttered interior. This is an intimate scene of Norwegian domesticity, made public by the privileged access and creative effort of another woman. It is possible that Backer's painting was finished during a summer trip to Norway's South Western district of Jæren where she was accompanied by the artist, Kitty Kielland (Lange 1996: 32). While Kielland would turn to the many moods of Norwegian nature as a subject from which to build a distinct mode of art, from around 1884 Backer's interest would lie in the domestic activities of her own gender (Lange 2013: 84-85). *En Vevstue* became one of several scenes by Backer that presented women in the confines of rural or urban lodgings, quietly weaving, sewing or embroidering. Inspired by *En Vevstue*, this article explores the visual representation of weaving women in and around Kristiania by looking at paintings as well as tapestries produced at the end of the nineteenth century by artists such as Backer, and the tapestry artist Frida Hansen. In doing so, it analyses the changing roles that the painted and woven image played in the construction of a consolidated nation in possession of a burgeoning modern industry, as well as an identifiably Norwegian culture. If mass produced and bespoke woven goods are to be understood as embedded with information concerning methods of production, circulation and consumption, we ask, to what extent might we challenge the visual relationship between labourer, artist, machine and nation? In short, how did engaging in textile work change women's lives in the modern Norway, and how did women weavers contribute to the economy and culture of a modern and independent nation?

Completed during an epoch of escalating nationalism, Backer's *En Vevstue* could be understood as a visual articulation of traditional pursuits taking place within the Norwegian household. The home was regarded as Norway's core productive unit as much as the domain of woman, thus, in 1884 when the art critic Andreas Aubert encouraged Norwegian painters to employ the interior as a subject as readily as they had the natural landscape (Lange 1995: 118), Backer was well placed to meet such a demand. By showing women engaged in 'feminine' pursuits, such as weaving, her career earned her recognition inside Norway as well as beyond. Backer's productivity could be analysed in terms of gender, but in a large, sparsely populated, Lutheran country ruled by Sweden, the contribution of female as well as male artists could be understood as participating in the blossoming of a modern and identifiably Norwegian cultural identity.[2]

A notoriously slow worker herself, it is possible that Backer perceived the methodical discipline of weaving as a visual metaphor for her own approach to painting. That we see a woman at the loom depicted by a jobbing painter working during the founding year of the *Norsk Kvinnesaksforening* (Norwegian Association for Women's Rights, NKF) deserves further comment. Kitty Kielland was amongst the 171 campaigning founders of the NKF, and her friendship with Backer would have led to exchanges concerning the efforts of the NKF to advance women's economic and legislative status (Lange 2013: 84). The 1880s was a decade of intense socio-political realignment, with growing numbers of Norwegian men and women in search of waged work using the extension of the railways to emigrate from rural provinces to cities such as Kristiania (modern day Oslo), or to travel by ship to America.[3] As it has been found, the jobs that were secured by young, single women were often connected to textiles. The lower classes might operate machines in textile factories to the east; whilst those of a more bourgeois background might become artisan weavers or practice handicrafts in suburbs to the west.[4] Divided as the workers were by way of background, age and employer, it would seem that weaving could be regarded as a unifying activity, as well as a skill that enabled a spectrum of women to advance their professional and political objectives. Between the date that Backer's painting was completed and the year 1905, when Norway achieved independence from Sweden, the loom could be regarded as a means for women to break out of the confines of domesticity into the public arena.

The industrial revolution came late to Norway, but when it arrived, it came hard and fast to a small, peripheral country seeking a status of her own.[5] In 1861, the textile entrepreneur and owner of the Hjula Weavery, Halvor Schou, underlined Norway's desire to build herself into a nation-state that was not only independent, but also technologically advanced. A letter was sent by Schou to the Scottish engineer, Sir William Fairbairn, in which Schou addressed the space allotted to Norwegian industry at London's Industrial Exhibition of 1862 (Bruland 1989: 26). Sweden and Norway were separate, Schou carefully explained, with distinct governments, finances and legislations. 'Neither of the two nations wish to have their industrial production mixed together' (Hjula Papers, Kopibok, 1861-1863, 28 June 1861).

By the early 1890s, Schou's Hjula Weavery had become one of Norway's largest textile factories with close to 800 employees divided between production facilities in Kristinia, Lillestrøm and Fredrikstad. By 1895, the Norwegian textile industry was providing jobs for as many as 8,805 employees (Konon and Fischer 1900: 395). A large proportion of these were unmarried women, whose numbers grew steadily as other firms, such as Nydalens Spinnery, were built along the Akerselva River as the quality, scale and transfer of equipment improved and as foreign imports of raw cotton increased. In an effort to promote Norway as a country equipped with a mechanised textile industry worthy of foreign, particularly British, investment, factory portraits were made and sometimes commissioned by artists such as Carl Emil Baagøe and the eminent painter, Frits Thaulow.[6] In addition, photographs of the workers at Hjula and Nydalens were taken by documentary photographers such as Anders Beer Wilse, one of the leading documentary photographers of the day, and Per Adolf Thorén. Photographs usually showed workers at their best with clean clothes, hands and faces and standing in neat lines wearing their identical uniforms outside the factory gates. Painters and photographers were tasked with promoting Norwegian industry abroad and at home, thus they would rarely have given access to the factory floor during working hours, where they might have observed the frenetic and filthy environment endured by female employees.

One exception was the painter Wilhelm Peters. After returning from Skagen in Denmark, where he had become imbued with ideas about French Naturalism and the notion that art, like the literature of 'det moderne gjennombrudd' (the Modern Breakthrough), should deal with contemporary social issues, Peters set about detailing the hard graft suffered by female and male members of Norway's industrial workforce.[7] Of particular interest to this article are two pictures finished in 1886 and 1888, both of which depict lower-class women operating mechanical looms inside the walls of the Hjula Weavery. At the time, Peters was Head Teacher at the Statens håndverks og kunstindustriskole (Norwegian National Academy of Craft and Art Industry), a role that perhaps bolstered his aim to critically represent the degenerative effects of modern manufacture on social wellbeing. Peters' first picture was finished in pastel and presents a cage of whirring cogs and protruding levers in which indistinct, drably-dressed female labourers stand back-to-back, hunched over monstrous looms. The suffocating atmosphere of noise, dust and smells that make Peter's painting so arresting contrasts drastically with the chaotic though quiet and soft homeliness presented in *En Vevstue*. Peters' picture is loud and forbidding, with electric light exposing a dense, ugly space littered with spun fibres and women who function as systematically as the contraptions that they drive. As they push and pull the levers, their responsibility is to churn out reams of nondescript cloth from morning until night. Peters' first representation of the Hjula staff was probably a preparatory sketch for his painting of 1888. The setting of both artworks is almost identical, but in the later version, the interplay of three female characters introduces a sentimental narrative to a scene that would otherwise be a straightforward portrayal of lower class labour. To the right of the frame, a bulky loom is controlled by a young woman while to the bottom left sits an elderly woman clutching a milk-can. Her presence absorbs the curiosity of a small girl who, standing with her back to the viewer, may be indicative of the child labour recruited by Norway's textile industry right up until the turn of the century (Konon and Fischer 1900: 387).[8] These three female figures could be representative of three generations of women, with the grandmother serving as a subtle reminder of the wisdom and liberty of a former existence now overshadowed by the modern, mechanical systems of city life.

Because Norway's emergent art market was largely driven by the demands of the affluent classes, the majority of painters who sought patronage avoided subjects that might magnify deprivation or destitution in their own country. Whereas the national romantic painter Adolph Tidemand created nostalgic paintings featuring the rural poor, and Bjørnstjerne Bjørnson's literature often dealt with the idea of the 'noble peasant', these could be evaluated as contrasting with the exacting, unsentimental portrayal of social injustice defining the visual and literary work of Christian Krohg. Krohg's visual and literary representations might present the lower-class, urban population as subjected to overcrowded, disease ridden hovels, whilst the lower-class rural population were shown to relish the freedom of fjords, forests and folk-tales. This was, however, a far cry from the truth. Life in the countryside was just as hard: farm girls regularly inhabited the same quarters as animals; women laboured long hours in isolation; and as Neil Kent has described throughout his book *The Soul of the North*, basic survival across all of Scandinavia was challenged by the effects of a very cold climate and very rocky topography. It is plausible that someone from Setesdal, where rocky ground made for exceedingly poor agricultural yields, would have been tempted to move into wage work in a municipality where his or her basic skills could secure paid employment and a better life. The archives of the Norsk Teknisk Museum (Norwegian Museum of Science and Technology), Arbeidermuseet (Workers Museum) and Arbeiderbevegelsens arkiv og bibliotek (Arbark, The Norwegian Labour Movement Archives and

Library) contain invoices, log books and domestic artefacts connected to the Hjula Weavery which highlight how, while some industrial firms offered little hope for a better life or promotion, others offered women exclusive, hygienic living quarters and wage increases in an attempt to prevent their core staff from absconding.

If during the 1860s and 1870s, most textile factory managers were male, towards the 1890s, the collections of Arbark reveal that women, such as Anna Pleym, were not only becoming managers, but factory inspectors and even union leaders who fought for better wages and conditions for women within their sector. Pleym began working for Nydalens Spinnery as a sixteen year old, foregoing her job upon marriage to raise a family. The death of her husband and ensuing economic hardship forced Pleym to give her children up for adoption and resume work with the Hjula Weavery. One might say that it was personal misfortune and tragedy that forced Pleym to take control of her own affairs. Accordingly, she became part of the female workers union in 1906, for which she was appointed chairwoman in 1910. Between 1908 and 1916 Pleym was a member of the Norsk Arbeidsmandsforbund (Committee of Norwegian Workers) and she played an active role in the Sagenes Politiske Kvinneforening (Sagenes Woman's Union) for which she served as leader from 1913 until 1916.

It must be noticed that public life in Norway did, however, privilege selected voices over others. Significantly, as far as we know, Pleym was never immortalised in portraiture in the way that some women of the NKF, such as Kielland, happened to be. Yet although working class women formed unions, and middle class women arranged group collaborations from the comfort of their homes, the intention of both segments of society remained the same: more legal rights for women and the right to vote in national elections. The strategies employed by each class, however, differed greatly. Industrial workers campaigned in marches and boycotts to demonstrate their contribution to the national economy. Their bourgeois counterparts opted for less militant means, stating their case though the publication of articles in women's magazines including *Urd* or *Nylænde*, public speeches or, in the case of Backer and Kielland, the exhibition of paintings at the Høstutstillingen

(Autumn Art Exhibition) that was founded in 1882.[9] By the 1890s, as the currents of the international Arts and Crafts movement ingrained themselves in the north, the fashion for anything that was hand-made or related to the cottage industries provided women with an alternative avenue through which they could make their mark (Ueland 2015: 63). New opportunities for women opened up as the artistic potential of Norwegian tapestry became apparent.

By the *fin-de-siècle,* some of the best examples of decorative tapestry were reported to be Norwegian-made (Röstorp 2013: 181). Encouraging reviews in southern Europe, particularly in France, fed a determination amongst Norway's cultural elite to reassess an aspect of their heritage which had hitherto held little sway beyond domestic quarters. Earlier disengagement with the idea that woven goods could be considered artefacts may be excused by a general miscomprehension of what constituted 'art' and what was fit for display in a country dominated by the remnants of Dano-Norwegian culture. Until the international art world started to reconsider ordinary, handmade crafts as extraordinary, Norway's art establishment was tentative about elevating something so mundane as a tapestry. By 1900, however, one of Norway's most respected art historians, Jens Thiis, admitted in Norway's official publication for the 1900 Paris Exhibition that the history of Norwegian painting was 'the youngest in Europe' (Konon and Fischer 1900: 525). But by way of compensation, Thiis's colleague Lorentz Dietrichson, art historian and promoter of the decorative arts, asserted that, 'at an early period, Norwegian people had begun to exercise their in-born artistic sense upon the articles employed in daily life' (Konon and Fischer 1900: 576). Such articles, he stated, included embroideries, woven items of wool and silk and picture weavings, all of which were traditionally made by women.

The vigour of Norway's tradition of home crafts, or what became known as *husflid,* was the product of any country enduring extensive winters and impenetrable geography. As such, women habitually spent up to nine months weaving, sewing and embroidering items for warmth, wear and basic survival. Thus, by positioning the figure in *En Vevstue* between icy hues of light blue and warm colours of yellow-brown, one might suggest, Backer hints that the time of year portrayed is mid-summer. As winter melts away, windows are thrown open and the products of domestic culture sold at market or distributed by tradesmen. Indeed, the passing of the Crafts Act (Håndverksloven) of 1839 and the Trade Act (Handelsloven) of 1842, which allowed widowed or single women to make and trade handicrafts, meant that at a relatively early period it was acceptable for some women to make their own money. This was, as the century progresses, a practice stimulated by the *fin-de-siècle* cross-continental enthusiasm for products made by hand, in the home.

Judging by convention, therefore, women were ideally placed to achieve commercial and artistic eminence as the art of tapestry became reinterpreted as a means with lucrative and patriotic potential. The idea that a portable, woollen picture could instil social cohesion as effectively as its painted equivalent was given impetus by the widespread belief that the traditional home industries faced obliteration through the rapid proliferation of cheap, manufactured goods. Wilhelm Peters' representations of life in the textile factory coincided with official endeavours to limit the passing of time and the death of convention via the establishment of consortia whose intention was to maintain, strengthen and extend what was believed to be the natural practice of Norwegian handicrafts (Glambek 2005: 288-291). By 1891, three separate associations were operating under Den Norske Husflidsforening (The Norwegian Handicraft Association). Eight years later, this was selling a range of tools for weaving, appliqué, quilting, inlays and figure embroidery through shops in Kristiania, Bergen, Trondheim, Stavanger and Kristiansand.[10] As noticed earlier, such a favourable situation led a number of Norwegian women to work for weaving businesses in the major cities. But others, such as Frida Hansen, went so far as to establish their own ateliers (Ueland 2015: 63-64). In urban areas it was not long before it was commonly accepted for handicraft to provide women with a job, wage and purpose. Women were responsible for the dying of yarn, the transference of cartoons, the weaving of tapestries and carpets, cushions and fabrics. In this way, women's work met local as well as national demands for private display as well as public exhibition. One of the biggest customers for handcrafted textiles was Den Norske Husflidsforeningen (The Norwegian Home Craft Association). And weavings were also collected by Norway's recently founded decorative arts museums, including Kristiania's Kunstindustrimuseet (Museum of Decorative Arts and Design) (1876) and Trondheim's Nordenfjeldske Kunstindustrimuseum (1893).

If a man could be seen to hold prominence in the realm of fine arts, one may assume that with their lives so intertwined with textiles, women would secure equivalent status in the decorative arts. The work of the art historian Anniken Thue has shown, however, that the obstacles encountered by female weavers like Frida Hansen during the establishment of her own career were no more easily navigated than those of her friend, Harriet Backer. For a female tapestry artist, professional success still depended on standards set by men. Professionalism remained the domain of the male. Weaving, like other domestic handicrafts, was still more widely regarded as a subsidiary activity intended for the embellishment of the domestic space. Furthermore, good ladies were not supposed to make money of their own out of a talent for home decoration, for handicrafts were meant to signify industriousness and perfect womanhood (Schaffer 2013: 27). As such, the recognition obtained by Frida Hansen's artworks did not grow without the shadow of Gerhard Munthe. He was an artist whose bright, block coloured tapestry patterns from the early 1890s onwards were made into pieces which, unlike Hansen's own, were readily celebrated as pieces of 'national' art and actively collected by museums (Glambek 2005: 292). Munthe's designs were, at times, inspired by women's tapestries from the middle ages, before being woven by women such as his wife, Sigrun, or the female employees of the Nordenfjeldske Kunstindustrimuseum or Det Norske Billedvæveri (DNB). But it was usually Munthe's name that was associated with pieces such as *Sorte Hæste* (Black Horse) from 1899, or *Nordlysdøtre* (Daughters of the Northern Lights) made in 1903 over and above the names of women who had helped him.[11]

Nevertheless, when hindsight allows us to fully review Frida Hansen's creative vision, the celebrity that Munthe achieved for his foray into tapestry art seems somewhat inflated. DNB was a functioning workshop established by Frida Hansen, who worked not only as a tapestry designer but also as the weaver and marketer of her own work (Thue 1986: 52-53). And yet the establishment of DNB underlines how a woman of exceptional talent still needed to rely on group force in order to instigate change. Moreover, as much as the climate for tapestry art was ripe, Hansen's achievements were, like those of Anna Pleym, to no small degree secured on the back of disappointing personal fortunes experienced early on in life. Hansen was born into one of Stavanger's most important shipping families, and married the merchant Hans Wilhelm Severin Hansen in 1873. But the bankruptcy of his firm, Plough & Sundt, in 1883 forced the couple to separate and the family house at Hillevåg to be sold (Beate Ueland 2015: 62-63). When two of their three children died, Frida turned to embroidery, before turning to tapestry, as a means to sustain herself. She set up business in Stavanger first, before founding a weaving studio at Tullinløkka and the DNB in Kristiania in 1892, the same year that Munthe started to become known for his tapestry designs. This coincidence perhaps propelled Hansen's determination to secure successes of her own. She and DNB would go on to participate in exhibitions in Scandinavia, southern Europe and America, advertise in newspapers and create what could be called a 'brand identity'. Frida also authored books, including *Home Industry and Art Industry in Norway* (Husflid og Kunstindustri i Norge), published in 1899.

In little less than a decade, Hansen went from novice to expert. One of her legacies was the revival of interest in Norwegian woven art through the reconstruction of ancient and nearly forgotten crafting traditions. But Hansen did not refrain from interweaving *avant-garde* influences, such as the floral art of William Morris, the whip-lash line of Art Nouveau or Symbolism into her large scale tapestries and transparent door hangings, or *portières*. It is sometimes impossible to detect technical differences between men's and women's ability with the brush (Lange and Aaserud 2013: 89). If we turn to Hansen, one may say that this was not the case with regard to men's and women's mastery with the loom, if only because tapestries started to assume conflicting meanings as repositories connected to national but also gendered sentiments at the *fin-de-siècle*. As designers and weavers of their own work, Hansen and the other women of DNB possessed a skill that superseded that of Munthe. As Backer's painting hints, the female gender had an inherited knowledge of fabric, yarn and loom work which created work of a more complex, ambitious standard.

Frida Hansen went to great lengths to fully comprehend the artistic potential of an already established national craft. She took courses with the feminist Randi Blehr and the weaver, Kjerstina Hauglum in Sogn, she discussed weaving techniques with farm women from Ryfylke county and Jæren, and founded the country's first organic dye works in Stavanger in 1889 (Beate Ueland 2015: 63). Six years later, a trip to Cologne taught Hansen about medieval art, and whilst in Paris, she studied life drawing and became familiar with the lucid, dream-inspired paintings by Puvis de Chavannes as well as structured poster art by designers like Eugene Grasset or Paul Brethon. Anniken Thue has discussed the distinctive style of flower ornamentation that emerged in Hansen's work, and the translucent but functional 'transparency' technique which she patented in 1897. The process of designing, dying, weaving and branding became, for Hansen, a language of endless possibilities.

It would seem that Hansen's enjoyment of botany and memories of her beloved rose garden from her family home at Hillevåg imbued her pieces with a unique style. Indeed, as Janne Leithe has conveyed, the delicacy of flowers and gardens, as well as the quality of light and shade, were motifs associated with conventional womanhood. But for Hansen, they also strongly communicated something of what it meant to be a modern woman struggling to have her voice heard during an era when it was by no means straightforward (Leithe 2015: 66-72). As for Hansen's monumental tapestry, *Melkeveien* (The Milky Way), finished in 1898, this was a breakthrough piece for the artist and DNB, as much as an ardent statement about gender. Six haloed women cascade from heaven, holding a veil of stars while hovering assertively above an inscription that reads, when translated from Hebrew: 'And let them be lights in the expanse of the sky to give light on earth' (Genesis 1:14-18 New International Version). This is but one example of how Hansen actively embraced concurrent arguments related to the

'Woman Question'. And we see this carried through to other pieces, such as her specially commissioned tapestry *Løvetand,* or *Dandelion,* 1893 (Gudmundson 2015: 73-84). In her youth, Hansen had been taught to draw and paint by Kitty Kielland, and the 1893 tapestry was initially made for the NKF before being subsequently reworked as a transparent *portière* (renamed *Hesteblomster*) then exhibited at the Paris Exhibition in 1900 along with *Salome's Dance.* In the former, the wild, robust plant that signified womanhood was sensationally transformed from its mistaken form as a weed, to a budding flower (Leithe 2015: 70). In the latter, close to seven metres of weave revealed a dramatic scene from the New Testament in which a pearl-clad but unusually unassuming Salome moves before flowers and snakes. Rather than being flanked by men, Salome is escorted by women.

Described as an artist adept in the main features of Art Nouveau, Hansen continued to explore the potential of wool and warp through the use of emblems specific to her sex. *Libellernes Dans* (Dance of the Dragonflies) was finished in 1901, *I Rosenhaven* (In the Rose Garden) in 1904 and *Semper Vadentes* in 1905. All were well received internationally, largely on account of their voluptuous hues, experimental forms and graceful lines. That out of all three, only *In the Rose Garden* was purchased by a Norwegian collector seems baffling, particularly given the reawakening of interest in Norwegian tapestry art both at home as well as abroad.[12] Just as Hansen had risen during the years before the turn of the century, as the twentieth century progressed, she gradually fell from public favour after 1900.[13] But this might be regarded as equally illuminating as it is perplexing, particularly with regard to comprehending how women, women's work and women's creative contribution was celebrated in a so-called egalitarian country struggling to assert itself. Hansen's artworks survived in their ability to transcend time and place, but it would seem that continentalism, timelessness and qualities connected to the highs and lows of being a female contributed to woven images that could seem, for some, illogical in content, even disturbing in composition. Perhaps her pieces were too far-reaching, whereas Munthe's tapestry designs were identifiably nationalistic with all their boldness and heroic, historic subject matter. Unlike Hansen, Munthe was not an artist who broke onto the scene like a firebrand. While the speed and emergent excellence of the textile industry in Kristiania's east worked in conjunction with the sprouting interest in the slow beauty of woven art to the west, Hansen, Backer and Pleym were women whose hands were expected to build a clear identity for a country first and foremost, rather than focus on autonomous celebrity for the sake of their gender.

These women would have to wait until 1913 to see universal suffrage granted. And while Norway's neutrality during the First World War may be assessed as noble, retrospective analysis reveals the extent to which economic as well as cultural facets were significantly disturbed and, in some respects, even reversed by such disengagement in world issues. Towards 1930, Norway was seen by many to be a peripheral and provincial country in terms of policies, expectations and art. It seems that weariness with this situation also drove Hansen's robust disposition, particularly, as Janne Leithe has shown in her work on the artist, with regard to altering unprogressive attitudes relating to women's work and contribution. 'Vevarbeidet er fremdeles mitt kjæreste arbeide' (Weaving is still my passion) (Rogstad 1926: 37), Hansen would state in an interview with the feminist Anna Rogstad in 1926 (Leithe 2015: 71). She then reminded her audience that, 'Jeg vet at den norske billedvevning er gjenvakt til liv, at den vil lev videre og være en faktor av verdi i vårt folks kultur. Jer er glad mitt livsverk ikke har været forgjeves' (Rogstad 1926: 37) (I know Norwegian tapestry has been resuscitated, that it will live on and be a factor of value in our culture. I'm glad my life's work has not been in vain).

## Endnotes

[1] Frida Hansen as quoted in (Rogstad 1926: 37).

[2] Anne Wichstrøm's research has revealed that a substantial proportion of exhibiting artists in Norway during the 1880s and 1890s were women.

[3] The history of Norwegian women's emigration to, and settlement in, the United States is most comprehensively covered in *Norwegian American Women: Migration, Communities, and Identities,* which consists of essays by a range of scholars. These are edited by Betty A. Bergland and Lori A. Lahlum and published by the Minnesota

Historical Society Press, 2011.

[4] *Norway: Official Publication for the Paris Exhibition 1900* offers a comprehensive statistical and descriptive overview of the main sorts of work that women did in urban Norway towards the end of the century. See also Ingeborg Glambek's work on *kunstindustri* (decorative arts) and *husflid* (home crafts), Anniken Thue's work on Frida Hansen and parts of Hilde Danielsen, Eirinn Larsen and Ingeborg W. Owesen's book *Norsk Likestillingshistorie 1814 - 2013*.

[5] Industrialisation began in Norway the 1840s, which was relatively late, through the establishment of steam powered saw and wood pulp mills, followed by textile mills, breweries, match factories, iron foundries and brick and tile works.

[6] British firms continued to support the growth of the Norwegian textile industry throughout most of the nineteenth century. A large number of British firms, particularly from the North of England, were active in Norway, both through the supply of machinery but also manual labour. Kristine Bruland has shown that a proportion of the workers were British women.

[7] For further discussion about how elements of the Modern Breakthrough, such as naturalism and debating literature influenced Scandinavian art, see D. Jackson's essay in *Nordic Art: The Modern Breakthrough 1860 - 1920*.

[8] According to the Norwegian census of 1891, among those working in industry were 1,880 children under the age of fifteen. 1,055 were engaged in manufacturing industries, which included 285 girls, 600 in artisan industries, which included 21 girls, and 230 in sewing and other minor industries, 70 of which were girls (Konon & Fischer 1900: 387).

[9] From 1884 the exhibition was in receipt of state funding, and renamed the *Statens Kunstutstilling (The National Art Exhibition)*.

[10] The three associations that merged were The Norwegian Arts and Crafts Association, the Association of National Textile Art and The Norwegian Handicraft Association.

[11] Before 1899, DNB was known as Norsk Aaklæde og Billedteppe -Væveri (NABV, Norwegian Åkle and Pictorial Weaving Studio). It was a share holding company established by Backer and Randi Blehr in 1897.

[12] *Melkeveien* ended up in the collection of the Museum für Kunst und Gewerbe in Hamburg, *Libellernes Dans* at the Nordiska Museet in Stockholm, and *Semper Vadentes* at Château de la Rochepót, Cote-D'ôr in France.

[13] Frida Hansen received the King's Medal of Merit in gold for her work as a textile artist in 1915. Between 1926 until her death in 1931, she worked on the *Olav Carpet* which now hangs in Stavanger Cathedral. Thereafter, Hansen remained largely

forgotten until Anniken Thue rediscovered her in the 1970s though the work on her Magister thesis of 1974.

# References

Anderson, B. R. O. (1991). *Imagined Communities: Reflections on the Origin and Spread of Nationalism*. London: Verso.

Arntzen, J. G. (2010). *Oslo 1900-1925*. Oslo: Kom Forlag.

Behrndt, H., H., & Veiteberg, J. (2002). *Women Painters in Scandinavia 1880-1900* [published in conjunction with the exhibition Women Painters in Scandinavia 1880-1900 organised and held by Kunstforeningen Copenhagen (10 August-27 October 2002), Niedersächsisches Landesmuseum, Hannover (21 November 2002-26 January 2003), Bergen Kunstmuseum (14 February-27 April 2003)]. Copenhagen: Kunstforeningen.

Berg, K. and Anker, P. (1981). *Norges kunsthistorie*. Oslo: Gyldendal norsk forlag.

Bergland, B. A. and Lahlum, L. A. (2011). *Norwegian American Women: Migration, Communities, and Identities*. St. Paul, MN: Minnesota Historical Society Press.

Bruland, K. (1989). *British Technology and European Industrialization: The Norwegian Textile Industry in the Mid Nineteenth Century*. Cambridge: Cambridge University Press.

Danielsen, H., Larsen, E. and Owesen, I. W. (2013). *Norsk Likestillingshistorie 1814-2013*. Bergen: Fagbokforlaget, 2013.

Derry, T. K. (1973). *A History of Modern Norway 1814-1972*. Oxford: Clarendon Press.

Glambek, I. (2005). 'Norway' in Livingstone K. and Parry., L. (eds.), *International Arts and Crafts*. London: V&A, pp. 286-293.

Glambek, I. (1988). *Kunsten, Nytten og Moralen: Kunstindustri og*

149

*Husflid i Norge 1800-1900*. Oslo: Solum forlag.

Goggin, M. D. and Tobin, B. F. (eds.) (2009). *Women and the Material Culture of Needlework and Textiles 1750-1950*. Farnham: Ashgate.

Gudmundson, I., M., L. (2015). 'Frida Hansens litterære billedtepper' in Ueland, H. B., *Frida Hansen: Art Nouveau i full blomst* [published in conjunction with the exhibition Frida Hansen: Art Nouveau i full blomst organised and held by Stavanger Kunstmuseum (12 June-18 October 2015)]. Stavanger: Stavanger Kunstmuseum, pp. 31-49.

Hadjiafxendi, K. and Zakreski, P. (eds.) (2013). *Crafting the Woman Professional in the Long Nineteenth Century: Artistry and Industry in Britain*. Farnham: Ashgate.

Hansen, F. (1899). *Husflid og kunstindustri i Norge*. Kristiania.

*Hjula Papers, Kopibok*, 1861-1863.

Hodne, F. (1975). *An Economic History of Norway 1815-1970*. Bergen: Tapir.

Jackson, D. (2012). 'Nordic Art: The Modern Breakthrough' in Jackson, D. (ed.), Nordic Art: The Modern Breakthrough 1860-1920 [published in conjunction with the exhibition Nordic Art: The Modern Breakthrough 1860-1920 organised and held by Groninger Museum, (9 December 2012-5 May 2013), Kunsthalle der Hypo-Kulturstiftung Munich (30 May-6 October 2013)]. Munich: Hirmer, pp. 11-25.

Kent, N. (2000). *The Soul of the North: A Social, Architectural and Cultural History of the Nordic Countries 1700-1940*. London: Reaktion.

Kokkin, J. and Munthe, G. (2011). *Gerhard Munthe: en radikal stilskaper*. Lillehammer: Lillehammer Kunstmuseum.

Konon, S. and Fischer, K. K. E. (eds.) (1900). *Norway: Official Publication for the Paris Exhibition 1900*. Kristiania: Aktie-Bogtrykkeriet.

Kunstindeks Danmark & Weilbachs Kunstnerleksikon. (2015). Wilhelm Peters. Available at: https://www.kulturarv.dk/kid/VisWeilbach.do?kunstnerId=4104&wsektion=alle (Accessed: 29 October 2015).

Lange, M. I. (1995). *Harriet Backer*. Oslo: Gyldendal norsk forlag.

Lange, M. I. (1996) *Harriet Backer, 1845-1932* [published in conjunction with the exhibition X organised and held by Bergen Billedgalleri (7 September-27 October 1996) and Nasjonalgalleriet (9 November 1996-2 February 1997)] Oslo: Nasjonalgalleriet.

Lange, M. I. and Aaserud, A. (2013). *Kvinnene kommer*. Rosendal: Baroniet Rosendal.

Leithe, J. (2015). 'Alltid Blomster – om Frida Hansens transparente portierer' in Beate Ueland. H. Frida Hansen: Art Nouveau i full blomst [published in conjunction with the exhibition Frida Hansen: Art Nouveau i full blomst organised and held by Stavanger Kunstmuseum (12 June-18 October 2015)]. Stavanger: Stavanger Kunstmuseum, pp. 19-30.

Lunden, M. S. (1944). *De frigjorte hender; et bidrag til forståelse av kvinners arbeid i Norge etter 1814*. Oslo: J.G. Tanum.

Lunden, M. S. (1948). *Den lange arbeidsdagen*. Oslo: J.G. Tanum.

*Norsk kunstnerleksikon*, bd. II (1983). Oslo: Universitetsforlaget.

Nunn, P. G. (1987). *Victorian Women Artists*. London: Women's Press.

Ohlsen, N. (2012). 'Women's Rooms: An Aspect of Nordic Interior Paintings' in Jackson, D. (ed.), Nordic Art: The Modern Breakthrough 1860-1920 [published in conjunction with the exhibition Nordic Art: The Modern Breakthrough 1860-1920 organised and held by Groninger Museum, (9 December 2012-5 May 2013), Kunsthalle der Hypo-Kulturstiftung Munich (30 May-6 October 2013)]. Munich: Hirmer, pp. 217-223.

Oltedal, A. and Skre, A. (2013). *Formødrenes stemmer: kvinneliv rundt stemmeretten.* Oslo: Pax Forlag.

Parker, R. (2011). *The Subversive Stitch: Embroidery and the Making of the Feminine.* London: I.B. Tauris.

'Pleym, Anna Karoline' in Friis, J. and Hegna, T. (1935). Arbeidernes Leksikon, bd. V. Oslo.

Rogstad, A. (1926). *Kjente menn og kvinne: Fra deres liv og virke,* vol. II. Oslo: Jacob Dybwads Forlag.

Röstorp V. (2013). *Le mythe du retour: les artistes scandinaves en France de 1889 à 1908.* Stockholm: Stockholms Universitets Förlag.

Sirna, G. C. (2006). *In Praise of the Needlewoman: Embroiderers, Knitters, Lacemakers, and Weavers in Art.* London: Merrell.

Store Norske Leksikon. (2015). Hjula Væverier. Oslo: Norsk nettleksikon. Available at: https://snl.no/Hjula_Væverier (Accessed: 29 October 2015).

Thue, A. (1974). *Frida Hansen: norsk tekstilkunstnerinne ved århundreskiftet.* Magister thesis: University of Oslo.

Thue, A. (1986). *Frida Hansen: en europeer i norsk tekstilkunst omkring 1900.* Stavanger: Universitetsforlaget.

Ueland. H. B. (2015). *Frida Hansen: Art Nouveau i full blomst* [published in conjunction with the exhibition Frida Hansen: Art Nouveau i full blomst organised and held by Stavanger Kunstmuseum (12 June-18 October 2015)]. Stavanger: Stavanger Kunstmuseum.

Visted, K. and Stigum, H. (1951). *Vår gamle bondekultur,* bd.1. Oslo: J.W. Cappelen.

Visted, K. and Stigum, H. (1952). *Vår gamle bondekultur,* bd. II. Oslo: J.W. Cappelen.

Wichstrøm, A. (1983). *Kvinner ved staffeliet: kvinnelige malere i Norge før 1900.* Oslo: Universitetsforlaget.

# The Compass of Nordic Tone: Jazz from Scandinavia

## Haftor Medbøe

This chapter aims to plot the development of jazz in Scandinavia while questioning widespread assumptions about Scandinavia as a geo-cultural construct and the relationship of each of its constituent countries to the genre. By exploring the history of jazz in the Scandinavian countries, it will be demonstrated that jazz has become an integral part of the region's cultural tapestry; a cultural export that has, in global jazz circles at least, become typically associated with essentialist conceptions of Scandinavia and the Nordic region. In doing so, the impracticalities inherent a single Scandinavian jazz narrative will be highlighted and a discursive approach proposed; one that provides a more holistic overview of actors and events that have influenced re-imaginings of the genre beyond contexts particular to its American origins. Such narratives will be unpacked alongside those more concerned with the preservation of canonical tradition.

The term *jazz* readily conjures up a narrative borne of twentieth-century-steeped stereotype and mythology. Its imagery is typified by the sharp-suited musician, shrouded in cigarette-smoke, reproduced in high-contrast monochrome, as imprinted on history through the iconic photography of Herman Leonard, Bill Claxton and others. Such representations are underscored by the recurring motifs of alcohol and narcotics abuse that defined and, in many cases, cut short the lives of a great many of the music's most cherished artists.

Forged in the tense dichotomy of a racially divided United States during the early twentieth century, jazz evolved to become an expression of empowerment, protest and subversion (Newton 1959; Pinheiro 2015; Knauer 2009) while, at the same time, appealing to a populist following. In its marriage of anti-establishment non-conformism alongside the groundswell of the emerging twentieth century zeitgeist, jazz ultimately found itself under a yoke of seemingly unassailable stylised iconography and convention. Chiming, as it did, with the prevailing spirit of modernity, jazz was quickly commoditised and popularised through burgeoning contemporary technologies of reproduction and dissemination. The massification, commercialisation and subsequent global reach of jazz has led to continuing, often racially framed, arguments over authenticity and guardianship of what William 'Billy' Taylor declared to be 'America's Classical Music' (1985: 21), as reenergised during the 1990s by Winton Marsalis and Stanley Crouch.

It may therefore seem incongruous that jazz, with its supposedly unique ethno-geographically rooted foundations and associated baggage of urban American narrative, trope and iconography, should have come to be located in the Scandinavian countries – a region typically imagined through a rather differently constructed prism of cultural and national stereotypes. History, however, has proved otherwise. Not only did jazz find a receptive audience in Northern Europe, especially amongst its younger generations, Scandinavia's musicians adopted the imported musical language with enthusiasm, ultimately reimagining the genre far beyond its erstwhile American conception. Stuart Nicholson describes the fruits of this stylistic reimagining through processes of transculturation (Wallis and Malm 1984), as a 'glocalised' jazz, and as 'one that is 'hybridized [...] in local and national contexts' (Nicholson 2005: 177).

Retrospective examination suggests that, following a period of imitation of the 'founding fathers' of American jazz, Scandinavia's jazz musicians arrived at a nationalist cultural awakening; one in which elements of indigenous high and low-art heritage were incorporated to concoct an unmistakeably Scandinavian reconceptualisation of the genre. This nationally-framed acculturation of jazz has come to be widely described as 'Nordic tone' or the 'Scandinavian sound' in international press and commentary.

What sets Scandinavian jazz apart from the rest of the world is the Nordic Tone, an exemplary example of the 'glocalization' effect, whereby the globalized 'American' styles of playing jazz have been reinscribed with local significance, be it folkloric influences, classical influences (Nicholson 2006).

While such a summation of aesthetic development in jazz from Scandinavia – from mimicry to ownership – is attractive in its linear simplicity, it falls rather short of acknowledging more intricately nuanced understandings of the complexities underlying: firstly, the self-identities of the three Scandinavian countries and disparities in their individual relationships to the genre and, secondly, the ever-broadening church that has been constructed to house the stylistic fracturing of jazz over the past century.

## A Brief History of Jazz in Scandinavia

Jazz, in all its forms, has occupied a significant space in Scandinavian cultural consciousness since the genre's heyday during the inter and post-war years. The tendrils of jazz spread quickly into Scandinavian music life from the roots of its American nascence through the early proto-jazz performances of visiting 'minstrel shows' and, later, the jazz-infused repertoire of US military bands during and following the First World War (Martin and Waters 2012: 124).

At the conclusion of the First World War, the rude exoticism of a music that (from a reductionist perspective) was purported to combine the 'primitive' rhythms of Africa with the 'free' spirit of the New World represented, to increasingly globally-aware younger generations, a timely emancipation from the austerity of Victorian values and the weighty traditions and lineage of Western classical music. The sonic embodiment of liberation, hope and rebellion, jazz was also at the vanguard of an increasingly dominant American worldview, as propagated through its military interventions alongside the cinema of Hollywood and the American recording industry. Hardly surprising, then, that jazz was perceived as a threat to the status quo in certain corridors of the establishment, and almost universally by contemporary and subsequent totalitarian regimes in Europe.

In 1925, the eminent Danish composer Carl Nielsen proffered in the magazine *Hjemmet* his belief that: 'Jazzmusikken vil dø hen af sig selv. Den har jo nemlig intet Indhold, og den har ingen Rødder i vor Kultur' (Wöldike 1925: 8) (Jazz music will die off of its own accord as it has no content and nor roots in our culture).

Five years later, Nielsen expanded his views on jazz warning against: 'den åndelige degradering af tidens musik' (the spiritual degradation of the music of the time), and continued: 'Aldrig før har Musikkens Kunst været så ilde stedt som i dette Øjeblik. Fra at være en Aandelig Værdi, som vi alle samledes om, er den blevet en Skøge, som tilbyder sig fra aabne Døre og Vinduer, fra Kælderhalse og stinkende Jazzbuler' (Jensen 1991: 9) (Never before has the art of music been in such a dismal place than at this moment. From being a spiritual worth on which we all agreed, it has become a whore that offers itself from open doors and windows from cellar openings and stinking jazz-dens).

Johan Fornäs, a contributor to *Afro-Nordic Landscapes* (2014: 58) highlights less palatable interpretations of Scandinavia's early fascination with the African-American roots of jazz, pointing out that Swedish press of the time described Louis Armstrong as 'cannibal offspring' and 'a gorilla from the deep jungle' in their reviews of his 1933 Swedish tour.

Any such dismissal and denigration did little to dampen a growing enthusiasm for this new music from America amongst young Scandinavians, however. By the 1930s, jazz had gained an unassailable foothold in Danish mainstream culture. Following the 1924 debut of Sam Woody's Chocolate Kiddies in Copenhagen, The Original Dixieland Jazz Band, Sidney Bechet, Louis Armstrong, and later Duke Ellington and Coleman Hawkins, all toured Europe during the 1920s and '30s, inspiring the domestic uptake of jazz. In Norway, the recordings of Paul Whiteman and Art Hickman, and live appearances at the Grand Hotel by Feldman's Jazz-band from England in 1921, and at the Bristol by The 5 Jazzing Devils from the USA, inspired Norwegian dance bands to incorporate jazz in their musical repertoire (Stendahl 1987). Following in Armstrong's footsteps, Joe Venuti, Coleman

Hawkins, Benny Carter, Jimmie Lunceford and Fats Waller were some of the American musicians to tour Sweden during the 1930s.

During the Great Depression of the 1930s, the new movement of Cultural Radicalism ('Kulturradikalisme') gained prominence in Denmark. To its followers '... jazz was seen as an alternative to a repressed, artificial and narrow-minded culture. Jazz, they thought, was rhythm, the body, eroticism and naturalness, and thereby carried with it a life-affirming rationality fit for the modern age', writes Dvinge, another contributor to *Afro Nordic Landscapes* (2014: 62). Pioneers of pedagogy, notably Bernhard Christensen (1906-2004), helped to introduce jazz into the public education system. The cover-all term 'rytmisk musik' (rhythmic music) was coined, leading to a music-pedagogy in schools and higher education that included 'improvisation and a rhythmic-bodily musical culture' (Pedersen 2011).

The 1930s honeymoon-period of jazz in Scandinavia was, however, soon curtailed by the outbreak of the Second World War and the subsequent Nazi occupation of Denmark and Norway in the years between 1940 and '45. The Nazis declared jazz 'Entartete Musik' (degenerate music), pejoratively labelling it 'Negermusik' (Negro music), prohibiting its live and radio performance and imposing a ban on both visiting American artists and on the import of jazz records. Nonetheless, the playing of, and dancing to, jazz in Denmark continued, not least as a symbol of resistance to the Nazi prohibition. The Nazi moratorium of jazz on the radio was eventually relaxed in order to discourage the Danish public from tuning in to broadcasts of jazz on the BBC. Even in the German homeland, despite the official Nazi distaste for jazz, Joseph Goebbels gave permission for the formation of Charlie and his Orchestra, a sponsored jazz band comprising Germany's best jazz musicians, as a tool for propaganda against the Allies (Willett 1989). Such wartime ambivalence surrounding jazz is illustrated in the Kongelig Teater (Royal Theatre) 1943 presentation of George Gershwin's Porgy and Bess, albeit with an all-white cast, in the face of fierce criticism from German and Danish Nazis (Pedersen 2013).

In Norway, jazz was forced underground during the Nazi occupation.

Official moves to de-Americanise jazz led to the renaming of 'swing' in Norwegian language as 'rytmemusikk' (rhythm music). Due to the banning of radio alongside the screening of American cinema during the occupation, live jazz enjoyed a significant, if covert, upsurge. Norwegian musicians under the Nazi censure were forced to develop cunning strategies in order to keep jazz hidden from the authorities, with jazz being performed in private and many jazz clubs masquerading as 'sewing circles' (exempt from Nazi restrictions) to avoid sanction and reprisal (Stendahl & Berg 1991).

Due to Sweden's neutrality during the conflict, jazz enjoyed an unrestricted rise in appeal despite the wartime scarcity of American record imports. This rise was not without its domestic critics. Although the genre had gained greater institutional acceptance following the Swedish Musicians' Union relaxing of its dim view of jazz during the 1930s, it was not until the 1950s (as retold in the 1976 film *Sven Klangs Kvintett* set during the period) that jazz became more embedded in Swedish cultural life.

The latter war years saw the emergence of bebop in America – an intellectualised development in the harmonic language of jazz with a focus on virtuosity that would ultimately prove crucial in elevating jazz from the preserve of entertainment to the status of art. In Scandinavia, however, the entertainment forms of swing and dance-band music continued to dominate, leading to the so-called 'golden ages' in Scandinavian jazz. It is interesting to note that the Danish golden age of jazz is generally accepted to have occurred, in spite of the German occupation, between 1940 – '45 (Büchmann-Møller n.d.), the Swedish in the first half of the 1950s (Bruér 2007) and the Norwegian, not until the 1970s (Kristiansen n.d.) – although the dates of these epochs are perhaps somewhat dependent on the stylistic tastes of the arbiter.

Following the conclusion of the Second World War, America instituted the $13 billion Marshall Plan (also known as the European Recovery Program), an aim of which was to create a sizeable free-trade zone for American 'goods, services and cultural products' (Nicholson 2014: 65). From its pre- and interwar beginnings as an exotic curiosity, massified jazz, by way of the technologies of radio and gramophone, had become the first popular music of an increasingly globalised world.

The energised sounds of bebop first took hold in Denmark following Don Redman's visit to Copenhagen in 1946, bringing with him the 'tricks of the trade' of this latest jazz variant. The Danish passion for bebop was further enlivened by the 1948 visit by Dizzie Gillespie's big band. Many of the most prominent American jazz musicians of the time made extended visits to Europe – with some setting up home and never returning to their home country. In Europe, American musicians found receptive audiences, better pay and a non-segregated society in which to work.

Dexter Gordon, Ben Webster, Stan Getz, Oscar Pettiford, Thad Jones, Yusef Lateef, Ed Thigpen, and Kenny Drew were some of the musicians that took up residency in Denmark during the post-war years. At Copenhagen's legendary Jazzhus Montmartre (established in 1959 and reopened in 2010 after a fifteen-year hiatus), American musicians performed alongside domestic sidemen that included pianists Thomas Clausen and Ole Kock Hansen, saxophonist Jesper Thilo, trumpeter Palle Mikkelborg, trombonist Erling Kroner, drummer Axel Riel, bassists Jesper Lundgaard, Mads Vinding, Bo Stief, and 'The Great Dane', Niels Henning Ørsted Pedersen. These sidemen were to become pillars of the post-war Danish jazz scene, many going on to enjoy international acclaim. The rise to prominence of these domestic musicians was in no small part due to the continuation of a 1927 Danish Musicians' Union rule dictating that concerts involving artists from abroad had to feature a corresponding number of Danish musicians (Dvinge 2014: 71).

During this period, jazz criticism was maturing in the emerging Europe through pioneering works by Belgian Robert Goffin (Aux Frontières du Jazz, 1932), Frenchman Hughes Panassié (Le Jazz Hot, 1934) and German Joachim-Ernst Berendt (Das Jazzbuch, 1952). Advances in historiography and critical writing coincided with the emergence of specialist Scandinavian publications and significant number of domestic jazz record labels. From the 1940s, critic and researcher Erik

Wiedemann (1930-2001) became an important figure in Danish jazz, arguing for the genre to be appreciated on a par with classical music. In Sweden, *Orkester Journalen* had come into being already in 1933 and now claims to be the world's longest running jazz periodical.

## The 'Nationalisation' of Jazz

The post-war years were a fertile period for jazz in Sweden with, again, considerable influence being taken from visiting American jazz musicians, many of whom recorded for the Swedish Metronome record label. It was during the 1960s, however, that a 'nationalising' of Swedish jazz took place, most notably through the 1964 recordings by pianist Jan Johannson (Jazz På Svenska) and singer Monica Zetterlund with the Bill Evans Trio (Waltz for Debbie). Johansson produced an album of Swedish regional folk songs in a 'chamber jazz' aesthetic, and Zetterlund collaborated with her American rhythm section to present an album featuring Swedish lyrics on an Evans composition 'Monicas Valse', a Swedish folk song 'Vindarna Sucka' and a work by Swedish songwriter, Olle Adolphson, 'Om Natten'. Alongside the jazz 'retellings' of Swedish folk songs by saxophonists Sven Arne Domnérus and Lars Gullin, these two recordings can be said to have introduced a sparseness and attention to timbral and tonal balance that have come to characterise a distinct aesthetic associated with jazz from Scandinavia. This 'nationalisation' process was not exclusive to jazz from Sweden. Niels Henning Ørsted Pedersen's 1973 album with American expat pianist, Kenny Drew featured two traditional Danish songs, 'Det Var En Lørdag Aften' and 'I Skovens Dybe Stille Ro'. More recently, Norwegian examples of the 'jazzification' of national music can be heard in trumpeter Arve Henriksen's collaboration with Oslo Chamber Choir's 2004 'Kyst Kust Coast' that features songs from the coasts of Norway and Sweden, or in Espen Eriksen and Gunnar Halle's 2014 album 'Psalms', in which Norwegian liturgical song is employed as a starting point for meditative improvisations. In the process of becoming a global music, jazz can thereby be said to have taken on distinctly supra-American dialects – dialects in which the local story can be retold.

It was following the 1969 establishment of Manfred Eicher's ECM (Editions of Contemporary Music) record label that a recognisably Norwegian jazz vernacular emerged (Hyldgaard 2009). Norwegian saxophonist Jan Garbarek spearheaded a new style that drew influence from the post-bebop fracturing of the jazz genre that had led to sub-styles that included modal jazz, free jazz, third stream, and jazz fusion. Elements of Norwegian and Sami folk musics were introduced into this stylistic melange, resulting in a regionally framed jazz with an ear to global music culture. Through the pioneering work of Garbarek and, amongst others, fellow Norwegians Arild Andersen, Terje Rypdal, Jon Christensen, and Karin Krog, jazz from Norway announced itself on the international scene. Marketeers and the press were quick to construct a quintessentially Nordic narrative around the music's aesthetic, one that liberally employed the imagery of fjord and fjell and lore of sagas and runes instead of the urban topography associated with American jazz. ECM, and its musicians to an extent colluded in this myth building, as is evidenced in album and song titles and associated cover art of the period (Lake and Griffiths 2007).

ECM's founder, Manfred Eicher, used Garbarek to establish the cliché of Nordic jazz being icily exotic and romantically gloomy, using tons of reverb and echo to suggest that Garbarek was playing up against a Norwegian fjord (Lewis 2012).

This new 'Nordic jazz' was, however, not as mono-culturally or nationally conceived as certain histories might lead us to believe. Eicher, whose attention to his unique aesthetic vision sets the benchmark for his Münich-based ECM label, likens himself to a film director:

> I'm not comparing myself with Bergman, of course, but when he worked with Liv Ulmann or Max Von Sydow or Erland Josephson, those people were fantastic. When they worked with someone else they were also very good, but not as good as they were with Bergman. (Williams 2010).

His directorial approach promoted a European aesthetic within jazz that has become a byword for Nordic tone. As Garbarek responded in interview:

> I don't think we were talking about a European approach before ECM, there is a something he hears, something he wants to mirror from musicians. (Nicholson 2010)

Garbarek's approach has firm roots in free jazz and the work of American pianist, composer and theorist George Russell, with whom he worked during Russell's sojourn in Sweden during the late 1960s. In the same interview with Stuart Nicholson, Garbarek cites prevailing musical influences:

> Don [Cherry] brought folk, Cecil Taylor brought dynamic flow, temperature; Ornette [Coleman], melody, developing melody. All these various parameters that make up our music, we got them from anywhere. (ibid)

The unquestionable folk elements present in Garbarek's music (Dickenson 2003) are representative of a wider appetite for 'back-to-source' materials amongst musicians of the time – whether in the cases of Dizzy Gillespie's inclusion of African musics or Don Cherry's interest in Indian folk forms. Furthermore, Garbarek does not limit himself to exploring the folk musics of Norway and the Sami culture of Northern Scandinavia in his use of *seljefløjte* (traditional Norwegian shepherd's flute) and recordings with Norwegian Sami singer Mari Boine Persen (Heffley 2005: 75). His collaborations with Zakir Hussain, Trilok Gurtu, and Lakshminarayana Shankar (India), Egberto Gismonti (Brazil), Miroslav Vitous (Czechoslovakia), and Manu Katché (France/Ivory Coast) point to a one-world view – one that is somewhat at odds with the cultural isolationism suggested by the use of the term 'Nordic tone'. Nor was the ECM label's artist roster limited to Norwegian musicians. Keith Jarrett, Ralph Towner, John Abercrombie, Bill Frisell, Jack DeJohnette, Carla Bley, Paul Motian and Pat Metheny (USA) alongside Dave Holland, John Surman (UK), Kenny Wheeler (Canada), Tomasz Stanko (Poland) Eberhard Weber (Germany), and many others, all contributed to the label's defining aesthetic.

## Boundaries and Infrastructures

There is a tendency amongst those beyond their borders to view the Scandinavian countries and their cultural offerings collectively (Schaad 2008), as borne out in the now-frequently bandied media constructs such as 'Nordic Noir', 'Scan-dram' and, as applied to jazz, 'Nordic tone' and 'Scandinavian sound'. Similarly, in political spheres, Scandinavia is typically imagined as a uni-cultural model of egalitarian utopia. Although it can be said that there exists a degree of consensus regarding welfare within the region (Alestalo et al. 2009) it seems that little attention is given to variances between the internal politics of the individual countries in non-Scandinavian press. Subsequent attempts at regional consolidation by the Nordic Council have further muddied the waters for those looking on from the outside. Where there is confusion surrounding which countries constitute Scandinavia (and even those that live there seem sometimes unsure), the demarcation of the Nordic region seems equally elusive to those beyond its constructs.

Geographic and cultural assumptions and confusions aside, it is precisely because of the co-operational spirit between three countries of relatively small population and their Nordic neighbours, that jazz from Scandinavia has been able to so successfully develop and sustain itself, albeit with distinct regional variations. Cultural activities in each of the three Scandinavian countries benefit from taking place within what Cloonan (1999) refers to as a 'promotional state' – a state that is proactively supportive of its national culture. Through investment in grassroots activity, co-operation and collaboration between member-states and coherent export strategies, state and local government fiscal support for jazz in Scandinavia is often the envy of jazz musicians living and working elsewhere in the world. The official report on cultural policy in 2014 (Norwegian Government 2015), by example, states the policy goal that one per cent of public spending should be allocated to the arts, in which jazz is explicitly included. This figure contrasts starkly with 0.1 per cent equivalent spending in the UK (Brown 2013).

In addition to the efficiencies afforded by the Scandinavian trade zone, jazz in the individual Scandinavian countries enjoys a high level of institutionalisation. Norsk Jazzforbund was established 1953 and has received continued state funding since 1980 through to its dissolution and rebranding in 1997 as Norsk Jazzforum. Jazz in Denmark has since 1997 been steered by JazzDanmark, the organisation that replaced both Den Danske Jazzkreds (established in 1956 and government supported since 1965) and Det Danske Jazzcenter which came into being during the early 1970s. Svenska Jazzriksförbundet has promoted jazz in Sweden since 1948 and, latterly, been bolstered by Svensk Jazz SJR, a network association of Swedish jazz clubs and prize awarding body for excellence on the domestic scene. Jazz in the Scandinavian region has also benefitted from monetary and organizational support from the Nordic Council through funding initiatives and prize-giving awards.

Scandinavia's jazz is supported academically through Norsk jazzarkiv (Norwegian Jazz Archive) established in 1981, Svenskt Visarkiv (Swedish Song Archive) established 1951 (an archive of folk songs and dance music, spelmansmusik, 'older' popular music and Swedish jazz) and the Center for Dansk Jazzhistorie (Centre for Danish Jazz History) at Aalborg University, established in 2006.

Successful lobbying for state funding and acceptance by academe in the Scandinavian countries points to jazz having become a 'naturalised' art form – one that has come to harmoniously coexist within an ostensibly deeper-rooted Scandinavian cultural tapestry. The imported language of jazz has afforded a musical common currency that crosses geographic and cultural borders with arguably greater ease than folk, or even classical, traditions. In its regional refinement, jazz has come to reflect a cosmopolitan 'Scandinavianism' that has the potential to express a sense of national grounding while simultaneously celebrating the global dimensions of the music's roots and reception.

We should return, however, to the problematic notion of a 'Nordic tone' or 'Scandinavian sound'. When discussing jazz, or for that matter any cultural product from the region, such constructed conflations elicit a number of significant issues. Firstly, jazz practitioners rarely align their activities with any promotion of nationhood or government. The jazz musician is traditionally identified, and self-identifies, as an outsider (Merriam and Mack 1960). Throughout the world, jazz musicians typically occupy the overlaps between cultural sectors. Neither part of the high-art classical world, nor the commercialised world of popular music, jazz is practiced across a range of social situations, from bar room to concert hall. A condition of 'otherness' is experienced by many jazz musicians, in plying a highly skilled art form that is, to an extent, enjoyed predominantly by a small number of cognoscenti, while often having to harness its underlying craft in less salubrious performance situations to address professional imperatives.

Secondly, in the jazz scenes of Oslo, Stockholm and Copenhagen (and those in the provinces), there are musical adherents to the range of the stylistic variants of the genre. These scenes, in tandem with their international counterparts, comprise co-existing factions that align themselves variously to New Orleans, swing, bebop, mainstream, free and fusion styles (and all their sub-variants and off-shoots). The scene, whether local, national or global, is imagined as a whole simply by virtue of the tenuous shared roots and philosophies of jazz. Jazz is, thereby, a complex construct that consistently confounds the practices of comparison and categorisation so often favoured in press and academia.

Undoubtedly, some jazz from Scandinavia might be said to bear quintessentially non-American hallmarks. One might even be so bold as to identify a Nordic or Scandinavian design sensibility or traces of Scandinavian folk cultures in aspects of its composition and performance (Frost Fadnes and de Bezenac 2014). But such examples comprise only one aspect of a multi-faceted practice of jazz in the region. Jazz in the Scandinavian countries is in excellent health despite the tightening of the government purse strings in recent years. The imposed label of *Nordic tone* is being peeled away by a post-ECM generation of musicians to reveal approaches that are informed not only by American and European jazz canons, intertwined as they are with folk and classical worlds, but equally by the sonic pallets and compositional forms closely linked to advancements in technologies associated with popular music over the past 30 years.

Frith may have rather overstated his case when he wrote that: 'The national no longer matters when every household has access to the global media flow' (1993: 23), but the 'national' has, during the intervening years, become an increasingly fractured construct into which feeds an near-inexhaustible profusion of cultural influences; one that brings into focus the complexity of contemporary identities as expressed through the arts.

## References

Alestalo, M., Hort, S.E.O & Kuhnle, S. (2009). *The Nordic Model: Conditions, Origins, Outcomes, Lessons.* Hertie School of Governance – Working Papers, No 41. [Online]. Available at: https://www.hertie-school.org/fileadmin/images/Downloads/working_papers/41.pdf

Bakriges, C. G. (2003). 'Musical Transculturation: From African American avant-garde jazz to European creative improvisation, 1962 – 1981', in E. T. Atkins (ed.), *Jazz planet.* Jackson, Mississippi: University of Mississippi Press, pp. 99-114.

Brown, M. (2013). 'Arts and culture worth more than £850m to UK export trade'. *The Guardian.* [Online]. Available at: http://www.theguardian.com/culture/2013/may/07/arts-worth-millions-uk-economy (Accessed: 21 October 2015).

Büchmann-Møller, F. (n.d.) *Dansk Guldalderjazz.* Det Kongelige Bibliotek [Online]. Available at: http://www.kb.dk/da/nb/samling/ma/fokus/guldalderjazz/ (Accessed: 14 October, 2015)

Bruér, J. (2007). *Guldår och krisår: Svensk jazz under 1950- och 60-talen* (Golden Years and Crisis Years Swedish Jazz in the 1950s and '60s). Svenskt visarkiv. No 19, 2007.

Bruér, J. et al (2003). *Nordisk jazzforskning: rapport fra den sjette konferansen i Oslo* (Nordic jazz research: report from the 6th conference in Oslo) 9-10 August 2002.

Cloonan, M. (1999). 'Popular Music and The Nation-State: Towards a Theorisation'. *Popular Music* 18/2, pp. 193-207.

Dickenson, J. W. (2003). *The Impact of Norwegian Folk Music on Norwegian Jazz, 1945-1995*. PhD thesis, University of Salford, UK.

Fadnes, P. F. and de Bezenac, C. (2014). 'Historical Overview of Jazz in Norway', *Rhythm Changes: Historical Overview of Five Partner Countries*. Available at: http://www.rhythmchanges.net/wp-content/uploads/2010/10/Historical-Report-WEBSITE.pdf (Accessed: 14 September 2016)

Frith, S. (1993). 'Popular Music and the Local State', in Bennett, T. et al. (eds.). *Rock and Popular Music: Politics, Policies, Institutions*. New York: Routledge, pp. 14-24.

Heffley, M. (2005). *Northern Sun, Southern Moon: Europe's Reinvention of Jazz*. London: Cambridge University Press.

Hyldgaard, S. J. (2009). *Den Nordiske Tone*. Masters Dissertation. Institut for Sprog og Kultur, Aalborg University, Denmark. [Online]. Available at: http://projekter.aau.dk/projekter/da/studentthesis/den-nordiske-tone(d5cfad0a-2b70-406c-95f9-49026570ac41).html (Accessed 18 October 2015)

Jensen, J. I. (1991). *Carl Nielsen. Danskeren*. Copenhagen: Gyldendal.

Kjellberg, E. (2009). *Svensk Jazz Historia: en oversikt*. (Swedish Jazz History: an overview) [Online]. Stockholm: Svensk visarkiv. Available at: http://carkiv.musikverk.se/www/epublikationer/Kjellberg_Erik_Svensk_jazzhistoria.pdf (Accessed: 5 October 2015)

Knauer, W. (2009). 'History or Histories: Why it is so difficult to draft a European jazz history'. *8th Nordic Jazz Conference: Conference Report*, pp. 1-29. [Online]. Available at: http://jazzconference.net/archive/2009/index_files/8th_njc_conference_report.pdf#page=7 (Accessed: 21 October 2015).

Kristiansen, S. (n. d.). 'Jazz i Norge Etter 1960' (Jazz in Norway after 1960). [Online]. Available at: http://www.jazzbasen.no/jazz. php?side=jazzhistorie.html (Accessed: 14 October 2015)

Kristiansen, S. (2005). 'Nordisk jazzsamarbeid – Nordjazz (1974–2000)', in: Frank Büchmann-Møller (ed.), *Nordisk Jazzforskning.* Rapport fra den syvende konference i Odense, 25–27 august 2004, Odense: Syddansk Universitet, pp. 45-52.

Lake, S. and Griffiths P. (eds.) (2007). *Horizons Touched: The Music of ECM*, London: Granta Books.

Lewis, J. (2012). 'London Jazz Festival. Where Has Garbarek gone? I miss him'. *The Guardian.* [Online] Available at: http://www.theguardian.com/music/musicblog/ 2012/nov/14/london-jazz-festival-2012-jan-garbarek (Accessed: 28 September 2016).

Martin, H. and Waters, K (2012). *Jazz: The First 100 Years.* 3rd ed. Boston: Shirmer.

McEachrane, M. (2014). *Afro-Nordic Landscapes: Equality and Race in Northern Europe.* New York: Routledge.

Merriam, A. P. and Mack, R. W. (1960). 'The Jazz Community'. *Social Forces.* 38(3) pp. 211-222.

Newton, F. (1959). *The Jazz Scene.* London: MacGibbon & Kee.

Nicholson, S. (2005). *Is Jazz Dead? (Or Has It Moved to a New Address).* New York: Routledge.

Nicholson, S. (2006). 'Scandinavian Jazz and the Global Jazz Explosion', in *Nordic Sounds, the magazine of NOMUS, the Nordic Music Committee*, no. 4, p. 18.

Nicholson, S. (2010). 'In conversation with Jan Garbarek'. *jazz. com* [Online]. Available at: http://www.jazz.com/features-and-interviews/archives/2010/1 (Accessed: 5 October 2015).

Nicholson, S. (2014). *Jazz and Culture in a Global Age*. Lebanon NH: Northeastern University Press.

Norwegian Government. (2015). *Official Norwegian Report On Cultural Policy 2014*. Oslo. Web. 21 Oct. 2015. [Online]. Available at: https://www.regjeringen.no/ globalassets/upload/kud/kunstavdelingen/rapporter_utredninger/ kulturutredningen_2014-official_norwegian_report_on_cultural_ policy_2014.pdf (Accessed: 18 October 2015)

Pedersen, P.K. (2011) 'Rhythmic Music' in *Danish music education* [Online]. Available at: https://www. academia.edu/2447441/_Rhythmic_Music_in_ Danish_Music_Education

Pedersen, P.K. (2013). 'Danish Music in the Years of the German Occupation 1940-1945'. Paper presented at the *International Musicological Colloquium*, Brno, September 2005. [Online]. Available at: http://www.academia.edu/4503985/ Danish_Music_in_the_Years_of_the_German_ Occupation_1940-1945 (Accessed: 5 October 2015)

Pinheiro R.N.F. (2015). 'Playing Out Loud: Jazz music and social protest'. *Journal of Music and Dance*, Vol 5(1), pp. 1-5.

Schaad, Eric. 2008. 'Perceptions of Scandinavia and the Rhetoric of Touristic Stereotype in Internet Travel Accounts'. *Scandinavian Studies* 80 (2). University of Illinois Press, pp. 201-238. Available at: http://www.jstor.org/stable/40920805 (Accessed: 16 October 2015).

Stendahl, B. (1987). *Jazz, Hot and Swing: Jazz i Norge 1920-1940*. Oslo. Norsk Jazzarkiv.

Stendahl B. and Bergh, J. (1991). *Sigarett stomp. Jazz i Norge 1940-1950*. Oslo. Norsk Jazzarkiv.

Stendahl B. and Bergh, J. (1997). *Cool kløver & Dixie: Jazz i Norge 1950-1960*. (Cool clubs and Dixie: Jazz in Norway 1950-1960). Publikasjoner fra Norsk Jazzarkiv nr. 6. Oslo: Norsk Jazzarkiv.

Taylor, W. (1985). 'Jazz: America's Classical Music'. *The Black Perspective in Music*. Vol. 14, No. 1. Special Issue: Black American Music Symposium. pp. 21-25.

Wallis, R. and Malm, K. (1984). *Big Sounds from Small Peoples*. London: Constable.

Ward, J. V. (2015). 'Discography, Preservation, and Cultural Crossings. The Role of the World Wide Web in the Underground Dissemination of Nordic Jazz Recordings', in *The Refereed Proceedings of the 9th Nordic Jazz Conference August 19-20, 2010*, Helsinki, Finland

Willett, R. (1989). 'Hot Swing and the Dissolute Life: Youth, Style and Popular Music in Europe 1939-49'. *Popular Music*, 8(2) (May 1989), pp. 157-163

Williams, R. (2010). 'Manfred Eicher: the sound man'. *The Guardian* [Online]. Available at: http://www.theguardian.com/music/2010/jul/17/manfred-eicher-ecm-jazz-interview (Accessed: 5 October 2015)

Wöldike, M. (1925). 'Jazzmusik og Revysang'. (Jazz music and Revue-song). *Hjemmet*, 17(6), p. 8.

# TRANSLATING SCANDINAVIA

# 'Fits and Starts': Chatto & Windus and Their British Translations of Maria Gripe[1]

## Charlotte Berry

### Introduction

This paper takes as its focus the labours of London publishing house Chatto & Windus to bring the works of Swedish children's author Maria Gripe to its juvenile audiences during the 1960s and 1970s under the auspices of editors Edite Graham and Norah Smallwood. Although several Gripe titles were published, the inner workings of the translation process proved problematic, and Chatto declined to pursue their Nordic interests in translated children's literature further.

Scholarly analysis of children's literature in translation has become increasingly common (Lathey 2006, 2016, Frank 2007, O'Sullivan 2005, Coillie and Verschueren 2006, Beckett and Nikolajeva 2006, Pinsent 2006). In contrast, scholarship of the literary and publishing settings in which translations are commissioned remains limited (Berry 2014b: 131). As a result, this case study is positioned within British publishing history and children's literature, and seeks to add to academic scholarship on translation in the mid-twentieth century (Edwards 2007, Heapy 2013, Reynolds and Tucker 1998a, Pearson 2013 and Lathey 2010). This can now be reviewed as a historical period where accessible archival sources are scarce and oral history interviews with living participants are becoming a problematic research tool as time passes.

This article will firstly place Chatto into a publishing context before addressing the development of Chatto's children's list. The remainder of the article will be dedicated to a detailed study of Chatto's endeavour to translate the work of Maria Gripe, firstly by commissioning its own translations from British-based translators, and then by working with an American publisher in collaboration with American translations. How were the translators selected, and what problems did the editors encounter throughout the translation and editing phases? It is hoped that this case study illustrates the extraordinary potential of modern publishing archives as a tool in researching the history of translation and children's literature. Only through utilising an archival-based methodology (as developed in Berry 2013 and her subsequent works) can text and author selection, translator selection and the role of the editor(s) be explored to the fullest degree.

## Chatto & Windus: 'Eccentric, Cultured' Publishing

Chatto & Windus remains one of the most well-known names in British publishing and survives today as an imprint within the Vintage Publishing Group of the Random House Group Ltd, which in turn has formed part of the Penguin Random House conglomerate since 2013 (Random House 2015). When Chatto announced its sale to Random House in 1987, the British publishing consortium was producing one hundred titles per year, representing 'many of the best-known authors of the twentieth century' (Schneller 1991: 117).

The firm was founded in Piccadilly in 1855 by 'one of the most colourful figures in nineteenth-century publishing' (Norrie 1982: 47), John Camden Hotten (1832-1873), who had interests in American authors and Romantic poets (Eliot 2004). In 1873 partner Andrew Chatto (1840-1913) bought the firm and poet W. E. Windus became a sleeping partner (Weedon 2004). Chatto reprinted British authors including Wilkie Collins and Ouida as successful 'yellow back' cheap editions as well as taking on major serials such as *Gentleman's Magazine; Idler* and *Belgravia Annual* (Taunton and Silva 2009: 109). Wilfred Owen and Aldous Huxley later joined the ranks, alongside H. G. Wells, Rosamund Lehmann, William Faulkner and Iris Murdoch (Schneller 1991: 114-115). As Norrie observes, Chatto became known as a medium-sized publisher with a 'strong literary bias', 'highly personalised, a type of medieval court, eccentric, cultured, autocratic and bristling with life and tension' (Norrie 1982: 107), delivering 'a list which was nicely balanced between what would sell and what deserved to' (1982: 48). During the 1950s, the company concentrated very strongly on British and American contemporary fiction, poetry and biography, all personal interests of chairman Ian Parsons (Curtis 2004). The firm subsequently followed the example of many British publishing mergers, maximising their financial resources by combining with Jonathan Cape in 1969 and the Bodley Head in 1973 (University of Reading 2015) before acquisition by Random House in 1987. It is regrettable within the context of this chapter that the one available company history is extremely succinct and does not cover any of the history of Chatto over the last forty years (Warner 1973).

## Translation and Children's Literature at Chatto

Chatto built their literary reputation on English and American authors and demonstrated only minimal interests in translation when compared to other British publishing houses. Their translation of Balzac's *Contes Drolatiques* was withdrawn from circulation following a scandal (Weedon 2004), although Baudelaire, de la Barca and Proust proved more successful (Eliot 2004). Their edition of Stig Dagerman's *A Burnt Child* in 1950 seems to have been a Swedish rarity until the appearance in the 1960s of *Doktor Glas [Doctor Glas]* and several titles by Nobel laureate Pär Lagerkvist.

Similarly, juvenile titles in translation were scarce as Chatto concentrated on English-language authors. However, a combination of bibliographical research and examination of the firm's seasonal catalogues (RH/CW, product catalogues, 1968-1974) makes it possible to gain an initial sense of the range of the publisher's juvenile authors and trends during the 1960s, a period when their authors Ursula Moray Williams and Penelope Farmer were major names in British children's literature.

Chatto were slow to follow an increasingly popular trend in translated

174

children's literature developed by Methuen who produced large quantities of French, German and other language translations during the 1950s and included several prominent Nordic authors such as Astrid Lindgren and Thorbjørn Egner in their list (Berry 2013: 112). Similarly J. M. Dent had made the most of the prolonged success of Selma Lagerlöf's *The wonderful adventures of Nils* (Berry 2014a) and Oxford University Press were working closely with Astrid Lindgren to capitalise on the success of the *Pippi Longstocking* trilogy (Berry 2014b). Ernest Benn were producing as many *Moomin* titles by Tove Jansson as they could persuade the author to write (Berry 2014c), and Hutchinson found themselves in a equally profitable position with Alf Prøysen's *Mrs Pepperpot* series (Berry 2014d). Certainly the extent of Nordic titles appearing in British translation could be termed a 'Golden Age' in its own right, with over 70 titles produced in nearly 350 issues during the period 1950-1975 by diverse group of publishers and by an increasing number of Scandinavian-specialist translators (Berry 2011: 80).

Chatto had not yet ventured into the translated children's market, which is surprising in light of the fact that it was one of the few British houses to boast specialist children's editorial staff who also had outstanding linguistic proficiencies. German-born Edite Graham (later Kroll) had moved to London to work in publishing at the age of eighteen, and had previously worked at Hutchinson (Arenstam 2012). She was Juvenile Editor at Chatto when Swedish author Maria Gripe was taken on but left sometime in 1965 (UR/CW 205/5) and thereafter relocated to the USA to continue her successful career in publishing.

Chatto partner and board member Norah Smallwood (1909-1984) displayed a keen interest in the juvenile list and undertook the Gripe editorial role during the late 1960s and early 1970s before Hugo Brunner and Jane Birkett took over. This was a busy time for Smallwood at a time of growth and expansion when she was running the company alongside Ian Parsons. She became chairman and managing director in 1975 before retiring in 1982 (Charlton 2004). She had joined the firm in 1928, served as head of typography and became a partner in 1945 (Schneller 1991: 115). Smallwood rose to become a director 'not only with only editorial flair but a deep concern for maintaining high standards of production' (Norrie 1982: 107), and remains known as one of the most successful figures in twentieth century British publishing. Her 'instinct for quality' was accompanied by a flair for 'working creatively with her authors' (Charlton 2004).

It is not clear how a Swedish author entirely unknown in the United Kingdom came to the attention of Norah Smallwood, who later claimed Gripe's 'discovery'. By the mid 1960s, Gripe was a prolific author in Sweden but her first eight books had entirely passed under the radar of the British literary establishment. Chatto can therefore take full credit for bringing her to a British readership through their translation of *Josephine* in 1961, the first title in a trilogy.

Gripe (née Walter, 1923-2007) was born in Vaxholm, grew up in Örebro and studied philosophy and religion at the University of Stockholm (Fagerström 1977: 245). She married set-designer and artist Harald Gripe (1921-1992) in 1945 and they made their home in Nyköping. Gripe published her first book in 1954 and went on to become one of Sweden's most prolific authors where she is highly regarded as a recipient of the Hans Christian Andersen Medal (1974) and the Nordic Children's Book Prize (1985). Gripe's breakthrough as a major Swedish children's author came in 1961 with the publication of *Josefin*.

Gripe has been described as the 'Karen Blixen of children's literature' due to her recurring pre-occupation 'that a person must follow his or her own purpose' through the search for or creation of personal identity and the quest for purpose in life (Jakobsen 1985: 19). Gripe achieves this through two main directions of writing, 'psycho-realistic' and 'mystic-fantastic' (Jakobsen 1985: 21) or 'psychological, realistic' and 'mystic, romantic' (Mannheimer 1973: 24). Both stylistic strands were of commercial interest to Chatto, who purchased the *Hugo and Josephine* trilogy and *Elvis* series representing the 'realistic' strand, and young adult novels *The Glassblower's Children* and *Pappa Pellerin's Daughter* representing the 'mystic' strand.

## Translations and the Role of the Editor

In the late 1960s and 1970s, Chatto published nine Gripe titles in total, but chose to commission their own translation only for the first title *Pappa Pellerin's daughter* (1966). The translations for the remaining eight titles, including the *Hugo and Josephine* trilogy (1971), were published elsewhere first. This strategy seems unusual, as British publishers producing Nordic children's fiction at this time either stuck consistently to their own commissions (as at Hutchinson for Tove Jansson, Berry 2014c), or mixed and matched with bought-in translations in a rather unpredictable pattern (as at Oxford University for Astrid Lindgren and Cecil Bødker, Berry 2014b). Senior partners and sales staff often contributed to the decision making process of author and text selection, but the commissioning of translations and the choice of translators were left to editorial preference and traditionally kept cheap and simple. Why this break in standard and accepted editorial practice at Chatto and with juvenile editors elsewhere?

The role of the editor within children's literature and within the process of translation in particular is only now beginning to attract concentrated research attention (see chapter 11 in Lathey 2010). Difficulties met in securing and accessing oral history and other supplementary primary sources are explored in Reynolds and Tucker (1998a, 1998b). In addition, the unpredictable survival rate of the publishing archives needed in original research such as editorial files and translation manuscripts is clearly apparent through the methodological and initial research phases of Berry (2013), Sturge (2004), Thomson-Wohlgemuth (2009) and Pearson (2010, 2013). However, editorial correspondence files constitute the only reliable means of re-constructing the publishing and translation history of a piece of literature.[2]

Fortunately the archival material surviving for Chatto's first four Gripe novels is rich and dense (UR/CW 205; UR/CW 232/14), enabling a detailed snapshot of editorial practice to be taken during the 1960s when editors Graham and Smallwood took on the task of bringing Maria Gripe into their juvenile list. This was no easy challenge since they had presumably little or no Chatto-based experience of working with children's literature in translation or, more significantly, with children's literature translators.

Graham was taking an interest in Gripe as early as 1963, when she was corresponding with major Swedish publisher Rabén & Sjögren about potential titles of interest. Rabén & Sjögren juvenile editor Sonja Bergvall offered two of the *Hugo and Josephine* titles and *Pappa* to Chatto the following year (UR/CW 205/5). Swedish-language expert Reginald Spink undertook the reader reports which were favourable only for *Pappa* (UR/CW RR/31554, 24 Feb 1964). As a result, Smallwood wrote to Paul Britten Austin at the Swedish National Travel Association in London in March 1964 to show him *Pappa* and to persuade him to take on the translation.[3] Austin was already known to Chatto as their translator of *Doktor Glas* and Smallwood was 'not so keen on commissioning an untried translator'. Time did not permit Austin to pursue the commission, but Austin referred Smallwood to Lars Warne at the Swedish Institute whose suggestions in May 1964 included Kersti French:[4]

> She is Swedish and has previously made translations of Swedish drama. Since she is a mother herself, I should imagine that she would have the proper "approach" (UR/CW 205/5).

French delivered two chapters as a sample, her translation was duly completed (UR/CW 232/14) and Graham herself was very content with the 'extremely polished' result. However, Smallwood, Spink and the Chatto board did not concur, with discussions following about whether the present translator 'would be able to make a good job of... putting it right' (UR/CW 205/5). In particular, the translation was felt to be unidiomatic, too literal and that the rendering of Swedish dialect had 'not come through satisfactorily'. Unusually a second native Swedish-speaking translator was brought in who confirmed the board's concerns and was then set about to 'put... [the] translation into order' (UR/CW RR/31554, 28 Oct 1964). As Graham (now Kroll) put it diplomatically to Bergvall when discussing other proposed Gripe titles in January 1965, 'we encountered some difficulties with the translation [which is...] now in order'. *Pappa Pellerin's daughter* duly appeared with illustrations by Harald Gripe in 1966, was favourably received (UR/ CW R/2/18) and was re-issued by Puffin in 1969, a sign of its success within the British juvenile market.

Kroll left her role at Chatto during 1965, having recently turned down Rabén's proposals of at least four Gripe titles and successor Judith Elliott followed the trend, rejecting *In the time of the bells*. By early 1968 Smallwood was again faced with challenge of producing a satisfactory translation, this time of the *Hugo and Josephine* trilogy. The editorial correspondence reveals that on this occasion the impetus for the project came from Seymour 'Sam' Lawrence, an American editor with a well-established passion for foreign-language children's literature.[5]

## American and Other Editions of Gripe

As an advocate of Gripe's authorship, Smallwood was tempted by the prospect of simply purchasing a completed translation from the USA, particularly as a successful film had just been released in Sweden which would generate British interest (Puffin brought forward their re-issue of *Pappa* as a result). Lawrence was keen to benefit from Smallwood's proven experience as Gripe's British editor and was happy to accept Smallwood's recommendation of Austin once more, partly on the grounds of Austin's 'superb translation of DR GLAS' which Lawrence had himself published in the USA in 1963 through Little, Brown and Co. With Austin's translation of the trilogy commissioned in March and delivered in July, both editors hoped for a smooth and trouble-free publication.

This time Smallwood left the bulk of the editorial work to Lawrence and had already noted that as Austin was 'being paid the highest rate... ever heard of for a translator...one would expect a first rate job' (CW 232/14). She was therefore dismayed to learn that Austin's manuscript was 'a real disappointment' and had required 'nearly four weeks of detailed editing and rewriting': Lawrence complained to Austin's agent in forceful terms, observing that 'it is difficult to believe that this is the same hand that produced DR GLAS with such skill and sensitivity' (CW

232/14). Lawrence specified in detail the translational issues he had identified. Repetitions, omissions, Swedish word order, transliterations and the unsuccessful translation of Hugo's dialect all required to be 'thoroughly edited and polished' in order to prevent the fact that 'the Swedish was constantly showing through' and 'the material... [was] unsatisfactory and unacceptable for publication'. Lawrence reported back at regular intervals to Smallwood, who was waiting for the completed version of the trilogy so that she could publish it in London with Chatto. Discussions with Austin's agent continued into August 1969 and then substantial American production delays and British re-editing and a different dust jacket slowed down publication further. Eventually the American and British editions appeared in 1969-1970 and 1971 respectively, completing an extraordinarily prolonged and complex editorial marathon on both sides of the Atlantic.

Given the problems that Gripe's works had posed for the firm, Chatto refused to take on any further options directly from Gripe's Swedish editor as British-commissioned translations, continuing instead to purchase American editions of *The Night Daddy* (1973), *Julia's House* (1975), *Elvis and His Secret* (1977), *Elvis and His Friends* (1978) and *The Time of Bells* (1978): these used American translators Sheila La Farge and Gerry Bothmer (Bothmer's translations of Astrid Lindgren were already being published by Methuen).

Although Chatto had done the hard work of introducing Gripe to a British readership, they declined to invest in Gripe's corpus to an exclusive degree, perhaps as a result of their unusually problematic editorial experiences with their first four Gripe titles. Abelard-Schuman instead took on Gripe's *The Glassblower's Children* and *The Land Beyond* in Lawrence-commissioned translations by Sheila La Farge. However, Chatto were able to see their translations of *Pappa* and the *Hugo and Josephine* trilogy re-issued by paperback specialists Puffin and Piccolo, the latter as a tie-in to the film.

Chatto published only two further Scandinavian children's titles, and opted to play it safe with established Scandinavian children's translators. Katja Beskow's *The Astonishing Adventures of Patrick the*

*Mouse* (1968) was translated by Florence Lamborn (another of Astrid Lindgren's translators at Methuen). Ann Mari Falk's *The Tree Hut* (1970) was undertaken by Gunvor Edwards, who had translated Edith Unnerstad and Astrid Lindgren for Oliver & Boyd prior to their later takeover by Chatto.

## A Typical Editorial Experience?

The history of Gripe's translations at Chatto & Windus is in many ways not representative of the practices of other major British publishing houses operating at the same time. The average British editor was reticent about taking on the additional expense and time involved in translating and editing a new work – this added considerable extra investment when compared to taking on home-grown British titles where the editor could collaborate intensively with the author as the work in question progressed, and could to some extent shape the final result with an eye to commercial viability and the current juvenile market. Many publishers would experiment with unknown translators (and their often cheaper fees), and would entrust their known language-specialist readers to comment on a translation's competency. However, it should be noted that Chatto's strategy to bring in a second translator to fix the problems inadvertently caused by the first in *Pappa* was extremely rare, both in terms of the implicit lack of confidence inferred in the first translator's work and also in terms of additional costs and delays to production.

British children's editors with either very limited or entirely absent linguistic and literary competency in Scandinavian (and many other) languages were forced to rely heavily on editor proposals, readers' reports and informal recommendations when selecting suitable texts and translators. Such editorial dependence on the linguistic expertise of others was not uncommon, but Chatto's issues in working with a respected translator following commission were indeed extremely unusual. They had been fortunate to have already on their books a British native-speaker of English such as Austin with his uncommonly good capabilities in Swedish and a proven track record in literature and broadcasting. In the 1960s and 1970s, the British and American worlds of Scandinavian translation were small. Similarly, the British publishing world at the same time was tightly knit and inter-connected, especially where children's editors were concerned.

Purchasing American translations was not at all uncommon practice in British publishing houses at a time when British editors were reluctant to take on the risk of a new and untried foreign author of any kind, even one such as Gripe with a good reputation already established in her homeland. Revising American translations (where a similar English-language market and readership had already been established successfully) was a popular editorial strategy in the context of Nordic translations. Once an author had proved their economic worth, the British editor would be more willing to take on their own commissioned translation where they could exercise more exacting editorial controls into the final version of the text.

With some quick changeovers in Children's Editors, Chatto moved their juvenile publishing interests on elsewhere. However, the firm was quick to take credit for discovering Gripe in the first place as Smallwood commented when writing to Gripe in May 1974:

> My firm has had the privilege of publishing your books for some years now... I have just heard the marvellous news that you have received the Hans Christian Andersen Award and I want to send you my warmest congratulations. It is indeed a great distinction... All of us at Chatto & Windus are very proud and pleased that you should have been honoured in this way, and I am particularly so because I personally bought the first book of yours that we published, *Pappa Pellerin's Daughter* (UR/CW 232/14).

Chatto's British publications had helped to bring Gripe's works to a wide-ranging English-language market and to encourage other houses to take on new Gripe and other Nordic titles and authors, particularly those falling into the ever popular fantasy genre which was well-established in the British juvenile market.

## Conclusion

The case study of British translations of Maria Gripe at Chatto & Windus demonstrates an atypical editorial experience in many respects to that found elsewhere in the Nordic-British juvenile publishing context. It was unusual to find a Children's Editor such as Edite Kroll who was a non-native English speaker and who had a wide experience of other literatures, and it was also unexpected that this proficiency and expertise was not exploited more by her British publishing house, which would usually struggle to establish such professional networks in a period prior to cheap international air travel and internet newspapers and communications.

It was common publishing practice in children's literature at this time to commission a translator through word of mouth and personal recommendation rather than through any formal recruitment and application procedure, and as a result the competency of the translator varied widely. However, it was extremely unusual to bring in a second translator to write a reader's report on another translator's finished work, as for *Pappa* and Kersti French. In addition, British editors very rarely were required to deal with a translator's agent, as for *Hugo and Josephine* and Paul Britten Austin. The case study of Maria Gripe at Chatto & Windus is therefore an intriguing one, tempting further archival research on her other titles produced elsewhere and on editorial practices in children's literature in Scandinavian translation at other British publishing houses.

## Endnotes

[1] Particular thanks are due to Jean Rose and Charlotte Heppell, former and current Librarians respectively, at the Random House Library and Archives, Rushden, Northampton, for assisting access to the archives and catalogues held by the company, and to Nancy Fulford, former Random House Archivist, University of Reading Special Collections. Permission to publish from unpublished archival sources was kindly granted by the University of Reading Special Collections.

It has not proved possible to locate the current copyright holder for Seymour Lawrence Inc as this does not appear to lie with Random House USA, the assumed owner. It is assumed that permission has been indirectly granted to publish from unpublished archival sources where copyright belongs to Random House UK as no response was garnered from a request to publish quotations within this chapter. The author is willing to secure permissions for future reprints of this chapter, should further information be made available to her on the matter of copyright owners.

[2] The available editorial files surviving for Chatto's publication of Maria Gripe's works relate to the *Hugo and Josephine* trilogy and *Pappa Pellerin's daughter*, although five other novels were published at a later date using American translations by Gerry Bothmer and Sheila La Farge. Given the much reduced editorial work involved in rendering the American versions suitable for a British market, the absence of dedicated editorial files is perhaps unsurprising but does leave a gap in the story of Gripe at Chatto.

[3] Austin (1922-2005) was Director of the Swedish Tourist Office in London. Married to a Swede, he had previously been head of English-language broadcasting for Radio Sweden in Stockholm and was already a published literary translator (Geddes 2005).

[4] French (née Molin) later translated Danish Kaj Himmelstrup's *Children of Tanacatcutli* for the Bodley Head (1969) and *Little Spook* (1969) for Methuen, the first in a long and successful Swedish children's series by Inger Sandberg. She continued to work for Chatto in a limited capacity as a reader eg for Gripe's *I klockarnas tid* in 1966 (UR/CW RR/33942). She had keen interests in film, writing criticism and translating with her film critic and journalist husband Philip French (1933-2015).

[5] Lawrence (1927-1994) started his independent imprint Seymour Lawrence, Inc. in 1965 in a co-publishing agreement with Dell (Delacorte label) which lasted until 1982 when it transferred to E P Dutton and in 1988 Houghton Mifflin (Lyons 1994). Lawrence was a particular advocate of Nordic children's literature in translation and worked regularly with British editors on co-editions.

# References

## Primary Sources – Archives

Random House Library and Archives. Chatto & Windus. (RH/CW):

--- RH/CW, product catalogues, Chatto & Windus, 1986-1974.

University of Reading Special Collections. Archives of Chatto & Windus Ltd. (UR/CW):

--- UR/CW 205/5, file, *Pappa Pellerin's Daughter*, Maria Gripe, 1963-1966.

--- UR/CW 232/14, file, *Hugo and Josephine* trilogy, Maria Gripe, 1967-1974.

--- UR/CW R/2/18, reviews, *Pappa Pellerin's Daughter*, Maria Gripe, 1966.

--- UR/CW RR/31554, reader's report, Reginald Spink, *Josefin, Hugo och Josefin, Pappa Pellerins dotter,* Maria Gripe, 24 Feb 1964.

--- UR/CW RR/31554, reader's report, Mrs [Paul Britten] Austin [née Margareta Bergström], *Josefin, Hugo och Josefin, Pappa Pellerins dotter,* Maria Gripe, 28 Oct 1964.

--- UR/CW RR/33942, reader's report, Kerstin French, *I klockarnas tid,* Maria Gripe, 1966.

**Primary Sources – Published (London: Chatto & Windus unless otherwise specified)**

Beskow, K. (1968). *The Astonishing Adventures of Patrick the Mouse.* Trans. F. Lamborn.

Dagerman, S. (1950). *A Burnt Child.* Trans. A. Blair.

Falk, A. M. (1970). *The Tree Hut.* Trans. G. Edwards.

Gripe, M. (1966). *Pappa Pellerin's Daughter.* Trans. K. French.

Gripe, M. (1969). *Hugo and Josephine.* Trans. P. B. Austin. New York: Delacorte Press.

Gripe, M. (1969). *Pappa Pellerin's Daughter.* Trans. K. French. Harmondsworth: Puffin.

Gripe, M. (1970). *Hugo.* Trans. P. B. Austin. New York: Delacorte Press.

Gripe, M. (1970). *Josephine.* Trans. P. B. Austin. New York: Delacorte Press.

Gripe, M. (1971). *Hugo.* Trans. P. B. Austin.

Gripe, M. (1971). *Hugo and Josephine.* Trans. P. B. Austin.

Gripe, M. (1971). *Josephine*. Trans. P. B. Austin.

Gripe, M. (1971). *The Night Daddy*. Trans. G. Bothmer. New York: Delacorte Press.

Gripe, M. (1973). *The Glassblower's Children*. Trans. S. La Farge. New York: Delacorte Press.

Gripe, M. (1973). *The Night Daddy*. Trans. G. Bothmer.

Gripe, M. (1974). *Hugo*. Trans. P. B. Austin. London: Piccolo (Pan Books).

Gripe, M. (1974). *Hugo and Josephine*. Trans. P. B. Austin. London: Piccolo (Pan Books).

Gripe, M. (1974). *Josephine*. Trans. P. B. Austin. London: Piccolo (Pan Books).

Gripe, M. (1974). *The Land Beyond*. Transl. S. La Farge. New York: Delacorte Press.

Gripe, M. (1974). *The Glassblower's Children*. Trans. S. La Farge. London: Abelard-Schuman.

Gripe, M. (1975). *Julia's House*. Trans. G. Bothmer.

Gripe, M. (1975). *Julia's House*. Trans. G. Bothmer. New York: Delacorte Press.

Gripe, M. (1975). *The Land Beyond*. Trans. S. La Farge. London: Abelard-Schuman.

Gripe, M. (1976). *Elvis and His Friends*. Trans. S. La Farge. New York: Delacorte Press.

Gripe, M. (1976). *Elvis and His Secret*. Trans. S. La Farge. New York: Delacorte Press.

Gripe, M. (1976). *The Glassblower's Children*. Trans. S. La Farge. London: Target.

Gripe, M. (1976). *The Time of Bells*. Trans. S. La Farge. New York: Delacorte Press.

Gripe, M. (1977). *Elvis and His Secret*. Trans. S La Farge.

Gripe, M. (1977). *The Green Coat*. Trans. S. La Farge. New York: Delacorte Press.

Gripe, M. (1978). *Elvis and His Friends*. Trans. S. La Farge.

Gripe, M. (1978). *The Time of Bells*. Trans. S. La Farge.

Gripe, M. (1990). *Agnes Cecilia*. Trans. R. Lesser. New York: Harper & Row.

Gripe, M. [2014]. *The Glassblower's Children*. Trans. S. La Farge. New York: New York Review of Books.

Himmelstrup, K. (1969). *The Children of Tonacatecutli*. Trans. K. French. London: The Bodley Head.

Lagerkvist, P. (1962). *Death of Ahaseurus*. Trans. N. Walford.

Lagerkvist, P. (1968). *Mariamne*. Trans. N. Walford.

Lagerkvist, P. (1971). *The Eternal Sea*. Trans. N. Walford.

Lagerkvist, P. (1984). *Pilgrim at Sea*. Trans. N. Walford.

Lagerlöf, S. (1950). *The Wonderful Adventures of Nils*. Trans. V. S. Howard. London: J M Dent.

Lindgren, A. (1950). *Pippi Longstocking*. Trans. F. Lamborn. New York: Viking.

Lindgren, A. (1954). *Pippi Longstocking*. Trans. E. Hurup. Oxford: Oxford University Press.

Sandberg, I. (1969). *Little Spook*. Trans. K. French. London: Methuen.

Söderberg, H. (1963). *Doctor Glas*. Trans. P. B. Austin.

Söderberg, H. (1963). *Doctor Glas*. Trans. P. B. Austin. Boston: Little, Brown and Co.

**Secondary Sources**

Arenstam, D. (2012). 'Saco literary agent begins career early', *Biddeford-Saco-OOB Courier*, 16 Aug 2012. Available at: http://courier.mainelymediallc.com/news/2012-08-16/Neighbors/Saco_literary_agent_begins_career_early_friend_of_.html (Accessed: 23 November 2015).

Beckett, S. and Nikolajeva, M. (eds.) (2006). *Beyond Babar: The European Tradition in Children's Literature*. Lanham and Oxford: Scarecrow Press and Children's Literature Association.

Berry, C. (2011). 'A golden age of translation? The publishing of Nordic children's literature in the United Kingdom, 1950-1975', *The Journal of Children's Literature Studies*, 8 (3), Nov 2011, pp. 77-95.

Berry, C. (2013). *Publishing, Translation, Archives: Nordic Children's Literature in the United Kingdom, 1950-2000*. PhD thesis. University of Edinburgh. Available at: https://www.era.lib.ed.ac.uk/bitstream/handle/1842/9450/Berry2014.pdf?sequence=2&isAllowed=y (Accessed: 23 November 2015).

Berry, C. (2014a). 'Journeys into English: an overview of the English-language versions of *Nils Holgersson* and Anglophone academic discourse', in: (eds) Forsås-Scott, H., Stenberg, L., and Thomsen, B. T. *Re-mapping Lagerlöf: Performance, Intermediality, and European Transmissions*. Lund: Nordic Academic Press, pp. 273-288.

Berry, C. (2014b). 'Pippi and the dreaming spires: Nordic children's literature and Oxford University Press', in: Epstein, B. J. (ed.) *True North: Literary Translation in the Nordic Countries*. Newcastle: Cambridge Scholars Publishing, pp. 130-148.

Berry, C. (2014c). '"Moomins in English dress": British translations of the *Moomin* series', *The Lion and the Unicorn*, 38 (2), Apr 2014, pp. 145-161.

Berry, C. (2014d). '*Mrs Pepperpot* rules Britannia: the British editions', in: Lassén, M. and Skaret, A. (eds.) *Empowering Transformations: Mrs Pepperpot Revisited*. Newcastle: Cambridge Scholars Publishing, 117-131.

Charlton, J. (2004). 'Norah Smallwood', *Dictionary of National Biography*. Available at: http://www.oxforddnb.com/view/article/31693 (Accessed: 23 November 2015).

Coillie, J. van and Verschueren, W. (eds.) (2006). *Children's Literature in Translation: Challenges and Strategies*. Manchester: St Jerome Publishing.

Curtis, A. (2004). 'Ian Macnaghten Parsons', *Dictionary of National Biography*. Available at: http://www.oxforddnb.com/view/article/62267 (Accessed: 24 November 2015).

Edwards, O. D. (2007). *British Children's Fiction in the Second World War*. Edinburgh: Edinburgh University Press.

Eliot, S. (2004). 'John Hotten', *Dictionary of National Biography*. Available at: http://www.oxforddnb.com/view/article/13859 (Accessed: 24 November 2015).

Frank, H. (2007). *Cultural Encounters in Translated Children's Literature: Images of Australia in French Translation*. Manchester: St Jerome Publishing.

Fagerström, G. (1977). *Maria Gripe, hennes verk och hennes läsare (Maria Gripe, her work and her readers)*. Stockholm: Albert Bonniers Förlag.

Geddes, T. (2005). 'Paul Britten Austin obituary', *Swedish Book Review*, 2005/2, autumn 2005, pp. 44-45.

Heapy, R. (2013). 'Children's books', in: Louis, W. R. (ed.) *The History of Oxford University Press. Volume III: 1896 to 1970*. Oxford: OUP, pp. 471-482.

Jakobsen, G. (1985). 'Nordic Children's Book Prize [Maria Gripe]',

189

*Book Bird*, 4/1985, pp. 18-23.

Lathey, G. (ed.) (2006). *Translation of Children's Literature: A Reader.* Clevedon: Multilingual Matters.

Lathey, G. (2010). *The Role of Translators in Children's Literature: Invisible Storytellers.* London: Routledge.

Lathey, G. (2016). *Translating Children's Literature.* London: Routledge.

Lyons, R. D. (1994). 'Seymour Lawrence, 67, publisher for a variety of eminent authors', *New York Times*, 7 Jan 1994.

Mannheimer, C. (1973). 'Highly commended author [Hans Christian Andersen Medal]: Maria Gripe', *Book Bird*, 11 (2), pp. 24-34.

Norrie, I. (1982). *Mumby's Publishing and Bookselling in the Twentieth Century.* London: Bell and Hyman.

OSullivan, E. (2005). *Comparative Children's Literature.* London: Routledge

Pearson, L. (2010). 'The making of modern children's literature: quality and ideology in British children's literature publishing in the 1960s and 1970s'. Unpublished PhD thesis. Newcastle: University of Newcastle.

Pearson, L. (2013). *The Making of Modern Children's Literature in Britain: Publishing and Criticism in the 1960s and 1970s.* London: Ashgate.

Pinsent, P. (ed.) (2006). *No Child is an Island: The Case for Children's Literature in Translation.* Lichfield: Pied Piper Publishing.

Random House (2015). *About the Random House Group Ltd.* Available at: http://www.randomhouse.co.uk/about-us/about-us/about-the-random-house-group (Accessed online: 23 November 2015).

Reynolds, K. and Tucker, N. (eds.) (1998a). *Children's Book Publishing in Britain since 1945.* Aldershot: Scolar/Ashgate.

Reynolds, K. and Tucker, N. (eds.) (1998b). *Oral Archives: A Collection of Informal Conversations with Individuals Involved in Creating or Producing Children's Literature since 1945.* London: Roehampton Institute.

Rose, J. and Anderson, P. J. (eds.) (1991). *British Literary Publishing Houses, 1881-1965. Dictionary of Literary Biography. Volume 112.* Gale Research Inc: Detroit.

Schneller, B. (1991). 'Chatto and Windus (London: 1873-1987). John Camden Hotten (London: 1855-1873)', in Anderson, P. J. and Rose, J. (eds.) (1991). *British Literary Publishing Houses, 1820-1880. Dictionary of Literary Biography. Volume 106.* Gale Research Inc: Detroit, pp. 110-117.

Sturge, K. (2004). *The Alien Within: Translation into German during the Nazi Regime.* Munich: Ludicium.

Taunton, M. and da Silva, S. G. (2009). 'Chatto & Windus (1873-1969)', in Brake, L. and Demoor, M. (eds.) *Dictionary of Nineteenth-Century Journalism in Great Britain and Ireland.* London: Academia Press and British Library, p. 109

Thomson-Wohlgemuth, G. (2009). *Translation under State Control: Books for Young People in the German Democratic Republic.* London: Routledge.

University of Reading (2015). *Special Collections. Archives of Chatto & Windus Ltd.* Available: https://www.reading.ac.uk/special-collections/collections/sc-chatto.aspx (Accessed: 23 November 2015).

Warner, O. (1973). *Chatto & Windus: a brief account of the firm's origin, history and development.* London: Chatto & Windus.

Weedon, A. (2004). 'Andrew Chatto', *Dictionary of National Biography.* Available at: http://www.oxforddnb.com/view/article/47445 (Accessed: 23 November 2015).

# Miss Smilla to Sarah Lund: The Key Agents in the Dissemination of Danish Literature in the United Kingdom (1990-2015)

## Ellen Kythor

Since 1990, just over one hundred literary books originally written in Danish have been published in English in the United Kingdom for the first time. Peter Høeg's *Frøken Smillas fornemmelse for sne* (1992. UK: *Miss Smilla's Feeling for Snow*, 1993) was the most significant Danish-English breakthrough novel in recent decades – both in terms of sales figures, with 400,000 copies sold in its first two years of publication (Bloom 2008: 99), and having been identified as a key paradigm shift in the Danish-English translation field by researchers over 20 years on (cf. Forshaw 2014: 132; Giles forthcoming). Yet the number of Danish titles entering the British market did not rise above a handful of books per year until much more recently – since after 2010, when the mean average of three books per year (1990-2010 inclusive) rose to around eleven books per year (2011-2015). This chapter will firstly outline the parameters and purpose of my corpus of Danish literature published in the UK since 1990, and then focus on the key findings – authors, translators, and emerging trends, such as those just introduced. The purpose of this chapter is to provide a descriptive overview of the field of Danish-English literary translation in the British book market.

Denmark is an example of a 'small nation' with a strong welfare state and a history of structured support for cultural production and circulation. I adhere to the definition of 'small nation' proposed by Hjort and Petrie in the field of Film Studies (2007: 4-6): within Europe and the wider global system, Denmark is linguistically, geographically, and culturally marginal by virtue of the size of its population and economy, despite its colonial history.

The UK holds key cultural capital in the Anglophone publishing market and the global literary system as a whole: it is a 'hyper-central' culture in the world system of translation constructed by Heilbron (2010: 309-10). According to Heilbron's hierarchical structure, Anglophone publishing markets in the USA and UK are 'hyper-central' in the global system because English is so dominant – three quarters of books in translation globally are translated from English into another language. After English, two languages are 'central' in the world system of translation: French and German – with around a ten per cent share each of all books translated globally – followed by 'semi-peripheral' languages, with one-to-three per cent of the total number of books translated worldwide, as confirmed by the UNESCO's *Index Translationum* data. 'Semi-peripheral' languages include Danish (Heilbron 2010: 310), which is one of the top ten languages translated from according to the *Index Translationum* (the latest statistics are from 2008) – although admittedly not into English. Truly 'peripheral' cultures in this system hold a tiny percentage of the global market – less than one per cent. This includes a number of widely spoken languages such as Chinese which has a large number of speakers but does not make up a large part of the translated book market (titles translated from Chinese); testament to how '[t]he size of language groups is clearly not decisive for their degree of centrality in the translation system' (Heilbron 2010: 310).

Using Denmark and the UK as the case study for this chapter therefore provides insight into the relationship between a small, 'semi-peripheral' culture and a 'hyper-central' culture in the global literary system.

## Corpus

The corpus of books I have collated is to enable an appraisal of the contemporary field of Danish-English literary translation in the UK, specifically to identify the key agents and how they participate in this 'hyper-central'/'semi-peripheral' relationship.

Firstly, I will provide an explanation of the parameters of the corpus. There is no pre-existing list of literary translations from Danish to English. In 2015, the Danish Agency for Culture (*Kulturstyrelsen*) began to collate the data of all literary books translated from Danish into any language as part of the Literature Department's International Strategy (2014-2017). Up to this point they had an incomplete list on their website (www.kunst.dk) based on contact with publishers and translators who had applied for translation grants. There are comprehensive (yet not flawless) databases I have drawn upon to collate my corpus data: in particular, the British National Bibliography (BNB) at the British Library. The BNB records all publications in the UK; it is very comprehensive but it relies on data supplied by publishers so it is incomplete (Donahaye 2012: 8). For additional bibliographical data to fill gaps on incomplete records, such as Danish titles or the names of translators, other online resources were used including UNESCO's *Index Translationum* – which attempts to provide a complete list of all books translated worldwide[1] – supplemented by Amazon, GoodReads, WorldCat, *Litteratursiden* and the *Danish Literary Magazine*.

Books included in the corpus are 'literature': novels, children's books, graphic novels, poetry and short story collections by a single author, and drama. Non-fiction books are excluded from the corpus as they circulate in such a different field from literary books. Here fiction and non-fiction are identified as separate 'fields' of cultural production (as per Bourdieu 1993). While both fiction and non-fiction books exist in the overall field of the British publishing market, the key agents (authors, literary agencies, publishers, booksellers, etc.) and corresponding interactions within the separate fields of cultural production for fiction and non-fiction are often different, as demonstrated by delineated newspaper bestseller lists and book review sections for each. Also excluded are books that were first published in the UK before 1990 regardless of whether they have been reissued – so 'classics' such as Isak Dinesen/Karen Blixen or Hans Christian Andersen are not included – in order to maintain the focus on the current process of transferring a book from Denmark to the UK for the first time.[2]

1993 in the USA and UK saw the biggest recent Danish breakthrough novel in English translation: *Frøken Smillas fornemmelse for sne* by Peter Høeg. By using 1990 as the start date for my corpus I can look at the immediate context of the publication of this pivotal book and what followed. The end date of the corpus is 2015, so the intention is to give an up-to-date appraisal of the field across a contained period of twenty-five years, during which the book market has encountered significant technological and commercial changes, such as the advent of internet commerce, and increasing dominance of large conglomerate publishers and retailers.

Identifying and analysing the corpus will act as a foundation for an understanding of the role of key agents in the dissemination of Danish literature in the UK - for instance, who are the most prolific translators, which book types are most readily transferred into the British market, and which titles received state funding from the Danish Arts Foundation to help with publication abroad. The following sections will provide an overview of the number of books in the corpus, text types/genres, authors, translators, and publishers.

## Corpus: Numbers and Timeline

At least 150,000 books are published in the UK every year (Booksellers Association report 2013). Most estimates - including the latest Literature Across Frontiers report (Büchler and Trentacosti 2015: 5) - tell us that fewer than five per cent of books in the British market are in translation. Translation Studies theorist Lawrence Venuti's well-documented criticism of the insular Anglophone book market and its 'aggressively monolingual readerships' (2013 [orig. 2008]: 159) seems borne out by numbers here.

At the time of writing, I have found 120 books that fit my parameters.[3] Over a period of twenty-five years, and taking into consideration the figures relating to the annual publication rates in the whole British book market and the percentage in translation, this is a very small number. Books first written in Danish then published in the UK in English are a tiny part of an already small subset. The Literature Across

Frontiers report confirms that Danish was the tenth most translated European language between 2000 and 2012 (Büchler and Trentacosti 2015: 15).

By arranging the corpus by year of publication on a graph or visual timeline,[4] it is easy to observe a drop-off in publications in the late 1990s, and a sharp increase in the number of publications from 2010 onwards. Yet it is hard to extrapolate data and draw conclusions from such small figures. There were two or three publications per year until the mid 2000s, then a (relative) 'leap' after 2010. More precisely: a mean average of three books per year until 2010, then around eleven books per year on average from 2011 onwards. This corresponds with increased state support for translation from the Danish Arts Foundation, but also correlates with the rise of the popularity of the Scandinavian crime fiction genre - primarily Swedish and Norwegian books in the UK by, for instance, Stieg Larsson, Henning Mankell, and Jo Nesbø - and related cultural exports. In fact, remarkably, three quarters of the crime fiction novels in the corpus were published after 2010. This date correlates with the release of other cultural products in the Nordic Noir 'brand' (cf. Broomé 2014: 270): Swede Stieg Larsson's bestselling *Millennium* trilogy was published in the UK between 2008 and 2010; Danish television series started being broadcast on BBC4 in a primetime Saturday evening slot with *The Killing* (Danish: *Forbrydelsen*) in 2011; the first Nordicana Expo was held in London in 2013; and 2013 also saw the first Petrona Award for Best Scandinavian Crime Novel available in English.

## Corpus: Text Types, Genre, Titles

The majority of books in the corpus are novels - 70 per cent - and around 40 per cent of those are in the crime fiction genre. 23 titles - 19 per cent of the corpus - are children's literature, including four graphic novels and one iPad app.[5] The remainder are six short story collections, five poetry books, and two plays. To reiterate: just over 40 per cent of the 83 novels are 'crime fiction', yet Danish literature is not the most strongly represented in the Nordic Noir genre in the

UK. Scandinavian crime fiction as a single genre has been called a misnomer, seeing as Denmark's outputs are outnumbered by Sweden and Norway's (Nestingen and Arvas 2011: 5) - although crime fiction is still the biggest single genre of novel represented in this corpus.

The corpus contains books published for the first time in English in the UK after 1990, excluding re-publications or re-translations of 'classics'. In the vast majority of cases these books have been published almost contemporaneously in Denmark, that is, first published within the previous decade in Danish. Notable exceptions are: Suzanne Brøgger Notable exceptions are: Suzanne Brøgger (*A Fighting Pig's Too Tough to Eat* [UK: 1997; Denmark: *En gris som har været oppe at slås kan man ikke stege*, 1979] and *The Jade Cat* [UK: 2004; Denmark: *Jadekatten*, 1997]), William Heinesen (Danish language titles first published 1934-1964; first published in UK 1992-2011), and Inger Christensen (UK: 2000 and 2007; Denmark: 1969 and 1981).

An author's books are not always published in the UK in the same order as in Denmark, especially when the success of one text has prompted the publisher to delve into that author's back catalogue and publish previous releases. Peter Høeg's *The History of Danish Dreams* (UK: 1996; Denmark: *Forestilling om det Tyvende århundrede*, 1988) and *Tales of the Night* (UK: 1997; Denmark: *Fortællinger om natten*, 1990) were published in Britain after the success of *Miss Smilla's Feeling for Snow* (1993) and likewise Jussi Adler-Olsen's *Alphabet House* (UK: 2014; Denmark: *Alfabethuset*, 1997) was first published following his Department Q series (UK: 2011-2014).

Sometimes texts in the corpus are translated and published for the American market first before being published in the UK. Some of these books have different titles in the USA and UK; almost certainly a decision by the publishing house. *Miss Smilla's Feeling for Snow* (1993) was published in the USA as *Smilla's Sense of Snow* (1993) and - notoriously in Danish-English translation circles (e.g. Satterlee 1996) - re-edited for the British market. Sara Blædel's *Call Me Princess* (USA: 2011) became *Blue Blood* in the UK (2013). All but one of Adler-Olsen's *Department Q* series have very different titles in the UK and USA, despite having the same translator for each corresponding American and British version (and only one of these titles is a 'word-for-word' translation of the Danish title):

| | Denmark | United Kingdom | United States |
|---|---|---|---|
| Volume 1 | *Kvinden i buret* (2007) [Literal translation: *The Woman in the Cage*] | *Mercy* (2011) | *The Keeper of Lost Causes* (2011) |
| Volume 2 | *Fasandræberne* (2008) [*The Pheasant Killers*] | *Disgrace* (2012) | *The Absent One* (2012) |
| Volume 3 | *Flaskepost fra P* (2009) [*Message in a Bottle from P*] | *Redemption* (2013) | *A Conspiracy of Faith* (2013) |
| Volume 4 | *Journal 64* (2010) [*Journal 64*] | *Guilt* (2013) | *The Purity of Vengeance* (2013) |
| Volume 5 | *Marco Effekten* (2012) [*The Marco Effect*] | *Buried* (2015) | *The Marco Effect* (2014) |
| Volume 6 | *Den Grænseløse* (2014) [*The Boundless*] | *The Hanging Girl* (2015) | *The Hanging Girl* (2015) |

**Table 1**: 'Department Q' book series titles (Jussi-Adler Olsen)

In 2014, the American title of the first in the series - *The Keeper of Lost Causes* - was chosen for the British circulation of the Danish film adaptation (2012), and the book was subsequently re-issued with this title in the UK as a tie-in. The use of different titles in the UK and USA exemplifies how the two literary fields are different (cf. Thompson 2010); the publishing imprint in each country chose a fitting title based on an understanding of their domestic literary market and how each book might be promoted. There is a commonality through volumes 1-5 of the British titles as they use distinctive one-word titles - this would have helped with paratextual materials; maintaining a theme and style with the book jacket design. Overall this is worth remarking on because it emphasises the nuances between these two Anglophone markets, and justifies my study being focused only on the British book market.

## Corpus: Authors

Peter Høeg – aforementioned starting point for the parameters of this research – is prolific in the corpus. Seven of his books have been published in the UK in this time period, and his latest (*Effekten af Susan*, Denmark: 2014) is scheduled to be in 2016. All have been released by the same publisher: Harvill. The most prolific authors are listed in Table 2. Lene Kaaberbøl has a varied catalogue of books in English: six children's books and one crime fiction book authored alone, and three crime fiction novels in partnership with another author, Agnete Friis. There are 59 separate author names in total in the corpus. Two thirds of books in the corpus are by male authors (individual members of co-authored books are counted to reach that total). Nearly a third of the books in the corpus are written by the same five authors (the first five authors in Table 2), followed by many authors with only a couple of books in the corpus including Danish bestsellers such as Sara Blædel and Helle Helle: precisely 30 authors have just one book in the corpus and 11 authors have only two books in the corpus.

| | |
|---|---|
| Lene Kaaberbøl | 10 |
| Jussi Adler-Olsen | 7 |
| Peter Høeg | 7 |
| Kim Fupz Aakeson | 5 |
| William Heinesen | 5 |
| Leif Davidsen | 4 |
| Stig Dalager | 4 |
| Jan Kjær & Merlin P. Mann | 4 |
| Henrik Stangerup | 4 |

**Table 2**: Authors and Number of Books in Corpus

## Corpus: Translators

Translators are crucial, although often overlooked, in the field of Danish-English translation: readers read the translators' words in the English-language edition, yet the translator's name is rarely included on the book cover. Translators with an appreciable proportion of books in the corpus include Charlotte Barslund (ten titles, three as co-translations), Anne Born (ten titles), Martin Aitken (ten titles), and Barbara Haveland (nine titles). Table 3 provides a good way of identifying 'established' translators in the field.

| Martin Aitken | 10 |
| Charlotte Barslund | 10 |
| Anne Born | 10 |
| Barbara Haveland | 9 |
| W. Glyn Jones | 7 |
| Lene Kaaberbøl | 7 |

**Table 3**: Translators and Number of Books in Corpus

Authors are not always translated by the same translator: Peter Høeg, for instance, has been translated into English in the UK by F. David (a pseudonym for Tiina Nunnally), Nadia Christensen, Barbara Haveland, and Martin Aitken, and translators of Jussi Adler-Olsen – whose *Department Q* series is outlined above in Table 1 – are Martin Aitken, William Frost, Lisa Hartford, Steve Schein, and K.E. Semmel. There are some 'self translators': Kaaberbøl has translated her children's literature and one crime novel into English, and crime author duo under the pseudonym Sander Jakobsen translated their novel *The Preacher* (2013).

There are 52 individual translators named in the corpus. Yet nearly 45 per cent of the books are translated by the same six translators (Table

3). By my estimate, around 70 per cent are native English speakers. 63 per cent are women – almost a reversal of the authors' gender ratio.

## Corpus: Publishers

Many imprints in the UK are actually owned by large conglomerates formed after mergers and acquisitions (cf. Schiffrin 2000: 109). For instance, Harvill Secker (its name in 2015) was formed by a merger; since 2002 it has been an imprint within the Vintage subsidiary of Random House, one of the largest publishers in the world. Publications by Harvill comprise 12 per cent of the corpus, but it is not as straightforward as labelling Harvill a 'large' publisher for the duration of the period of the corpus because at the start it was a smaller independent concern. There is a strong presence of small independent publishers including Boyars (four books) and the Nordic-specialist not-for-profit academic publisher Norvik Press (eight books).

As well as publishing imprints, it is important to identify the people behind the imprint who have made key decisions that resulted in publication – for instance, Christopher MacLehose appears to have had a direct connection to many books from Denmark in the UK via his position at Harvill where he worked from 1979, and then MacLehose Press: an imprint of Quercus since 2008. His intervention brought Høeg's *Smilla* to the United Kingdom (Pihl 1996: 111), and later MacLehose introduced Swedish crime authors Henning Mankell and Stieg Larsson to the English-language market, key authors in the Nordic Noir 'craze'.

## The Role of State Support: An Example

A prevailing theme in the translation of Danish literature into English is state support for this cultural endeavour from Denmark. Denmark gives consistent and high state support for cultural production and dissemination. The Danish Arts Foundation (*Statens Kunstfond*) plays an important role in the publication of literature in Denmark as well as in the translation, publication, and dissemination of Danish literature abroad. Administered by the Danish Agency for Culture (*Kulturstyrelsen*), the Danish Arts Foundation has seven financial support schemes for literary translation projects, five of which have a direct relationship with translation from Danish to English. Authors, translators, and publishers all have the potential to get financial support from these grants. The International Research Programme (*Det internationale researchprogram [Litteratur]*), the Literary Exchange Fund (*Litteratur- og personudvekslingspuljen*), and the Literary Events and Marketing Abroad Programme (*Litterære arrangementer og markedsføring i udlandet*) all support a variety of activities to further intercultural relationships and the promotion of Danish literature worldwide. The Sample Translation Fund (*Tilskud til Prøveoversættelser*) - paid to translators - and the Translation Fund (*Oversætterpuljen*) - paid to publishers to fulfil their contract with translators - both have clear parameters and a delineated, standardised application process. In addition to these five relevant funds, the Danish Arts Foundation also awards an annual Translators' Prize to one translator from Danish into any language, and career stipends (*Arbejdslegater*).

I have ascertained through fieldwork (in particular, interviews with key agents at both *Statens Kunstfond* and *Kulturstyrelsen*, including chairs of the literature departments: Thomas Harder and Anne Lise Marstrand-Jørgensen) that 'quality', non-market-led books tend to receive funding for translation over 'mainstream' genres or authors. State grants for non-mainstream books enable types of literature other than popular genres to enter the British market: larger publishers seem especially willing to fund books in translation that they believe will do well commercially and recoup costs, and they seek assistance (state funding or other sources) for less marketable books. Sample Translation Grants and the Translation Fund from the Danish Arts Foundation are - according to official criteria - awarded to books with 'literary quality' rather than those that might hold their own in the market without additional assistance, yet the notion of 'quality' is difficult to quantify.

The publication history of a recent book from Denmark in the UK will be used here to demonstrate the role of agents discussed above, thereby placing some of the corpus data into socio-historical context as well as demonstrating the role of state support agencies. Firstly, the value judgement bestowed by cultural gatekeepers, that is highly-regarded critics, publishers, cultural awards and prize committees, leads to an unspoken definition of 'quality' within the industry and with readers. Literary awards and prizes of particular relevance to the field of Danish-English literary translation include the Nobel Prize for Literature, the Nordic Council Literary Prize, the Golden Laurels (*De Gyldne Laurbær*) and the Petrona Award. Kim Leine's *Profeterne i Evighedsfjorden* (2012) (*The Prophets of Eternal Fjord*, UK: 2015) received the Nordic Council Literature Prize in 2013 and Denmark's Golden Laurels in 2012. Both of these prizes were named on the application form to the Danish Arts Foundation's Translation Fund by Liveright Publishing Corporation (USA), an imprint of W.W. Norton & Company. Liveright stated the funding from the Translation Fund would enable British independent publisher Atlantic Books to publish in the UK at the same time as Liveright published the American edition. Despite – or perhaps because of – the limited space on the Translation Fund application form, the prizes were named as they are considered shorthand for the significance and cachet of this novel. The publisher was appealing to the Danish Arts Foundation's mutual understanding of 'quality' and cultural value by including the prizes in the application.

Martin Aitken, a native British-English speaker who resides in Denmark, was selected as the translator for *Profeterne i Evighedsfjorden*. Aitken is named on copyright pages for both the American and British editions, and named by Liveright on the application form to the Translation Fund, as required by the application criteria. Aitken has been very active as a literary translator in recent years: as mentioned above, ten books in the corpus are translated by him, the first in 2011. Aitken has received various grants for his translation work from the Danish Arts Foundation, including career stipends in 2014 and 2015, perhaps a self-fulfilling marker of success and 'quality' as perceived by the Arts Foundation itself when considering other grants. For funders, publishers, and – in some cases – readers, the names of prolific and well-regarded translators can become shorthand for a good book and a good translation; their name becomes a marker of good quality. The cultural prestige of these translators means that it is assumed by cultural gatekeepers that they would not put their name to a 'bad book' and that their work in the target language will be of high quality, so it sometimes becomes valuable to name the translator in marketing materials and especially – as in this example – funding applications. Evidence that Aitken's personal 'brand' is growing comes on the cover of the American hardback publication of this book, where – unusually for any translated title in the Anglophone market – his name appears prominently on the front, and he even receives accolade in the 'about the author' section of both the American and British editions: 'Martin Aitken is an acclaimed translator of Danish literature'.

According to records on the Danish Arts Foundation's website, Atlantic Books was awarded DKK 50,000 from the Translation Fund in 2013 to enable publication of this novel in English. This amounted to 50 per cent of the overall fee described in the application form by Liveright, in keeping with the Danish Arts Foundation's usual practice of supporting 30 to 50 per cent of the translation fee (the publisher covers the remainder). *The Prophets of Eternal Fjord* was published in 2015.

## Conclusion

My research has identified that only 120 translated books of Danish literature were published for the first time in the UK between 1990 and 2015, yet given the small size of the whole field of literary translation in the British market, it is nonetheless interesting to identify trends and key agents involved in this particular relationship between these 'semi-peripheral' and 'hyper-central' cultures in the global system of translated literature. For instance, the changing landscape over time: the number of books published annually in this field between 1990 and 2015 only rose into double figures in 2011. The data also indicate a pattern of some regularly-occurring authors and translators followed by a succession of one-offs and outliers. Nearly 30 per cent of the 120 books are written by the same five authors and nearly 45 per cent are translated by the same six translators. These are followed by many authors and translators with only one or two books in the corpus. The example of Leine's *The Prophets of Eternal Fjord* brings the corpus data to life and demonstrates the process, agents, and values involved in bringing a translated book from Denmark to market in the UK. Further examples exist and a deeper analysis of the role of the agents identified above – especially within Danish state support mechanisms – can be found in Kythor (forthcoming).

## Endnotes

[1] The *Index Translationum* receives its data directly from the BNB (Donahaye 2012: 10). Yet in some cases the records have provided additional data to supplement information from the BNB records.

[2] Andersen's popular fairy tales arguably stand apart as their own genre or 'brand'; they are still the most (re-)translated and published books from Denmark in the UK, as evidenced by BNB records.

[3] The data for 2015 included in this article may be incomplete. The full corpus will be available as an appendix to Kythor (forthcoming) and is currently available as an unpublished working document on request.

[4] For instance using the web-based tool Tiki Toki, demonstrated here: http://www.tiki-toki.com/timeline/entry/179923/Danish-in-the-UK/

[5] The iPad app *Wuwu and Co.* (Merete Pryds Helle et al. 2014) is considered children's literature for the purposes of the corpus, yet it is not in a typical bound book format.

## References

Adler-Olsen, J. (1997). *Alfabethuset.* Copenhagen: Cicero.

Adler-Olsen, J. (2014). *Alphabet House.* Trans. S. Schein. London: Hesperus.

Adler-Olsen, J. *Department Q* Series (Denmark; UK; USA editions):

Volume 1

Adler-Olsen, J. (2007). *Kvinden i buret.* Copenhagen: Politiken.

Adler-Olsen, J. (2011). *Mercy.* Trans. L. Hartford. London: Penguin.

Adler-Olsen, J. (2011). *The Keeper of Lost Causes.* Trans. L. Hartford. New York: Penguin Random House.

Volume 2

Adler-Olsen, J. (2008). *Fasandræberne.* Copenhagen: Politiken.

Adler-Olsen, J. (2012). *Disgrace.* Trans. K.E. Semmel. London: Penguin.

Adler-Olsen, J. (2012). *The Absent One.* Trans. K.E. Semmel. New York: Penguin Random House.

Volume 3

Adler-Olsen, J. (2009). *Flaskepost fra P.* Copenhagen: Politiken.

Adler-Olsen, J. (2013). *Redemption.* Trans. M. Aitken. London: Penguin.

Adler-Olsen, J. (2013). *A Conspiracy of Faith.* Trans. M. Aitken. New York: Penguin Random House.

Volume 4

Adler-Olsen, J. (2010). *Journal 64.* Copenhagen: Politiken.

Adler-Olsen, J. (2013). *Guilt.* Trans. M. Aitken. London: Penguin.

Adler-Olsen, J. (2013). *The Purity of Vengeance.* Trans. M.Aitken. New York: Penguin Random House.

Volume 5

Adler-Olsen, J. (2012). *Marco Effekten.* Copenhagen: Politiken.

Adler-Olsen, J. (2015). *Buried.* Trans. M Aitken. London: Penguin.

Adler-Olsen, J. (2014). *The Marco Effect.* Trans. M Aitken. New York: Penguin Random House.

Volume 6

Adler-Olsen, J. (2014). *Den Grænseløse.* Copenhagen: Politiken.

Adler-Olsen, J. (2015). *The Hanging Girl.* Trans. W. Frost. London: Quercus.

Adler-Olsen, J. (2015). *The Hanging Girl.* Trans. W. Frost. New York: Penguin Random House.

Bloom, C. (2008). *Bestsellers: Popular Fiction since 1900.* Basingstoke: Palgrave Macmillan.

Blædel, S. (2011). *Call Me Princess.* Trans. E. Macki and T. Chace. New York: Pegasus.

Blædel, S. (2013). *Blue Blood.* Trans. E. Macki and T. Chace. London: Sphere.

Booksellers Association report (2013). 'UK Titles Published 2001-2013' Available at: http://www.booksellers.org.uk/BookSellers/media/SiteMediaLibrary/IndustryNews/UK-Titles-Published-2001-2013.pdf (Accessed: 26 September 2015).

Bourdieu, P. (1993). *The Field of Cultural Production.* Cambridge: Polity Press.

Broomé, A. (2014). 'The Exotic North, or How Marketing Created the Genre of Scandinavian Crime' in Epstein, B.J. (ed.) *True North: Literary Translation in the Nordic Countries.* Newcastle-upon-Tyne: Cambridge Scholars, pp. 269-282.

Brøgger, S. (1979). *En gris som har været oppe at slås kan man ikke stege.* Copenhagen: Rhodos.

Brøgger, S. (1997). *A Fighting Pig's Too Tough to Eat.* Trans. M. Allemano. Norwich: Norvik Press.

Brøgger, S. (1997). *Jadekatten*. Copenhagen: Gyldendal

Brøgger, S. (2004). *The Jade Cat*. Trans. A. Born. London: Harvill.

Büchler, A. and Trentacosti, G. (2015). 'Publishing translated literature in the United Kingdom and Ireland 1990 – 2012 – statistical report.' [Report for Literature Across Frontiers] Aberystwyth: Mercator Institute for Media, Languages and Culture.

Donahaye, J. (2012). 'Three percent? Publishing data and statistics on translated literature in the United Kingdom and Ireland.' [Report for Making Literature Travel – Literature Across Frontiers] Aberystwyth: Mercator Institute for Media, Languages and Culture.

Forshaw, B. (2014). *Euro Noir: The Pocket Essential Guide to European Crime Fiction, Film and TV*. Harpenden: Pocket Essentials, Oldcastle Books.

Giles, I. (forthcoming). *Tracing the Transmission of Scandinavian Literature to the UK 1917-2017*. PhD thesis, University of Edinburgh.

Heilbron, J. (2010). 'Towards a Sociology of Translation' in Baker, M. (ed.) *Critical Readings in Translation Studies* London: Routledge. pp. 304-316.

Helle, M. Pryds. et al. (2014). *Wuwu and Co* [iPad app].

Hjort, M. (2005). *Small Nation, Global Cinema: The New Danish Cinema*. Minneapolis/London: University of Minnesota Press.

Hjort, M. and Petrie, D. (2007). 'Introduction' in Hjort, M. and Petrie, D. (eds.) *The Cinema of Small Nations* in Edinburgh: Edinburgh University Press. pp. 1-19.

Høeg, P. (1988). *Forestilling om det Tyvende århundrede*. Charlottenlund: Rosinante.

Høeg, P. (1990). *Fortællinger om natten*. Copenhagen: Rosinante

Høeg, P. (1992). *Frøken Smillas fornemmelse for sne*. Copenhagen: Rosinante.

Høeg, P. (1993). *Miss Smilla's Feeling for Snow*. Trans. F. David. London: Harvill.

Høeg, P. (1993). *Smilla's Sense of Snow*. Trans. T. Nunnally. New York: Farrar Straus & Giroux.

Høeg, P. (1996). *The History of Danish Dreams*. Trans. B. Haveland. London: Harvill.

Høeg, P. (1997). *Tales of the Night*. Trans. B. Haveland. London: Harvill.

*Index Translationum*: http://www.unesco.org/culture/xtrans/ (Accessed 8 October 2015).

Jakobsen, S. (2013). *The Preacher*. Trans. D. Winther and K. Degnbol [S. Jakobsen]. London: Sphere.

Kythor, E. (forthcoming). *The Dissemination of Danish Literature in the UK 1990-2015*. PhD thesis, UCL.

Leine. K. (2012). *Profeterne i Evighedsfjorden*. Copenhagen: Gyldendal.

Leine, K. (2015). *The Prophets of Eternal Fjord*. Trans. M. Aitken. London: Atlantic Books.

Nestingen, A. and Arvas, P. (2011). 'Introduction' in Nestingen, A. and Arvas, P. (eds.) *Scandinavian Crime Fiction*. Cardiff: University of Wales Press. pp. 1-17.

Pihl, T. (1996). *The Publishing of Translated Fiction and Cultural Funding System in Britain and Denmark. A Cross-Cultural Study and Assessment*. PhD thesis, University of North London.

Satterlee, T. (1996). 'A Case for Smilla'. *Translation Review*, No. 50: pp. 13-17.

Schiffrin, A (2000). *The Business of Books*. London: Verso.

Thompson, J. B. (2010). *Merchants of Culture*. Cambridge: Polity Press.

Venuti, L. (2013). *Translation Changes Everything*. Abingdon: Routledge.

# CROSSING CULTURES

# Coastal Cultures in Scotland and Norway:
## Narratives, Affinity, Contact[1]

## Silke Reeploeg

This article investigates transnational cultural encounters that cross the established research areas of Northern European, Nordic, and Scandinavian Studies. Using approaches from Scandinavian research on coastal communities and cultural spaces, the article examines cultural transfer between Norway and Scotland through trade and exchange during the eighteenth and nineteenth centuries. The interdisciplinary and transnational approach adopted throughout the paper suggests new perspectives in researching coastal communities in Britain, as part of a wider understanding of cultural encounters between the communities of the North (Thisted *et al.* 2013).

### Coastal Communities and Regional Identities

Responses to globalisation, climate change, and independence processes have seen established Northern European relationships and spatial metaphors transformed during the twentieth century. Coastal communities, in particular, have adapted to political, social, and economic changes which resulted in opportunities for self-determination as well as new intercultural encounters. As a result, established research paradigms are renegotiated, creating new areas for reflection and critical examination. One example of this type of research is exemplified in the study of coastal culture (*kystkultur*) in Norway, which has already added valuable new perspectives to existing, land-based research into regional cultural identities. The term *kystkultur*, in Scandinavia, is perceived in different ways. On the one hand it encapsulates the life and activities in the days before industrialisation, in the form of material culture, such as structures and buildings. On the other, it also forms the basis for contemporary coastal heritage (Holm 1995). This ongoing creation of heritage selectively rediscovers and reinterprets coastal traditions and folklore, and plays an important role in how our perceptions of coastal landscapes are shaped.

At the root of the term lies the belief that life along the coast is not the same as life inland, or even along the fjords or other waterways that connect the land with the sea. So, coastal culture can mean a collection of artefacts that relate to living in this unique environment (where, for example, fishing may be as important as farming), such as work descriptions, stories, and artistic production. A similar approach can also be applied to the history and culture of Scotland's coastal communities, which should not be studied in isolation, nor only in relation to the other British Islands. Other regional and transnational perspectives need to be added – with the sea not seen a barrier but as 'more of a bridge, a link to the world beyond' (Smith 2003 [1984]: 323), an opportunity for intercultural contact. Coastal culture, created and communicated via maritime spaces, presents opportunities for intercultural contacts that lead to a variety of cultural identities, as well as a tool for demonstrating regional variety or even autonomy (Reeploeg 2012 and 2016).

Historically, coastal societies have differed from those inhabiting inland areas in that their culture is shaped by a combination-economy of farming and fishing, but also by their intensive use of coastal land- and seascapes (i.e. the area between high and low tides). This sea-focused cultural landscape exists across the coastal communities of the North, and informs the way in which regional cultural identities are formed and maintained (Rian 1997). It also forms the basis of ways in which coastal communities interact across the North Sea and other oceans, in transnational cultural regions or 'sub-national regions crossing international boundaries' (Winge 2001: 48). Parts of the British Isles, but in particular coastal Scotland, such as the Western and Northern Isles, have long been part of a wider Nordic territory, with political transfer of the islands of Orkney and Shetland from the Norwegian to the Scottish

Crown occurring as late as 1468 and 1469 respectively (Crawford 2013). The archipelagos of Shetland and Orkney therefore stand out as particularly evident areas of intercultural influences. Archaeological, historical and cultural evidence suggest regional communities that are far from isolated by their geographical position, but connected via maritime links both across the North Sea and the North Atlantic.

## Cultural Regions Rediscovered

Historical regions (geopolitical or cultural) have often been seen as representing the first state in an evolutionary progression from region to nation to global village, or outdated remnants of a pre-globalised world. Little attention has been given to what happens to historical links, regional cultural identity, and cross-national regions in new, globalised, geographical spaces which are still 'impregnated with administrative boundaries' (Häkli 1997: 9). This includes transnational regions, which manifest themselves in concrete policy such as through the implementation of European structural funds. The roles of local, regional and national boundaries, symbols and identity narratives in the production and reproduction of regions seems altogether less obvious. Both Sven Tägil (1995) and Christopher Harvie (2000 [1997]) have provided useful contextual introductions to the issues of regionalism and regionalisation within Northern Europe and the British Isles, where they describe regionalism as the dynamics of being part of a nation, but also being part of a network of transnational European regions (Jönsson, 2007 [2000]). Regional narratives then become a significant factor in terms of providing a basis for self-determination and de-centralisation projects that are an alternative to reactionary forms of regionalism based on essentialist geographical, ethnic, or racial notions of identity (Råberg 1997).

Anssi Paasi (2009) has explored a range of critical approaches to analysing regions which link human geography with other social sciences, in order to escape traditional and ahistorical centre-periphery models. He sees regional identities much more as products of cultural and social dynamics, influenced by global, national, and transnational ideas and processes:

> [R]egions should be seen as complicated constellations of agency, social relations and power. Regions are institutional structures and processes that are perpetually 'becoming' instead of just 'being'. They have a material basis grounded in economic and political relations. Various time scales come together in such processes. Similarly social institutions such as culture, media and administration are crucial in these processes and in the production and reproduction of certain 'structures of expectations' for these units. (Paasi 2009: 131)

It is clearly important to break down historiographical barriers that restrict intercultural contact to political histories, connecting the study of cultural history and historical context to that of everyday lives and material culture. These represent tangible and continuous intercultural links between North European regions on an interregional, rather than national, level. Cultural legacy or inheritance is therefore not simply a process of documentation and transmission across time, but also of renegotiation of what is meaningful to specific contemporary historical and political situations. The historical flow of material, cultural and narrative production between Scotland and Norway, for example, have clearly left their mark in the form of a regional Nordic cultural heritage, particularly in the Scottish Northern Isles of Orkney and Shetland. This ranges from language and literature to maritime knowledge and boat building. Many of these activities cross established discursive or geopolitical boundaries, creating intercultural narratives that adapt and renegotiate national and regional identities over time (Reeploeg 2015). An interdisciplinary approach therefore enables the consideration of both historical and cultural material side by side. From this perspective 'Nordic' and 'European' discourses and narratives can be better understood, and linked to their respective historical and economic realities.

## Intercultural Dialogue and Cultural Transfer: The North Atlantic Rim

A useful sea-based approach using an intercultural stance lies in the study of the North Atlantic Rim. As a conceptual tool for political economy the North Atlantic Rim has allowed Northern marginal regions to be compared and policies to be developed (Leroy 1999). Within the social sciences, Atlantic history emerged from a network of economic, geo-political, and cultural exchanges between the British, French, Dutch, Spanish, and Portuguese empires, and the Americas. Atlantic historians argue that the continents and societies bordering the Atlantic Ocean can therefore be studied as a shared, regional sphere (Armitage and Braddick, 2009 [2002]). As an emerging academic field, North Atlantic Rim studies can thus be seen to follow Bernard Bailyn's *Atlantic History: Concepts and Contours* (2005), which focuses on cosmopolitan and multicultural elements. This encourages a critical engagement with issues such as (mainly British) colonial studies, imperialism, and other spheres often neglected or considered in isolation by traditional historiography dealing with Europe or the Americas. In this context, the study of the North Atlantic region offers the opportunity to compare North American historical and cultural perspectives with those of the Northern European and Nordic countries.

The North Atlantic, as a historical and cultural region, is thus an equally complex spatial concept. When looking at the history of the North Atlantic Rim area, it becomes apparent that the societies within this region have had strong historical connections through trade, migration, and political unions/divisions. The movement of Norse explorers and settlers, for example, stretches over parts of the North Atlantic region and Northern Europe, with archaeological finds indicating cross-regional communities with a shared sense of identity and beliefs (Magnusson 1980; DuBois 1999).

## Space, Identity, and Organisation in Coastal Regions

Both tangible and intangible cultures are rich sources in terms of considering the European 'trialogue' between space, identity, and organisation (Jönsson, 2007 [2000]). Northern European and Atlantic coastal communities share a set of environments and cultures that are different from their respective inland areas. As already mentioned, coastal regions are shaped by a combination-economy of farming and various ways of using the sea and coast. So, for example, underwater topographies, together with seasonal changes in temperature, determine the production of plankton, which affect the quantity of fish in a particular area. A shared, cross-cultural vocabulary of intangible knowledge about both the sea and the land (i.e. offshore fishing grounds and the seashore) is therefore a critical part of the economic and cultural capital of coastal communities (Klepp 1992). Coastal culture is visible in not only tangible objects such as harbours, boats, and coastal buildings, but also the less tangible knowledge about the cultural landscape of the coast such as fishing meds (a combination of inland and offshore orientation to located fishing grounds), safe anchorages, and other underwater landscape features. Shared traditions and narratives thus connect coastal communities in their diverse, but similarly sea-focused cultural landscapes that exist across the oceans of the world. Narratives, in turn, inform the way in which regional cultural identities are formed and maintained (Rian 1997). They also form the basis of ways in which coastal communities maintain communal memories (Aronsson 2009), constructed through cultural traditions, which maintain 'sub-national regions crossing international boundaries' (Winge 2001). Seen in a wider context, island cultures, such as the British Isles, are also essentially coastal cultures, and need to be approached as a network of diverse identities that include intercultural features:

> Although islands have a very easily defined border, between sea and land, the cultural identities of the islanders neither define themselves in isolation or only in relation to their nearest national centre. In view of an intercultural analysis of cultural practices and historical narratives, the sea that surrounds the British Isles is therefore not a barrier, that somehow keeps Britishness contained […]. (Reeploeg 2012)

## Trade and Cultural Exchange across the North

Coastal maritime and economic links are fruitful areas for the investigation of coastal cultures in areas with long coastlines and relatively small populations. These small societies are said to be marked by a particular mentality characterised by not only a combination of strong individualism, but also a sense of community and solidarity (Holm 1995: 219). Mercantile links are essential to societies living in areas with limited resources or opportunities for agriculture. Norway, for example, has had a long tradition of interregional encounters along the Norwegian coast based on fishing and trading in economic resources. Both 'obvious and hidden regions' (Winge 2001) have been the result of these economic, social, and political/administrative regional relationships, with complex cultural encounters occurring. These are used as the basis and context for the formation of identities, both on a sub- and transnational level (Reeploeg 2012).

Economic and social relationships are important when studying transnational coastal cultures, as well as the possibility of 'hidden' regions, where cultural elements can be detected via the analysis of both contemporary and historical material. So, for example, when considering the cultural links between Scotland and Norway, earlier contacts, such as the Hanseatic trading networks into Europe and the Baltic are often good starting points. Historical analysis allows us to look at the development of trade and cultural exchange between Norway and countries across the North Sea, especially centred on not only the supply of resources such as timber, grain, and salt, but also migration and the creation of cultural networks stimulated by trade (Andersen *et al.* 1985; Bjørklund 1985).

Regular trading links between Scotland and Norway meant the opportunity for people to not only maintain and extend a variety of commercial networks, but also to engage in cultural contact (Murdoch and Sher 1988). In Norwegian history the Dutch period (1550–1750) or *Hollendartida* is connected with a triangular trade in timber, dried fish, grain, and commodities to and from the Norwegian port of Bergen. However, it also links into regional trade along the whole northern and southern coast of Norway (Løyland 2012) and the subsequent Scottish Trade, which continued existing timber imports between Norway and Scotland, and across Northern Europe (Næss 1959 [1920]). Scottish traders often bought timber directly from coastal regions such as Ryfylke, and later directly to the fjords of Sunnhordland, the area between Ryfylke and Bergen, Western Norway's main port. This led to the Western Norwegian region of Sunnhordland becoming 'the leading source for timber exports to Scotland' (Thomson 1991: 15). The commercial networks created by the timber trade also instigated a new, semi-official, triangular trade between the Dutch/Northern German coast, Norway, and the eastern coasts of the United Kingdom, which revolved around the trade of dried stockfish, salted-dried cod (*klippfisk*), and imports of commodities from mainland Europe (Bjørklund 1985).

It is hard to measure the impact of the cultural exchange that took place during both the Dutch and Scottish periods in Norwegian history. Margit Løyland points out the cultural influence the Dutch period had on West Norwegians, focusing on Dutch place- and family names, as well as lexical additions to the Norwegian language (Løyland 2012). She provides a list of words and phrases from historical documents that have been retained in both languages, or were mutually intelligible at the time. Equally, on the other side of the North Sea, eighteenth century Shetlanders, for example, were said to speak a dialect that continuously accommodated other contact languages from across the North Sea area. This was the result of pragmatic, but also dynamic choices by the population in response to ongoing social and economic change (Knooihuizen 2010). Other, more specific terminology seems to have developed around regular trading objects such as timber and boats, but intercultural exchange is also found in coastal folklore, literature, regional traditions, and music (Anttonen and Kvideland 1993; Shaw 2007). So, for example, Andreas Næss studied the place names along the Norwegian coast that commemorate the connection with the Scottish Trade, with the existence of *skotteferdsla* or traffic routes (both by land and sea) previously used by Scots, and specific coastal promontories where the Scots loaded timber appearing as 'Skòtanese' (Næss, 1959 [1920]). Harbours and beaches are named *Skottavik, Skottasund, Skottaflua*, or *Scotland Anes*. Næss also notes the name of 'Skòtøyo' and 'Skòtasonde' found in Os (Tysnes), south of Bergen, which, he argues, have the same origin in the Scottish Trade, rather than any interpretations connecting them to the Old Norse term for shooting (*skot*) (Næss 1959 [1920]). More recently, Nina Østby Pederson has traced the remains of Scottish place names, particularly in Bergen and along the coast between Bergen and Stavanger (Pederson 2005). As in other areas around the world, trade and cultural exchange can thus be seen to be closely connected. Both document and mediate specific relationships between humanity, the coastal landscape, and the sea. As mentioned above, these practices give rise to tangible culture such as buildings or different types of constructions along the coast (including settlements and towns) and transport and commercial networks, as well as intangible cultural knowledge about navigation and fishing. They both form the basis for an understanding of the sea as a practical resource, as well as the basis for a unique mentality or way of life (Holm 1995).

## Coastal Cultures: Narratives, Affinity, Contact

Coastal culture, as a heritage experience, can be found along the Norwegian coast in a range of coastal heritage museums and organisations such as *Forbundet Kysten*, a national network of coastal heritage associations. Here, a lot of work is devoted to preserving tangible cultural heritage, such as restoring boats, buildings, cultural landscapes, farm animals, and artefacts, while intangible knowledge is transmitted by providing, for example, access to training in traditional craft to new generations of Norwegians. This gives value to coastal culture as a fluid and changeable part of Norwegian identity and provides a counterbalance to traditional historical foci on farmers, mountains and fixed cultural identities. It also means a move away from larger, land-based monuments, such as churches, and a deliberate distancing from a national-romantic search for the 'urnorske' essence found in the Viking sagas and antiquarian historiographies (Klepp 1992: 9). Instead, the focus is on the diverse and changing cultural landscape of the coast.

Coastal culture is shaped by four important factors: the sea; the effects of the climate (weather, temperature, and wind, as well as sky- and sea-states, such as visibility, ebb, and flow); topography (the materials and formations of the earth's surface, both above under underneath the water) and the production of organic materials (resources, basic to human life). These diverse influences vary according to time and place, which means we can never really speak about a defined coastal culture 'but more like a series of adaptations to variable conditions – and elastic or flexible lifestyle that is intimately connected to the coastal environment' (Klepp 1992: 11). Coastal culture thus provides a valuable field for research on the relationships that exist between the coastal communities across the North Sea and the North Atlantic region. As Jarle Bjørklund has suggested, studies of North Sea culture can provide us with 'a key to a richer understanding of the present world and explain the feelings of mutual relationship among the coastal inhabitants of the North Sea' (Bjørklund 1985: 151).

## Tangible and Intangible Encounters:   Boats and Cultural Transfer

The wooden boat, in particular, represents 'an important part of the technological basis for a Europe and a world in transition. The ships and their men brought with them not only goods but also new technology and cultural impulses' (Bjørklund 1985: 151). Wooden boats were exported from Western Norway to Scotland until the mid-nineteenth century, with Norwegian boat builders adapting regional styles to those required by buyers, and Scottish boat builders, in turn, adapting Norwegian boat designs for specific regional conditions (Christensen 1984; Thowsen 1970). Imports of boats and other wooden objects thus led to trans-regional innovation. So, for example, an adaptation of a local boat-design in Western Norway led to the development of 'Shetland boats' (*Hjeltabåtane*) a boat-type initially built to the south of Bergen, in the coastal communities around Os, Tysnes, Fusa, Strandvik, and Samnanger (Fenton 1997 [1978]: 554).

It is important to note that later contacts between Scottish and

Norwegian coastal communities were quite varied and differed from one region to another. Norwegian historian Arne Odd Johnsen, in *Den Britiske Innflyttingen til Nordmør på 1700-tallet* (Johnsen 1938-1941), for example, describes the impact of what effectively were headhunting activities by the Danish monarch for protestant merchants to come to the area. A variety of advantages were offered to the migrants including freeing them from normal obligations, such as taxes and civic duties. As a result, the dried and salted cod industry along the coast around the Nordmøre region in Western Norway, originally started by a Dutch migrant, was commercialised by migrants from Scotland such as John Ramsey (1701-1787) (Bryn 2009). Originally from Banffshire on the North Eastern coast of Scotland, Ramsey migrated to Fosna (now Kristiansund), buying the fishing village Grip on Veidholmen in 1737. Both Scottish and English migrants brought their own regional business networks with them, as well as their particular brand of entrepreneurship and religious and cultural norms (Vollan 1956). Working with two other Scottish associates William Gordon (1669-1755) and George Leslie (1713-1751), both also from North-East Scotland, Ramsey ran a successful business in exporting salted and dried cod for the next twenty years, laying the foundation for what is still today the region's main export industry.

The second half of the eighteenth century was a significant period for international trade within Northern Europe. This offered many young men an opportunity to apply their talents abroad, using the developing networks that connected international merchant communities. Hans Carl Knudtzon, for example, came from Northern Friesland in Schleswick to Trondheim as a sixteen-year-old in 1767 (Williamsen 2012). He later married Karen Mueller, the daughter of the head of the Trondheim garrison, Major Frederik Mueller. Knudtzon took over a company from his patron Hr. Hofagent Lysholm, naming it Hans Knudtzon and Co., which the family ran until the 1870s. This shipping and wholesale company dealt with the import of corn, salt, hemp, sugar, and coffee, and the export of fish, wood, and copper.

The largest export market was to Britain, followed by Ireland, France (wood), Holland (copper and fish), the Mediterranean countries, and the Baltic (Knudtzon 1993). The years 1814 to 1820 saw Hans Knudtzon & Co. grow into the biggest trading house in the region, with interests in foreign trade, finance, and shipping. However, the family was also very influential in the areas of art, culture, and science, maintaining a network of associates that played an important role across other parts of Norway and Northern Europe (Knudtzon 1993). One of Hans Knudtzon's sons, Christian, was for many years the director of the Røros copper mine in the centre of Norway, and the family also had interests in Trondheim's sugar refinery, regional trading, and fisheries. His other son, Jørgen (1784-1854), enjoyed an independent income and, like many young men of his class, travelled widely. In 1806 he joined an English ship on its way to Jamaica and met one of the other passengers, the Scot Alexander Bailie from Aberdeenshire. They started a lifelong friendship and travelled together over large parts of Europe and the Orient, spending the winters with Jørgen's family in Trondheim (1806-1807) and maintaining extensive cosmopolitan personal networks which included the poet Byron. Jørgen's brother, Lysholm Knudtzon, assembled an impressive private library of over 2000 books. These included works in French, English, German, Italian and Danish, which were donated to the Royal Norwegian Scientific Society of Trondheim (*Det Kongelige Norske Videnskabers Selskab*) in 1860 (Williamsen 2012). From the examples above it is clear that migrant networks in the coastal communities of Northern Europe increasingly merged with each other during the eighteenth and nineteenth centuries, with a variety of formal and informal cultural exchanges taking place. As a personal friendship such as that between Knudtzon and Bailie shows, the social and cultural impact of the cosmopolitan coastal merchant on the developing urban regions cannot be underestimated. With it came the formation of scientific and literary collections that passed into the public sphere of Norway during the late nineteenth century. Their heritage forms part of a national patrimony that had a firmly cosmopolitan basis (Byrne 2013).

To sum up, the transnational links described above resulted in transient networks of intercultural regional identities that have connected the coastal communities of Northern Europe during certain historical periods. The investigation of eighteenth and nineteenth century cultural networks between the coastal communities of Scotland and Norway, for example, has offered useful areas for the investigation of cultural transfer. This applies especially to the way in which both tangible and intangible culture has been mediated, adapted, and recontextualised over time. It is clear that the shared, maritime cultural landscape inhabited by the coastal communities of the North Sea and the North Atlantic region informs how regional identities are constructed and maintained (Thompson *et al.* 1983; Klepp 1992). The socio-historical experiences that create coastal cultures can thus be investigated as part of the field of transnational studies. This enables us to investigate the complex and dynamic product of multiple regional, ethnic, and institutional identities, rather than the traditional focus on the nation-state or geo-political region as central and defining frameworks. The historical and cultural analysis of coastal cultures also opens up important new areas for the investigation of how cultural transfer occurs. Links between coastal communities can be investigated using the construction and transmission of both tangible and intangible coastal culture. The shared, diverse, but similarly sea-focused cultural landscape that exists across the coastal communities of the North clearly informs the way in which regional cultural identities are formed and maintained (Rian 1997). As such, coastal cultures form a complex new area of research, offering opportunities to cross the boundaries between Northern European and Nordic area studies by investigating cultural encounters and transnational 'regions of culture' at the Nordic peripheries.

## Endnotes

[1] Parts of this paper have been published in a slightly different form in Reeploeg 2016.

## References

Andersen, A. B., Greenhill, B. and Grude, E. H. (1985). *The North Sea: A Highway of Economic and Cultural Exchange, Character-history.* Stavanger: Norwegian University Press.

Anttonen, P. and Kvideland, R. (1993). *Nordic Frontiers: Recent Issues in the Study of Modern Traditional Culture in the Nordic Countries.* Turku: Nordic Institute of Folklore.

Armitage, D. and M. J. Braddick (2009 [2002]). *The British Atlantic World, 1500-1800.* Basingstoke and New York: Palgrave Macmillan.

Aronsson, P. (2009). 'National cultural heritage – Nordic cultural memory: negotiating politics, identity and knowledge', in Henningsen, B. *et. al.* (eds.), *Transnationale Erinnerungsorte: Nord- und südeuropäische Perspektiven.* Berlin: BWV Verlag, pp. 71-90.

Bailyn, B. (2005). *Atlantic History: Concept and Contours.* Cambridge: Harvard University Press.

Bjørklund, J. (1985). 'Trade and Cultural Exchange in the 17th and eighteenth Centuries', in Bang-Andersen, A., Greenhill, B., and Grude, E. H. (eds.), *The North Sea, A Highway of Economic and Cultural Exchange.* Stavanger, Oslo, Bergen, Tromsø: Norwegian University Press, pp. 151-166.

Bryn, K. (2009). John Ramsay. *Norsk biografisk leksikon. Norwegian biographical encyclopedia [online].* Available at: http://snl.no/.nbl_biografi/John_Ramsay/utdypning (Accessed: 29 January 2016).

Byrne, A. (2013). *Geographies of the Romantic North: Science, Antiquarianism, and Travel, 1790-1830.* New York: Palgrave Macmillan.

Crawford, B. E. (2013). *The Northern Earldoms. Orkney and Caithness from AD 870 to 1470.* Edinburgh: John Donald at Birlinn.

Christensen, A. E. (1984). 'Boats of the North. Boats and boatbuilding in Western Norway and the islands', in Fenton, A. and Palsson, H. (eds.), *The Northern and Western Isles in the Viking World: Survival, Continuity, and Change.* Edinburgh: John Donald Publishers, pp. 885-895.

DuBois, T. A. (1999). *Nordic Religions in the Viking Age.* Philadelphia:

University of Pennsylvania Press.

Fenton, A. (1997 [1978]). *The Northern Isles: Orkney and Shetland.* Edinburgh: John Donald Publisher.

Harvie, C. (2000 [1977]). *Scotland and Nationalism, British Society and Politics 1707 to the Present.* New York: Routledge.

Holm, P. (1995). 'Kystkultur som forskningsemne', in *Kystsamfunnets Materielle Kultur.* Oslo: Norges Forskningsråd, pp. 7-13.

Häkli, J. (1997). 'Borders in the Political Geography of Knowledge', in Landgren, Lars-Folke and Häyrynen, Maunu. (eds.), *The Dividing Line, Borders and National Peripheries.* Helsinki: The Renvall Institute for Area and Cultural Studies, pp. 9-16.

Johnsen, A. O. (1938-1941). 'Den Britiske Innflyttingen til Nordmør på 1700-tallet', in *Heimen* V, pp. 299-324.

Jönsson, C. *et. al.* (eds.). (2007 [2000]). *Organising European Space.* London: Sage Publications Ltd.

Klepp, A. (1992). 'Hva er kystkultur?', in Løseth, A. and Sæther, P. (eds.), *Kystkultur, Særpreg og mangfald.* Volda: Høgskulen i Volda, pp.7-16.

Knooihuizen, R. (2010). 'Perspectives on the Norn-to-Scots language shift in Shetland' in Sigurðardóttir, Turið and Smith, Brian (eds.), *Jakob Jakobsen in Shetland and the Faroes.* Lerwick : Shetland Amenity Trust, pp. 85-98.

Knudtzon, H. J. (1993). 'Knudtzon i Trondhjem – merkantilt og kulturelt', in Giertsen, Anette and Knudtzon, Hans Jørgen (eds.), *Norsk købmandskultur fra Thorvaldsens tid.* Copenhagen: Knutdtzons Bogtrykkeri A/S, pp. 21-48.

Leroy, M. (ed.) (1999). *Regional Developments around the North Atlantic Rim.* Conference Proceedings. Tenth International Seminar on Marginal Regions. Cape Breton: Canada.

Løyland, M. (2012). *Hollendartida i Norge – 1550-1750.* Spartacus: Oslo.

Magnusson, M. (1980). *Vikings!* London: The Bodley Head Ltd.

Murdoch, A. and Sher, R.B. (1988). 'Literary and Learned Culture', in Devine, T. M. and Mitchison, R. (eds.), *People and Society in Scotland, 1760-1830*. Edinburgh, John Donald, pp. 127-142.

Næss, A. (1959 [1920]) *Skottehandelen på Sunnhordland* (The Scottish Trade in Sunnhordland). Sunnhordland Årbok 1920, Stord: Sunnhordland Museum.

Paasi, A. (2009). 'The resurgence of the 'Region' and 'Regional Identity': theoretical perspectives and empirical observations on regional dynamics in Europe', *Review of International Studies*, 35(S1), pp. 121-146.

Pederson, N. Østby. 2005. 'Scottish Immigration to Bergen in the Sixteenth and Seventeenth Centuries', in Grosjean, A. and Murdoch, S. (eds.), *Scottish Communities Abroad in the Early Modern Period*. Leiden: Brill, pp. 135-167.

Reeploeg, S. (2012). 'The Uttermost Part of the Earth: Islands on the edge ... and in the centre of the North Atlantic', in Matthews, J. and Travers, D. (eds.), *Islands and Britishness: A Global Perspective*. Newcastle upon Tyne: Cambridge Scholars Publishing, pp. 207-217.

Reeploeg, S. (2015) 'Northern Maps: Re-negotiating Space and Place in Coastal Scotland and Norway after 1707', *Northern Scotland*, 6 (46), pp. 24-48.

Reeploeg, S. (2016) 'Nordic Border Crossings : Coastal Communities and Connected Cultures in Eighteenth-Century Norway, Scotland, and Canada', *Scandinavian-Canadian Studies / Études Scandinaves au Canada*, Volume 23 (in press).

Rian, Ø. (1997). 'Regionens rolle i historien', *Heimen*, 34, pp. 283-288.

Råberg, P. (1997). *The Life Region: The Social And Cultural Ecology Of Sustainable Development*. London: Routledge.

Shaw, J. (2007) '(E)Migrating Legends and Sea Change', *Folklore:*

*Electronic Journal of Folklore* [*online*] Estonia: Estonian Folklore Institute. Available at: https://www.folklore.ee/folklore/vol37/shaw. pdf (Accessed: 29 January 2016).

Smith, H. (2003 [1984]). *Shetland Life and Trade 1550-1914*. Edinburgh: John Donald Publishers Ltd.

Thisted, K., Nielsen Gremaud, A.-S., Moberg, B.R., Volquardsen, E., Jørgensen, A.M., (2016). *Denmark and the New North Atlantic* [*online*] Copenhagen: University of Copenhagen. Available at: http://tors.ku.dk/forskning/forskningpaafagene/minoritetsstudier/ denmarkandthenewnorthatlantic/ (Accessed: 18 April 2016).

Thomson, A. (1991). 'The Scottish Timber Trade, 1680 to 1800.' PhD diss., Department of History, University of St. Andrew.

Thompson, P., Wailey, T. and Lummis, T. (1983). *Living the Fishing*. London: Routledge & Kegan Paul.

Thowsen, A. (1970). 'The Norwegian Export of Boats to Shetland, and its Influence upon the Shetland Boatbuilding and Useage', in Pettersen, L. and Thowsen, A. (eds.) *Sjøfartshistorisk Årbok 1969, Norwegian Yearbook of Maritime History*. Bergen: Bergens Sjøfartsmuseum, pp. 145-201.

Tägil, S. (1995). *Ethnicity and Nation Building in the Nordic World*. London: Hurst & Co.

Vollan, O. (1956). *Den norske klippfiskhandels historie*. Førde: Øens Forlag.

Williamsen, O. W. (2012). *Nicolay Heinrich Knudtzon III. Klippfisk, verdiskaping og samfunnsbygging*. Nordmøre: Nordmøre museum.

Winge, H. (2001). 'Regions and regional history in Norway', in Eliassen, F.-E., Mikkelsen, J. and Poulsen, B. (eds.) *Regional Integration in Early Modern Scandinavia*. Odense: Odense University Press, pp. 41-55.

# Imagining a City on Film: Dreams of the Øresund Region in *Drømme i København* (2009)[1]

## Pei-Sze Chow

> Cities are not simply material or lived spaces – they are also spaces of the imagination and spaces of representation (Bridge & Watson 2000: 7).

Max Kestner's *Drømme i København* (*Copenhagen Dreams*, 2009) is a 'city symphony' documentary that depicts images from the everyday environments of Copenhagen's inhabitants and, more explicitly, the forms and surfaces of the city. The film is an intimate portrait of the Danish capital, but it is also one that largely ignores Copenhagen's material and imaginative connections with the transnational Øresund region, an EU-supported economic region and cross-border conurbation that Sjælland in Eastern Denmark shares with Skåne in Southern Sweden, and that was imagined into existence by politicians and brand experts.[2] Only two scenes briefly attempt to address the Øresund project: one features a young family considering moving to a housing development in the Ørestad district, and another takes place atop the Radisson Blu hotel where a couple dine with a clear view of the Øresund strait. Despite these fleeting references to the Øresund, Copenhagen remains a resolutely national space in Kestner's film.

*Drømme i København* premiered in Denmark as part of the CPH:DOX festival in late 2009, and was screened in cinemas (January 2010) and on television (June 2010) shortly after (Danish Film Institute n.d.). The documentary was funded by the Danish Film Institute (DFI) with support from Danmarks Radio, Realdania, and the Dreyer Fonden, making this an emphatically Danish production. The director Max Kestner, a graduate of the National Film School of Denmark, is very much a significant name in the Danish film industry, and continues to make his mark as a documentary filmmaker primarily interested in Danish stories. The conspicuous absence of the Øresund region in Kestner's documentary is worth investigating further as it suggests that the ambitions of the Øresund project and its attendant rhetoric have failed to become a part of the urban identity and the everyday lives of the local inhabitants. Thus, the fact that the Øresund project fails to become a prominent feature in a documentary exploring the collective experience of the city space of Copenhagen points towards the broader challenge of how to bolster a sense of a regional identity amongst local communities whose identities are more nationally rather than regionally inflected – a challenge the supporters of the Øresund project are still grappling with.

In this article, I therefore reflect on what this absence means. Why does a documentary about Copenhagen in 2009 omit – whether by design or not – such a significant element of the city's larger spatial identity? Through a close reading of the film with a particular focus on the two scenes mentioned previously, I draw attention to the spatio-political significance of the film's portrayal of Copenhagen. I argue that this representation evokes a particular disconnect between the ideal of an equally shared Øresund identity and the reality of a bi-national project where one partner is assuming an increasingly dominant role over the other. My intention is to show how Kestner's framing of urban Copenhagen from a pedestrian perspective invites a deeper reflection on what the spectator can and cannot perceive about the city and the region, and to show how the city mediates – architecturally and cinematically – the sense of a larger transnational region.

## The Øresund Project

The transnational Øresund region spans the southern region of Sweden, Skåne, and the eastern region of Denmark, Sjælland. As a result of several wars between the two kingdoms in the seventeenth century, contact across the Øresund strait diminished and the body of water came to be perceived by politicians as an 'iron curtain' rather than a space of exchange (Löfgren 2008: 198). In the late nineteenth and twentieth centuries, the Øresund strait continued to be broadly perceived as a 'blue wall' and a barrier that represented strict national borders and unused economic potential (Pedersen 2004: 81). Now, regional administrators and urban planners imagine the strait as a porous and liminal space that joins the two lands. Linked by the iconic Øresund Bridge, the economic and political activities of the 'mega-city' conurbation centre on Denmark's capital, Copenhagen, and the postindustrial city of Malmö that has since become the unofficial capital of Southern Sweden (Olshov 2010: 77).

While some elements of spatial change within Copenhagen can be seen as consequence of the larger Øresund project, such as the Ørestad district that I will discuss later on, *Drømme i København* shows us a Copenhagen that has not incorporated the region's spatio-cultural ambitions into its self-perception. Where the Øresund strait and the everyday experience of Copenhagen briefly intersect, the result is a community that will only identify with the regional, transnational identity of Øresund for specific ends. Kestner's documentary shows that the planned visions of the Øresund region instead form an additional 'layer' on top of quotidian experience, one that does not penetrate into the inhabitants' core self-experience of the city.

## Imagining a Region

*Drømme i København* is a paean to the buildings and streets of Copenhagen, and examines the way peoples' lives are shaped by urban spaces, and vice versa. Elements of the Lefebvrian triad of the city as material, lived, and imagined run throughout the film, and the documentary's main narrative concern is with how these three modes interweave to 'produce' Copenhagen.[3] Walls, windows, and façades are shot in sharp focus, no longer the backdrop to the people in the frame. The latter move in and out of focus within the frame while the camera remains fixed on the physical surroundings. Sequences of banal conversations between Copenhageners are interspersed with shots of streets and outdoor spaces. These images are overlaid with an energetic voiceover describing the minutiae of everyday life in each sequence. The pace of the voiceover is quick, commenting on particular elements in the shot or details about the people or place in one image before jumping to the next without pause.

Throughout the documentary, the sense of a larger transnational region or, indeed, the Øresund strait itself, is neither mentioned nor directly visualised. It is only hinted at in the final voiceover commentary which describes a man who dreams of houses being built over the sea, toward Sweden:

> There is a man in Copenhagen, who dreams of taking on the sea itself. He imagines the city, growing out into the ocean, grasping towards Sweden. He sees people in the future, living where the sea wind whips over the houses, and you row to your neighbour, if the elements permit. He dreams of a city that belongs to everyone, but is always and forever its own. (*Copenhagen Dreams*)[4]

In Kestner's documentary portrait, Copenhagen's inhabitants are dreaming and imagining the present and future spaces of the city. The film presents us with a city performing itself to viewers who see the capital of Denmark as a self-contained urban space marked by small spatial changes throughout its past, present, and future. Apparently, this is an image of the city that is not just being torn down and built up and over, but it is also a city that imagines a more horizontal growth, opening up, spreading outwards, and extending its reach across the Sound towards her neighbouring territories.

The film shows different levels and scales of imagining: the totalising, future-oriented gaze of urban planners and architects is contrasted with the subjective, social, and present-oriented activity of the inhabitants' everyday lives. The imagining of the former group results in physically reconfiguring space and potentially altering urban relations, in contrast to the inhabitants of the local community who simply move, adapt, and re-articulate the spaces they traverse on an everyday basis. Both groups are just as involved as one another in 'building' the city and negotiating their respective social identities via continuities with the past and projections of their immediate future.

I argue that the documentary makes visible this disconnect between the different levels of imagining by the different groups of Copenhageners. City planners and inhabitants each have their own dreams of the capital, and each vision forms a small part of a much larger tapestry of the city. However, I suggest that, when reading the documentary in the context of the transnational region, its narrative points towards a larger, and more fundamental clash between cosmopolitan visions of the Øresund project and local realities of the city. On an acutely individual and local level, the regionalist and transnational aspirations of the Øresund project are barely registered. In my view, this absence is significant. It is therefore my argument that *Drømme i København* functions on two levels. First, as a visual document and cross-section of the city, the film registers the disconnect between the planned and the lived as a defining characteristic of a city in the midst of urban change and growth. Second, the documentary critically nuances the grand notion of the city as a site of transnational flows and globalised spaces. What is articulated instead is an ambivalence of local perspectives toward the new transnational urbanity advanced by the Øresund project. The city, as imagined by its inhabitants and by the film script, remains a resolutely national space.

## Aerial Shots, Planners, and Perspective

Peppered throughout the documentary are aerial, top-down shots which are juxtaposed with eye-level shots that travel, track, and pan across the horizontal space of the city. These are two perspectives that Kestner utilises in order to critically reflect the disconnect between the planned and the lived. At various stages in the film, Kestner employs the aerial and establishing shots to 'look down' on the city and frame sections of Copenhagen as idealised spaces from a position of privilege and power – the 'planner's gaze' (Vidler 2011; Webb 2014). In these particular shots, the viewer is suddenly dangled above the city and invited to study the clean lines, shapes, and forms of the city's urban layout. The opening shot, for example, presents an orderly and functionally spaced intersection in the Nørrebro neighbourhood. In one long take, the camera focuses its gaze on the empty road junction while the narrator reels off banal statistics about the city: 'Copenhagen has 109 football fields. 395km of bike lanes, and 3591 benches painted a special colour called "Copenhagen green". Gradually, the frame fills up with people, cars, and bicycles, all crossing the junction in a burst of movement in specific directions as determined by the rational logic of urban traffic management.

The aerial viewpoint activates both the 'utopian and projective' visions of planners (Vidler 2011: 656), which not only allows for an enlarged field of vision, but is also suggestive of a certain power over the space. From this perspective, the framing does not draw our attention to any particular person or group of people. Instead, the movement of inhabitants through the space is only one variable in the larger project of urban city planning. In various scenes, the documentary foregrounds the figure of the architect or urban planner involved in such positions of power, who dreams ambitiously and continually attempts to distinguish the city as a node in a global network of urban centres through the modification of the 'spatial texture' of the city (Thacker 2003: 20). These architects and planners are depicted in teams, clustered in their offices, discussing the spaces of the city over cardboard models and posters in technical jargon. As planners, they debate, plan, design, imagine, calculate, and quantify the urban fabric of the city, diagramming and dissecting Copenhagen into abstract forms or 'representations of space' linked to certain ideologies, codes, and signs. The place of the planners in the film, however, is always subordinate to the images, sounds, and presence of the city outside of their offices. One sequence features a group of planners and architects in a seminar room discussing the value of public squares. Meanwhile the camera is focused on the windows, the view outdoors, and the sound of seagulls squawking mingle with the human voices, at times even distracting from them.

Yet these technocrats are not the only planners in the city. Inhabitants are also shown as actively making plans for their own urban environments, albeit on much smaller and personal scales. For example: a couple discuss their plans to move to a new district, Ørestad; a pair of friends are depicted in the midst of remodelling a flat; and another couple negotiate the cost of buying a houseboat with an agent. The contrast between such scenes of earnest planning at different levels asserts the agency of the individual: urban space is being profoundly shaped by individuals on their own terms, and with greater meaning and material consequence in contrast to the architects and planners whose dreams for the city remain unrealised in the form of sketches or miniature models.

The film shifts between the general and the particular, cross-cutting between aerial shots and close-up interior tableaux, and at no point asserting a definitive statement nor image as representative of Copenhagen's form or spirit. As Danish critic Kim Skotte notes, the film is emphatically 'not a tourist film' nor does it attempt to push certain political agendas (2009). Instead, Kestner offers glimpses of places and people with the goal of producing a composite portrait of the city with a greater focus on visualising the material, concrete landscape of the city.

## Insular Tendencies

One remarkable aspect of this documentary is the way in which it visually depicts a Copenhagen that is insular. For all the interconnectedness of the urban condition that the documentary's narrator suggests, the city remains self-contained, even cloistered. The film largely depicts its inhabitants alone and within the walls of their own spaces, minding their own business. Verticality is generally not part of the city's aesthetic, where most buildings – particularly in the city centre – are no higher than six storeys. Moreover, there are only a handful of locations from which people can grasp a sense of the city's expanse and, crucially, of what lies beyond the city. Copenhagen's skyline, after all, is predominantly horizontal. A scene in the middle of the film shows a couple having lunch in a restaurant on the top floor of the historic Radisson Blu Royal Hotel, formerly known as the SAS Royal Hotel, which is located at the heart of the city in the Vesterbro district. The couple, in the foreground of the shot, are blurred while the camera focuses on the view outside of Copenhagen's rooftops and the striking blue horizon of the Øresund strait framed by the window. As the young couple gaze out of the window, they comment on how they had previously never noticed the row of offshore wind turbines just at the eastern edge of the city. After a few seconds' pause their conversation turns to where they live and their favourite streets in the city centre. While they speak, the camera leaves them and tracks to the left, following the row of windows that continues to frame the panorama of wind turbines and the water.

For most Copenhageners, a paucity of high-level vantage points means that people navigate the city in an insular manner on a quotidian basis, leaving them somewhat unmindful of the city's wider reach across the Øresund. The couple's comment points to a certain nescience of Copenhagen's relationship with spaces beyond the city limits. This is surprising because the Øresund strait is certainly not an unknown entity among inhabitants. The suggestion is that the Sound is not part of Copenhagen's visual and urban identity, at least not from the point of view of this Copenhagen couple. On a quotidian level, it is not visible to the person on the street, nor is it thought of as forming a part of the everyday landscape of the city: 'A sight from the situated context of a body in the world may not always see things that are visible to a "high-altitude" or "God's-eye-view"' (Jay 1988: 19). At twenty stories high, the Radisson building is hardly a skyscraper in the contemporary sense. Yet the top floor provides one of the few actual vantage points in the city – what Henri Lefebvre calls 'the *elsewhere* where the urban reveals itself' (2003 [1970]: 116). It is high enough for one to see not just a consolidated view of the city but also the marine hinterland that Copenhagen shares with Malmö. At the time of its completion in 1960, the SAS Royal Hotel was the tallest building in Denmark. It was the first downtown hotel in Europe to incorporate an airport terminal, and the capital's first skyscraper. But more importantly, it was a hotel that was built to function as a gateway (and globalised 'non-place' in Marc Augé's view) to Scandinavia for foreign tourists travelling across the Atlantic (Agerman 2011).[5]

However, this vantage point and the access to a broader view of the city was, and still is, only available to a specific, even exclusive, group of urban *bons vivants* who have the means to dine in one of the city's top restaurants. In other words, a slightly different version of the 'planner's gaze' (Vidler 2011; Webb 2014). I interpret this restricted and exclusive ability to even perceive the Øresund strait from within the heart of Copenhagen as a reflection of the Øresund project being an *additional* and exclusive layer on top of the quotidian.

## Ørestad Is Ahead Of Schedule

So far, I have suggested that the Øresund strait is largely omitted from the documentary's portrayal of the city. Yet it must be noted that the ethos of the region manifests itself in an altogether different way in the documentary. In a scene shot just outside a show-flat attached to a construction site, a sales representative for a new residential complex in the developing Ørestad district persuades a young family to imagine themselves as pioneering settlers forging a new path through an unknown land. The people are framed standing on the balcony of a show-flat next to a building clearly still under construction, while a green field is visible in the background.

The Ørestad district, located on Amager island, is only a short distance to the south of the central part of the city and was, until the late 1990s, composed of green, open fields (By og Havn 2011: 5). It benefits from a strategic location, only minutes away from both Kastrup airport and the city centre. Prior to the 1990s, spatial planning was driven to a large degree by the public sector as part of the welfare state philosophy. However, an abrupt change of spatial planning policy in the 1990s led to a market-oriented 'entrepreneurial' philosophy that resulted in the Ørestad development. This was a plan to build a 'city annex' to central Copenhagen in conjunction with the construction of the bridge between Copenhagen and Malmö (Majoor 2008: 123). The Ørestad development therefore appears as a key element in the Øresund agenda since not only is it couched in the same discourse of European integration and regional competition but, more importantly, it was framed by city developers and the Ørestad Development Corporation as forming a strategic part of the emerging cross-border region (Majoor 2008: 127). The development also constitutes the most visible physical representation of the Øresund agenda after the bridge itself.

The scene with the couple visiting the show flat captures the particular moment when the Ørestad development is already under way, and the remaining work is to convince people to actually live in this space. In some ways, this is a microcosm of the larger Øresund 'problem' to convince local people to buy into the notion of region-building. The scene of the young family considering a move to Ørestad records the space in the midst of its transformation. The sense of a *tabula rasa* upon which a new social and urban dynamic is being written. The planning of the Ørestad project was conducted in a top-down manner, and throughout its development it attracted much controversy for a number of political and economic reasons that Majoor recounts in his detailed case study (2008). As a part-publicly and part-privately funded endeavour, the Ørestad project was criticised for over-running budget limitations and for the lack of transparency in decision-making, which resulted in social and civic communities having difficulties in identifying with the project (Majoor 2008: 131). New buildings and the new metro transport line were eventually built, albeit at an inflated cost, and commercial development had been slow to take root. The mixed reception of the Ørestad plan can therefore be related once again to the disconnect and misunderstandings between the planned and the lived, between the ambition of commercial interests on the one hand and the interests of the local community on the other. The fleeting appearances of the Øresund strait in these scenes could therefore be interpreted as the repressed memories in the city's subconscious, which only momentarily resurface in instances of ordinary lives. As much as the documentary – or Kestner – avoids engaging with the regional dynamic to instead focus on a national space, elements of the region's dreams and aspirations still creep into the space of the city and the film.

## Conclusions

In conclusion, I argue that the documentary mode is a powerful way of exploring the dynamics of urban places undergoing spatial and social transformation. Each documentary is a cinematic act of memory-construction that intervenes, through its production and exhibition, in wider conversations about the changing spaces of the region. The significance of the documentary also lies in the fact that it is a material and indexical fragment of the places and social practices that it depicts, and of the respective historical moments in the larger story of the Øresund region.

In *Drømme i København*, the dreams of the city are characterised by a degree of solipsism – instead, the filming of the architecture emphasises the insularity of the inhabitants' experiential realms rather than engaging with dynamics beyond the city's boundaries. The documentary's aesthetic places an intense focus on the surfaces and particularities of urban living, while also dipping into personal spaces. The city's multiple layers of history are expressed through a spirited and spellbinding narration that seeks to draw the viewer deeper into the spaces of the city and the dreams of its people. Yet these acts belie a pronounced sense of ambivalence and distance. That is, like a dream, the film can only hint at a sense of the city's identity, unable to define what it is. In this reverie, one can only just make out the Øresund vision appearing in certain places and from certain perspectives. Otherwise, the quotidian realm remains ignorant of transnational gestures from across the Sound.

## Endnotes

[1] This essay has been adapted from a chapter of my doctoral thesis, completed in September 2015: 'A Symptom of Something Real': The Øresund Region on Film and Television, 1999–2014.

[2] While Denmark and Sweden are meant to be equal partners in the Øresund regional project, the fact that Copenhagen is a capital city while Malmö is peripheral city means that this is an asymmetrical relationship. This asymmetry has become even clearer when we consider that, as of January 2016, the Øresund is now renamed 'Greater

Copenhagen and Skåne. For a further discussion of the region's complexities, see Chow (2015).

[3] See Henri Lefebvre, *The Production of Space* (1991).

[4] In this essay, quotations from the documentary come from its official English version, titled *Copenhagen Dreams* (2009).

[5] The building, including all the details of its interior furnishings down to the tableware and cutlery, was designed by Arne Jacobsen, and has since been declared one of Jacobsen's major works and an example of *Gesamtkunstwerk* (Tøjner and Vindum 1999: 10). A large part of the hotel's international appeal at its inception was its design element and the notion that the structure (and its interiors) were a bastion of mid-century Danish modernism.

## References

Agerman, J. (2011). 'SAS Royal Hotel', *Icon: International Design, Architecture and Culture*. Available at: http://www.iconeye.com/opinion/icon-of-the-month/item/9180-sas-royal-hotel (Accessed: 16 June 2015).

Augé, M. (1995). *Non-Places: Introduction to an Anthropology of Supermodernity*. Trans. John Howe. London: Verso Books.

Bridge, G. and Watson, S. (2000). 'City Imaginaries', in Bridge, G. and Watson, S. (eds.), *A Companion to the City*. Oxford: Blackwell, pp. 7-17.

By og Havn (2011). *Copenhagen Growing: The Story of Ørestad*. Copenhagen: By & Havn. Available at: http://www.orestad.dk/~/media/images/copenhagen-growing_web.pdf (Accessed:   8 June 2015).

Chow, P. (2015). 'A Symptom of Something Real': Film and Television in The Øresund Region, 1999-2014. PhD Thesis. University College London.

*Copenhagen Dreams/Dromme i København* (2009). Directed by Max Kestner [DVD]. Denmark: Upfront Films.

Danish Film Institute (n.d.). 'Drømme i København', *Fakta Om Film*. Available at: http://www.dfi.dk/faktaomfilm/film/da/63999. aspx?id=63999 (Accessed: 3 September 2015).

Jay, M. (1988). 'Scopic Regimes of Modernity', in Foster, H. (ed.), *Vision and Visuality*. Seattle: Bay Press, pp. 3-23.

Kestner, M. (2005). 'Jeg er en af dem, der tror, at sandheden er min', *Filmmagasinet Ekko*, (28). Available at: http://www.ekkofilm. dk/artikler/jeg-er-en-af-dem-der-tror-at-sandheden-er-min/ (Accessed: 11 June 2015).

Lefebvre, H. (1991). *The Production of Space*. Malden, MA: Blackwell Publishing.

Lefebvre, H. (2003 [1970]). *The Urban Revolution*. Minneapolis; London: University of Minnesota Press.

Löfgren, O. (2008). 'Regionauts: the Transformation of Cross-Border Regions in Scandinavia', *European Urban and Regional Studies*, 15(3), pp. 195-209.

Majoor, S. (2008). *Disconnected Innovations: New Urbanity in Large-scale Development Projects: Zuidas Amsterdam, Ørestad Copenhagen and Forum Barcelona*. Delft: Eburon.

Olshov, A. (2010). 'Denmark-Sweden Øresund Mega-City Region and the Øresund Bridge', in Korea Transport Institute (ed.), *Sustainable Transport Development Strategy of the Mega-City Region in Europe and China*. The Emerging Cross-Border Mega-City Region and Sustainable Transportation. pp. 50-81.

Pedersen, S.B. (2004). 'Place Branding: Giving the Region of Øresund a Competitive Edge', *Journal of Urban Technology*, 11(1), pp. 77-95.

Skotte, K. (2009). 'Cool Copenhagen', *FILM*, (67). Available at: http://www.dfi.dk/Service/English/News-and-publications/FILM-Magazine/Artikler-fra-tidsskriftet-FILM/67/Cool-Copenhagen. aspx (Accessed: 13 July 2015).

Thacker, A. (2003). *Moving Through Modernity: Space and Geography in Modernism*. Manchester: Manchester University Press.

Tøjner, P.E. and Vindum, K. (1999). *Arne Jacobsen: Architect & Designer*. Copenhagen: Danish Design Centre.

Vidler, A. (2011). 'Photourbanism: Planning the City From Above and From Below', in Bridge, G. and Watson, S. (eds.), *The New Blackwell Companion to the City*. Chichester: Wiley-Blackwell, pp. 656-666.

Webb, L. (2014). 'Remapping The Conversation: Urban Design and Industrial Reflexivity in Seventies San Francisco', *Post45*. Available at: http://post45.research.yale.edu/2014/06/remapping-the-conversation-urban-design-and-industrial-reflexivity-in-seventies-san-francisco/ (Accessed: 5 September 2015).

# NARRATIVES OF IDENTITY

# Viking Age Scandinavian Churchyard burial in Scotland, c. 850-950 CE.

## Shane McLeod

Despite the relative abundance of culturally Scandinavian burials in present-day Scotland, only five Christian cemeteries are known with certainty to be associated with Scandinavian burials, although there are another three possible examples. Of the five certain sites, there is one each in Orkney and Shetland, and three are in southern Scotland. This paper provides a brief overview of all eight sites before concentrating on the five certain examples. It considers the possible reasons for the choice of this burial location, what it may say about the religious affiliation of the deceased and those who buried them, and relations between the immigrants and local populations. The different political circumstances in the regions of the sites are also examined. The paper concludes that there is no single answer to explain the phenomenon, and that it may point to the deliberate adoption of multiple burial locations by an incoming population wanting to fulfil multiple objectives: demonstrating their legitimacy, remembering their cultural heritage, and adapting to the practices and practicalities of their new home.

There are currently over one hundred culturally Scandinavian burials in Scotland where the location of the site is known with a reasonable degree of certainty. These burials occur at forty-three sites: in the Northern and Western Isles, and the northern, western, and southern mainland (McLeod 2015a). Almost all of these sites are on the coast (Harrison 2007: 175), and all are either certainly or potentially close to Viking Age settlements (Graham-Campbell & Batey 1998: 145). Of these, only five sites (containing a minimum of twenty Scandinavian burials) are associated with Christian cemeteries, although burials at another three sites are possibly in Christian cemeteries. This low number may in part be due to many Viking Age cemeteries still being in use today, and therefore unlikely to be subjected to excavation or (hopefully) metal-detecting. However, two of the burials (St Ola's, Shetland, and Kirkcudbright, Dumfries and Galloway) were found due to grave-digging and extending the cemetery respectively. Yet despite this caveat, the relative paucity of Scandinavian burials at Christian cemeteries in comparison with burials in other locations indicates that the immigrants rarely used the local burial place.

The present study is concerned with culturally Scandinavian burials, by which I refer to burials that were unlike those of the pre-Viking Age population. That is cremations, which was not an option for Christian burial at the time, and inhumations, usually accompanied by artefacts, which were not consistent with contemporary indigenous burial practices. The use of mounds (newly constructed, natural, or re-used) and boats in the ninth and tenth centuries was also a Scandinavian burial tradition. Consequently, this study is concerned with the period c. 850-950 when it is thought that most 'pagan' burials occurred (Graham-Campbell & Batey 1998: 154). It excludes churchyard sculpture with runic inscriptions or Scandinavian art motifs, including the so-called 'hogback' monuments, as I consider these to be primarily post-950 when the Scandinavian population had adopted Christian burial practice. The term 'Scandinavian' is meant in the sense of 'culturally Scandinavian' as not all of those buried in a Scandinavian manner in Scotland had emigrated from Scandinavia. This has been demonstrated by isotope analysis of three individuals from one of the cemeteries discussed below, Westness (Rousay, Orkney). The results suggest that two males had grown up in Scandinavia but a female had spent her childhood in either the Midland Valley of mainland Scotland or north-eastern Ireland (Montgomery et al 2014: 64). For distribution maps, photographs, and summaries of all Scandinavian burial sites see McLeod 2015a.

## Scandinavian Burials Associated with Christian Cemeteries

Proceeding from north to south:

1) In 1938 an axe-head was found with unsexed bones in a grave at St Ola's churchyard in Whiteness, Shetland (*Inventory* 1946: *no* 1527). As no mention was made of the orientation of the grave it seems likely that it was the same as the others, i.e. in standard Christian alignment.[1] Ninth and tenth-century sculpture has also been found at the site, suggesting that the burial was placed in an existing cemetery (Stevenson 1981: 285-87). Such burials are often thought to be 'transitional' as communities began to acculturate to the local burial practices (in simple graves in a churchyard with Christian alignment) but also incorporate some aspects of their own burial tradition (the use of grave-goods).

2) Until the site of Westness on Rousay, Orkney, is fully published any certainty is impossible. It appears that, in the ninth and tenth centuries, nine graves containing ten Scandinavian burials (three male, three female, one infant, one unsexed and two for which I cannot find information) discovered in 1963, 1968-1984, and 1997, were added to an existing cemetery in use from the seventh century.[2] The pre-Viking Age burials did not include grave-goods, were in rectangular graves, and were all aligned roughly east-west. The Scandinavian graves all included grave-goods (including five graves with multiple items), were in boats, boat-shaped, or rectangular graves, and most were aligned SE-NW (Barrett & Richards 2004: 262; Graham-Campbell & Batey 1998: 135-138; Kaland 1993: 312-317; Sellevold 1999: Fig. 2; Wilson & Moore 1997: 60).

3) At Auldhame in East Lothian a male burial was found in 2005 in a monastic cemetery. The burial included a spear, spurs, and belt, but was otherwise like the neighbouring Christian graves (Crone & Heald 2015: 19).

4) On a hill overlooking a pre-Viking Age cemetery in Kirkcudbright, Dumfries and Galloway, an unsexed burial containing a Viking Age sword, ringed pin and a bead was discovered in the 1880s (Graham-

Campbell 2001: 13-15).

5) Near the probable mortuary chapel of the former monastic centre and bishopric at Whithorn, Dumfries and Galloway, a most unusual collection of burials was discovered during excavations between 1984 and 1991. An infant was buried with two beads, possibly on a necklace, in Christian alignment. Next to them in a single grave on the same alignment was a collection of disarticulated bones belonging to an adult male and a female, though neither skeleton was complete. Above these three individuals was a cremation layer containing the remains of at least four unsexed individuals (Hill 1997: 189). Although these burials do not include grave-goods, other than the beads with the infant, the use of cremation in particular makes it likely that they belonged to a Scandinavian cultural group. The discovery of adults of both sexes and an infant suggest a settled community.

In addition to these burials there are another three Scandinavian burial sites in Scotland that may be associated with Christian cemeteries. At Reay on the north mainland coast, three unsexed Scandinavian burials were discovered in 1912 (with a buckle and a horse-bridle), 1913 (with a pair of oval brooches, bronze buckle, steatite spindle whorl, ringed pin, and bridle bit) and 1926 (with an axe, shield, knife, sickle, buckle, ringed pin, and whetstone). None of these burials can be located with any accuracy. Undated unaccompanied burials and pre-Viking Age Christian sculpture have also been discovered in Reay, suggesting that the Scandinavians added their dead to an existing cemetery (Batey 1993: 152-154; Stevenson 1949-50: 218).

A similar situation exists at Cnoc nan Gall on the island of Colonsay in the Inner Hebrides, where in 2010 a male was found accompanied by a ringed pin and a strap end (Becket & Batey 2013). In 1978 a female burial accompanied by a small dog, re-used sheet metal, ringed pin, and a knife in a sheath was discovered close to four small houses dated to the early ninth century (Ritchie 1982). In 1891 a boat burial containing a horse, sword, axe, spear, shield, ladle, amber bead, and a penannular brooch was found (McNeill 1892). A second boat burial was possibly discovered in 1902 or 1904 (Becket & Batey 2013: 315).

Numerous unaccompanied burials have also been found in the area, making it possible that it was a pre-Viking Age Christian cemetery, although no sculpture or church remains have been uncovered (Becket & Batey 2013: 315-316).

Finally, in 2005 at Midross south of Luss, Argyll, six or eight accompanied burials (unfortunately the two preliminary reports do not agree on the number of burials) were found in a circular enclosure. Artefacts with the burials included knives, a finger ring and bracelets (including a child's), a whetstone from Norway, a tool, and a coin of Aethelred I of Wessex, England (d. 871). A shield-boss found in the ditch around the enclosure may represent another burial. Unaccompanied burials were also found in the enclosure, as was a rectangular timber building (Buchanan 2012: 21; MacGregor 2009: 11). Unaccompanied burials in a circular enclosure with a rectangular building suggest a churchyard, but this remains speculation until the full report is published.[3]

Although all three of these sites may represent Scandinavian burials being added to Christian cemeteries, the current uncertainty surrounding the sites excludes them from further discussion. There are also two or three probable Scandinavian 'transitional' burials in the Christian cemetery at Newark Bay, Orkney mainland, that will be discussed below.

## Discussion

The distribution pattern of the five certain Christian burial sites associated with Scandinavian burials is rather stark, with three occurring south of the Forth and Clyde rivers and two in the northern isles. None occur in Western Scotland (including Scandinavian burials in the Inner and Outer Hebrides, Isle of Arran, and Ardnamurchan peninsula) despite that region having fifteen Scandinavian burial sites. Neither are there Christian burial sites associated with Scandinavian burials in the northern Scottish mainland, but there are only four certain Scandinavian burial sites known in this region and one of these (Reay) may have been a Christian cemetery. Despite the relatively high concentration of accompanied Scandinavian burial sites in Orkney (twelve sites with at least thirty-eight burials excluding the new unpublished finds on Papa Westray), only one (Westness) is in a Christian cemetery, while on Shetland there is also only one, but this actually represents twenty per cent of the Shetland corpus as there are only five certain burial sites that can be located with any certainty.

Scandinavian burial sites in southern Scotland have been discussed at length elsewhere (McLeod 2015b), where it was noted that in the ninth and into the tenth centuries the region was the northern extreme of the Anglo-Saxon kingdom of Northumbria. Consequently, the burials need to be considered in relation to Scandinavian activity in northern England, specifically the relationship between Scandinavians and the Community of St Cuthbert following the treaty made between the Community and the Scandinavian king of Northumbria, Guthfrith, in c. 883. That three of the four certain Scandinavian burial sites in southern Scotland are associated with Christian cemeteries is certainly striking.[4] All three of them having a probable association with St Cuthbert is surely more than mere coincidence.[5] I have suggested that the burials may represent warriors, and in the case of Whithorn a community, used to protect the churches on behalf of the Scandinavian kings based in York, who also appear to have had a good working relationship with the Archbishop of York from 866 (McLeod 2014a: 178-180; 2015b: 99-101). Many of the Scandinavian settlers in England appear to have come from Scandinavian communities established in Frisia and Dublin and were therefore probably familiar with churchyard burial. This may have been a factor in the choice of burial site (McLeod 2014a: 109-158, 259-269). In present-day England there are eight churchyards associated with Scandinavian burials despite England having far fewer known Scandinavian burial sites than Scotland. This highlights the importance of churchyard burial in this region to the immigrants (McLeod 2013).

Orkney has a high concentration of Scandinavian burials yet the relative lack of burials associated with Christian cemeteries is in contrast to southern Scotland, indicating very different circumstances. Despite the paucity of burials associated with Christian cemeteries, the one certain example, Westness on Rousay, has the highest number of Scandinavian burials associated with a Christian site in Scotland. The burials include two in boats and at least two in boat-shaped graves, so that the forms of the burials, along with the many grave-goods, mark them very firmly as culturally Scandinavian. Even after the graves were closed, the use of a different alignment than the Christian graves would have continued to mark out their difference above ground as all of the burials in the cemetery are thought to have been marked (Kaland 1993: 312-315). Despite these clear differences the Scandinavian graves respected the earlier Christian graves, unlike an example at Balladoole, Isle of Man (Wilson 2008: 385-386). This does not suggest an anti-Christian (or anti-local) stance and may instead signal a degree of respect. The burial of men, women, and children in the accompanied graves indicates a settled Scandinavian group, one who either superseded the earlier inhabitants or lived alongside them. This of course does not mean that the immigrants and indigenous populations were not hostile to each other at different times, and indeed that one of the men in a boat burial was probably killed by arrows is a reminder of the violence of the Viking Age (Sellevold 1999: 44). There are two potential burials in the Christian cemetery at Newark Bay which fit the 'transitional' model more comfortably than most of those at Westness. However, it is debatable if the bracelet found in one burial really counts as a grave-good, and it is not certain that a comb found 40 cm from a skull was definitely in the other burial (Barrett et al 2000: 12). It is thought that a single 'flexed' burial found at Newark Bay may also represent lingering non-Christian practice in the Christian cemetery (Barrett et al 2000: 12). There is convincing evidence for some Christian churches in Orkney in the mid-tenth century, and for the likelihood that Christianity managed to survive Scandinavian immigration (Barrett et al 2000: 13-14). The survival of a native Christian community is likely to have been a major factor in the adoption of Christian burial practices, which is not necessarily the same as conversion to Christianity. Barrett et al (2000: 15) suggest that competing political factions may have also been important.

Along with the burial at Auldhame, and perhaps the two at Newark Bay, the burial closest resembling 'transitional' burials is the one with an axe at St Ola's, Shetland. The burial is quite different from the ostentatious burials added to the Westness cemetery. Despite the discovery of Northumbrian-influenced sculpture in the churchyard dating to the same period as the burial (Stevenson 1981: 286), it stretches the evidence too far to suggest that the Northumbrian influence came about due to Scandinavians emigrating from their settlements in Northumbria. However, the female buried at Westness is a pertinent reminder of 'Scandinavian' migration within the British Isles, and migration between Northumbria and Shetland is certainly possible. Regardless of the origin of the person buried at St Ola's, the Bressay cross-slab features an ogham inscription with two Gaelic and one possible Norse word, plus word division in the form found in runic inscriptions. It indicates the likely survival of the pre-Scandinavian population, including perhaps a Gaelic-speaking ecclesiastical community, and assimilation between groups at some point in the Viking Age (Gameltoft 2004: 45; Stevenson 1981: 284-285).[6] The earliest phases indicating Scandinavian material culture at the multi-period settlement at Old Scatness have also been interpreted as demonstrating interaction between the indigenous population and incoming Scandinavians (Dockrill et al 2010: 361-362), although dating such sites is problematic (Barrett 2008: 418-419). Such interaction would have been a factor in Scandinavians acculturating to indigenous (i.e. Christian) burial customs. Radiocarbon-dating of the earliest burial associated with a church at Kebister, Shetland mainland, produced a date range of 890-1021, so this evidence for Viking-Age Christianity may post-date the burial at St Ola's (Barrett 2003: 214). Consequently, the St Ola's transitional burial may be the earliest evidence for the Scandinavian population starting to adapt to local burial practices in Shetland.

## Conclusions

The five certain Scandinavian burial sites in Scotland associated with Christian cemeteries make it clear that different circumstances prevailed in different regions. In particular, the three southern sites should be considered in relation to developments in northern England. However, all of the sites demonstrate that burial rites with non-Christian aspects could occur in or near Christian burial grounds. This in turn suggests that Scandinavians were in control of those five regions when the burials took place, or at least that their wishes could not be ignored. It is easy to accept that a Christian community and local church hierarchy (if present) accommodated transitional burials like those found at St Ola's and Auldhame as a way of encouraging good relations between communities and of hopefully aiding in the conversion process. The same may be said of the Kirkcudbright burial overlooking a Christian cemetery. Of course in 'normal times' such burials would not have been accepted, so the burials represent both the accommodation of the Christian community and the power of the Scandinavian community who could force such concessions.

However, it is difficult to accept such a degree of negotiation at Westness or Whithorn. Although the respect shown to the Christian graves at Westness may be significant, it is hard to imagine the non-Scandinavian community welcoming the addition of boat and boat-shaped graves using a different alignment and containing extensive grave-goods to their cemetery. In this instance it would appear that the Scandinavian incomers took over the existing cemetery (Barrett et al 2008: 12-13) and any remaining locals had little chance of objecting. The failure to discover a contemporary church or chapel associated with the site suggests that there was not a church hierarchy present. In terms of Christian sites, Whithorn is of an entirely different magnitude to Westness. Whithorn was an important monastic site at which the Northumbrians had established a bishopric by 731 when Bede completed his *Historia Ecclesiastica Gentis Anglorum* (v.23) (Hill 1997: 16). Although a fire destroyed much of the church in c. 845 it was soon rebuilt, and continued Christian burial and the production of Christian sculpture indicate that Whithorn remained an important Christian centre (Hill 1997: 21-22, 54). This Christian activity makes the Scandinavian burials that occurred sometime after the fire all the more extraordinary. The burials, dated to c. 900, were inserted close to the outer wall of a high-status mortuary chapel which may have recently been repaired (Hill 1997: 167-170). Despite the Christian alignment of the two graves, the lack of grave-goods, and even the Christian parallels for burying disarticulated bones,[7] it is difficult to imagine the hierarchy at an important Christian centre condoning cremation unless they were under extreme pressure. Although cremation cannot have been officially sanctioned there was no doubt still a degree of pragmatism involved in gratifying the wishes of the local Scandinavian community. The absence of other pagan burials suggests that the adoption of Christian burial occurred soon after these burials, or that the Scandinavian community left.[8]

The paucity of Scandinavian churchyard burial in Scotland indicates that it was just one of many options available in terms of burial location. That three quarters of Scandinavian burial sites in southern Scotland are associated with Christian cemeteries demonstrates that in that region using the burial place of the local population was considered to be important. Although this may point to a degree of domination of the local population, it also signals acculturation and helps to explain the relative lack of 'pagan' burials in southern Scotland. By contrast, the lack of Scandinavian burials associated with Christian cemeteries in Orkney suggests that any interaction which took place between the populations did not extend to shared burial grounds, except in the case of Westness where Scandinavian domination of the local population may be inferred. In Orkney the other certain well-located Scandinavian burials are associated with pre-Viking Age monuments (Styes of Brough, Broch of Gurness) and settlement mound (Bay of Skaill), pre-Christian burial grounds (Brough Road), a Viking-Age house (Buckquoy), Viking-Age middens (Brough Road), and two possible 'virgin' sites (Sand of Gill, Scar) (McLeod 2015c and references therein). This array of locations highlights the burial options available to Scandinavian communities, and each burial location is likely to have been chosen for a specific reason. For example, the association with pre-Viking Age monuments may be due to their resonance with practices in Scandinavia and the use of ancient monuments to signal land-ownership and legitimacy (cf. Thäte 2007). The paucity of burials in contemporary indigenous cemeteries could suggest that the intended audience for the location of Scandinavian burials was primarily other Scandinavians. The same array of burial locations is found in Shetland where burials were found in a re-used burial mound (Weisdale), close to a settlement (Sumburgh), and possible 'virgin' sites (Clibberswick, Wick of Aith) (McLeod 2015a and references therein). The low number of Scandinavian burials, including no known cemeteries, in Shetland is unusual considering the other evidence for Scandinavian settlement (Graham-Campbell & Batey 1998: 39, 63-67), suggesting that very different circumstances prevailed there than on Orkney. For example, as well as signalling land-ownership and legitimacy, ostentatious burial has been linked to societies under threat, and competition between elites (Halsall 2000: 270-271; Richards et al 1995: 66). Thus the few ostentatious Scandinavian burials in Shetland may represent foundation burials of the new community/ies, after which further ostentatious burials were not considered necessary in a stable and peaceful society, as has been suggested for the lack of elaborate burials in fifth to ninth-century Denmark (Hedeager 1992: 282-300).

This paper demonstrates the variable nature of Scandinavian burials, even those associated with Christian cemeteries. There is no single way to explain the decision to utilise Christian cemeteries across such a large geographic and cultural area as Scotland, and even the notion of acculturation to Christian burial practice is hard to sustain at some sites. Instead, Scandinavian burial sites should be considered regionally, and where possible individually.

## Endnotes

[1] I would like to thank James Graham-Campbell for discussing the particulars of this burial with me.

[2] A double burial of a female and infant accompanied by multiple grave-goods was discovered in 1963, seven accompanied burials (three male, two female, two unstated) were discovered in excavations between 1968-1984 (Graham-Campbell & Batey 1998: 136; Barrett & Richards 2004: 262), and a single unsexed burial with a Viking Age comb was found in 1997 (Wilson & Moore 1997: 60).

[3] I would like to thank Colleen Batey for bringing this cemetery to my attention.

[4] The burial not associated with a Christian cemetery was at Carronbridge, Dumfries and Galloway. It was in/on top of a pre-Viking Age enclosure, over-looking the River

Nith, and close to a prominent road (McLeod 2014b and references therein).

[5] Auldhame belonged to the Community; Kirkcudbright is named after St Cuthbert and a chapel to the Saint is thought to have existed in the churchyard; Whithorn may have been visited by the Community during its period of wandering prior to their agreement with Guthfrith (McLeod 2015b: 99 and references therein).

[6] For a more cautious approach see Barrett 2003: 209. For theories regarding Pictish and Gaelic-speaking communities on Shetland before the Viking Age see also Grant 2003: 2-4.

[7] Disarticulated bones were stored in the adjacent mortuary chapel (Hill 1997: 169, 189).

[8] For example, there is evidence of resident Hiberno-Scandinavian crafts-people in the late-tenth and eleventh centuries, but no culturally Scandinavian burials from that period (Hill 1997: 55-59).

# References

Barrett, J. H. (2003). 'Christian and Pagan Practice during the Conversion of Viking Age Orkney and Shetland', in Carver, M. (ed.), *The Cross Goes North: Processes of Conversion in Northern Europe, AD 300-1300*. York: York Medieval Press, pp. 207-226.

Barrett, J. H. (2008). 'The Norse in Scotland', in Brink, S. with Price, N. (eds.), *The Viking World*. London: Routledge, pp. 411-427.

Barrett, J. H., Beukens, R., Simpson, I., Ashmore, P., Poaps, S. and Huntley, J. (2000). 'What Was the Viking Age and When did it Happen? A View from Orkney', *Norwegian Archaeological Review* 33 (1): pp. 1-39.

Barrett, J. H. and Richards, M. P. (2004). 'Identity, gender, religion and economy: new isotope and radiocarbon evidence for marine resource intensification in early historic Orkney, Scotland, UK', *European Journal of Archaeology* 7 (3), pp. 249-272.

Batey, C. E. (1993). 'The Viking and late Norse graves of Caithness and Sutherland', in Batey, C. E., Jesch, J. and Morris, C. D. (eds.),

*The Viking Age in Caithness, Orkney and the North Atlantic: Select Papers from the Proceedings of the Eleventh Viking Congress, Thurso and Kirkwall, 22 August-1 September 1989.* Edinburgh: Edinburgh University Press, pp. 148-164.

Becket, A. and Batey, C. E. (2013). 'A stranger in the dunes? Rescue excavation of a Viking Age burial at Cnoc nan Gall, Colonsay', *Proceedings of the Society of Antiquaries of Scotland* 143, pp. 303-318.

Buchanan, C., (2012), 'Scandinavians in Strathclyde: Multiculturalism, material culture and manufactured identities in the Viking Age', in Ritchie, A. (ed.), *Historic Bute: Land and People.* Edinburgh: Society for Northern Studies, pp. 17-32.

Crone, A. and Heald, A. (2015). 'Auldhame: in search of a Viking King', *British Archaeology* 141, pp. 16-21.

Dockrill, S. J., Bond, J. M., Turner, V. E., Brown, L. D., Bashford, D. J., Cussans, J. E. and Nicholson, R. A. (2010*). Excavations at Old Scatness, Shetland Volume I: The Pictish Village and Viking Settlement.* Lerwick: Shetland Heritage Publications.

Gameltoft, P. (2004). 'Among Dímons and Papeys: What kind of contact do the names really point to?'. *Northern Studies : The Journal of the Scottish Society for Northern Studies* 38, pp. 31-49.

Graham-Campbell, J. (2001). *Whithorn and the Viking World.* The Eighth Whithorn Lecture, 11 September 1999. Whithorn: Friends of the Whithorn Trust.

Grant, A.E. (2003). Scandinavian Place-Names in Northern Britain as Evidence for Language Contact and Interaction. Unpublished PhD thesis, University of Glasgow. Available at http://ethos.bl.uk/OrderDetails.do?uin=uk.bl.ethos.399826 (Accessed: 24 March 2016).

Graham-Campbell, J. and Batey, C. E. (1998). *Vikings in Scotland: An Archaeological Survey.* Edinburgh: Edinburgh University Press.

Halsall, G. (2000). 'The Viking Presence in England? The Burial Evidence Reconsidered', in Hadley, D. M. and Richards, J. D. (eds.), *Cultures in Contact: Scandinavian Settlement in England in the Ninth and Tenth Centuries*. Turnhout: Brepols, pp. 259-276.

Harrison, S.H. (2007). 'Separated from the Foaming Maelstrom: Landscapes of Insular 'Viking' Burial', in Semple, S. (ed.), *Anglo-Saxon Studies in Archaeology and History 14: Early Medieval Mortuary Practices*. Oxford: Oxford University School of Archaeology, pp. 173-182.

Hedeager, L. (1992), 'Kingdoms, ethnicity and material culture: Denmark in a European perspective', in Carver, M. (ed.), *The Age of Sutton Hoo*. Woodbridge: Boydell, pp. 279-300.

Hill, P. (1997). *Whithorn and St Ninian: The Excavation of a Monastic Town 1984-1991*. Stroud: Sutton Publishing.

*Inventory*. (1946). *An Inventory of the Ancient Monuments of Orkney and Shetland, Vol III: Inventory of Shetland*. Edinburgh: Royal Commission on the Ancient Monuments of Scotland.

Kaland, S. H. H. (1993). 'The Settlement of Westness, Rousay', in Batey, C. E., Jesch, J. and Morris, C. D. (eds.), *The Viking Age in Caithness, Orkney and the North Atlantic: Select papers from the proceedings of the eleventh Viking Congress, Thurso and Kirkwall, 22 August-1 September 1989*. Edinburgh: Edinburgh University Press, pp. 308-317.

MacGregor, G. (2009). 'Changing People Changing Landscapes: excavation at The Carrick, Midross, Loch Lomond'. *Historic Argyll*, pp. 8-13.

McLeod, S. (2013). 'The Acculturation of Scandinavians in England: A Consideration of the Burial Record'. *Journal of the Australian Early Medieval Association* 9, pp. 61-87.

McLeod, S. (2014a). *The Beginning of Scandinavian Settlement in England: The Viking 'Great Army' and Early Settlers, c. 865-900*.

Turnhout: Brepols.

McLeod, S. (2014b). 'A traveller's end?? – a reconsideration of a Viking Age burial at Carronbridge, Dumfriesshire', *Transactions of the Dumfriesshire and Galloway Natural History and Antiquarian Society* 88, pp. 13-20.

McLeod, S. (2015a). *Viking Burials in Scotland: Landscape and burial in the Viking Age*. Available at https://vikingfuneralscapes.wordpress. com/ (Accessed: 23 September 2015).

McLeod, S. (2015b). 'The *dubh gall* in southern Scotland: the politics of Northumbria, Dublin, and the Community of St Cuthbert in the Viking Age, c. 870-950 CE', *Limina* Special Edition: Festschrift in Honour of Philippa Maddern, pp. 83-103.

McLeod, S. (2015c). 'Legitimation through Association? Scandinavian accompanied burials and pre-historic monuments in Orkney', *Journal of the North Atlantic* 28, pp. 1-15.

McNeill, M. (1892). 'Notice of the discovery of a Viking internment, in the Island of Colonsay', *Proceedings of the Society of Antiquaries of Scotland* 26, pp. 61-62.

Montgomery, J., Grimes, V., Buckberry, J., Evans, J. A., Richards, M. P. and Barrett, J. H. (2014). 'Finding Vikings with Isotope Analysis – the view from the wet and windy islands', in Douglas Price, T. (ed.), *Viking Settlers of the North Atlantic: An Isotopic Approach, Journal of the North Atlantic* Special Volume 7, pp. 54-70.

Richards, J. D., Jecock, M., Richmond, L. and Tuck, C. (1995). 'The Viking Barrow Cemetery at Heath Wood, Ingleby, Derbyshire', *Medieval Archaeology* 39, pp. 51-70.

Ritchie, J. N. G. (1982). 'Excavations at Machrins, Colonsay', *Proceedings of the Society of Antiquaries of Scotland* 111, pp. 263-281.

Sellevold, B. J. (1999). *Picts and Vikings at Westness: Anthropological investigations of the skeletal material from the cemetery at Westness,*

*Rousay, Orkney Islands*. Oslo: NIKU.

Stevenson, R. B. K. (1949-1950). 'Pictish sculpture from Reay', *Proceedings of the Society of Antiquaries of Scotland* 84, pp. 218.

Stevenson, R. B. K. (1981). 'Christian sculpture in Norse Shetland', *Fródskaparrit* 28/29, pp. 283-292.

Thäte, E. S. (2007). *Monuments and Minds. Monument Re-use in Scandinavia in the Second Half of the First Millennium AD*. Lund: Dept. of Archaeology.

Towrie, S. (2015). 'Another Papay burial hints at possible Viking cemetery', *The Orcadian*, 27 August, p. 9.

Wilson, D. M. (2008). *The Vikings in the Isle of Man*. Aarhus: Aarhus University Press.

Wilson, G. and Moore, H. (1997). 'Westness Cemetery (Rousay parish), Viking cemetery', *Discovery and Excavation in Scotland*, p. 60.

# 'Dette er ingen rekreasjonstur.'[1]
## Surviving Auschwitz:
## Voices from Norway

## Karianne Hansen

At least 1.3 million people were deported to Auschwitz in the four and half years that the camp operated, of which the largest number were Jews from various European countries, including Norway. Some 736 Jewish individuals deported from Nazi-occupied Norway found themselves at the centre of the Final Solution, together with Poles, criminal prisoners, Soviet prisoners of war and others.[2] The focus of this article is a comprehensive analysis of survival in Auschwitz, taking as its basis a case study of Jewish individuals deported from Norway in the years 1942-1945. The value of such a detailed case study is the capacity to demonstrate conditions which could determine the death or survival of prisoners. This research will demonstrate that the timing and location of the deportation of the Norwegian Jews appear to have determined the fate of this national group, which experienced a mortality rate of 97 per cent. Out of 736 individuals there were some 20 survivors.[3] By focusing on the survival of two of these individuals, it is possible to examine how survival could become possible in this context. The Norwegians arrived in the camps at a time when the collaboration between concentration camp and industry meant that genocide and economic needs came together, culminating in the concept of extermination through labour. It will be argued that survival in Auschwitz was intrinsically linked to the overall development of the camp complex and Nazi policies towards slave labour. How did these changes manifest themselves inside the camp, and under what conditions could survival be achieved in this context?

In order to explore survival, I analyse two narratives that present the memoirs of two Norwegian survivors, Herman Sachnowitz's *Det angår også Deg* (It concerns you too) and Robert Savosnick's *Jeg Ville ikke Dø* (I didn't want to die). They both arrived in Auschwitz at the same time, yet their stories differ substantially. These two individuals came from two fundamentally different backgrounds, which is also reflected in their writings, and they represent different experiences of Auschwitz. This must be made explicit as it is now recognised that survivor biographies not only reflect on the suffering in the camps, but also on the life story of the author (Kushner 2006: 179-180). Therefore, to approach the concept of survival requires the acknowledgment that these individuals reinterpret events in the camp in the attempt to place their Auschwitz experience within the wider context of their lives.

## To Auschwitz by Sea: November 1942

The ship *Donau Aus Bremen* departed from Oslo harbour in late November 1942. On board were 532 Jews. The arrest and deportation of the Jews took approximately one month, and was carried out between late October and November 1942 by various branches of the Norwegian police force, as well as the paramilitary unit of *Nasjonal Samling* (National Unity) led by the infamous Vidkun Quisling. The motivations and politics of Nazi designs against the Jewish people have been discussed elsewhere, but it is worth mentioning in the context of this article that the motivations for the deportation of Jews from a country where, as it was discussed during the Wannsee conference of January 1942, such an operation would cause 'unnecessary societal resistance', remains unclear.[4] Nevertheless, the operation in Norway commenced and Herman Sachnowitz and others were headed towards Poland. Less than one week later, not knowing where they would end up, they were subjected to screams and segregation upon arrival in in the Polish village of Brzezinka, Birkenau. They were separated into groups based on sex, and were examined by an SS guard. As a result of this examination, 354 individuals, mostly the elderly, women and children were escorted onto trucks that would drive them to the destination known as 'Little White House' just outside the newly built Birkenau camp, the second improvised gas chamber. Oblivious to the fate of their loved ones, the remaining individuals underwent rituals which had been designed by the Germans to annul any links to previous lives and to collapse any notions of identity. Personal names were replaced by tattooed numbers and coloured triangles, which also worked as the social signifier in the camp. (Suderland 2013: 119-120) The Jews received a double triangle, red and yellow, to create the Star of David, while other camp categories included the green triangle for criminals and red for political prisoners. After the additional trauma of shaven heads and the white and blue striped uniform, they were now the prisoners of Auschwitz.

## Newcomers: Winter 1942

Approximately 220 Norwegians were registered as prisoners in Auschwitz in December 1942.[5] After a few days, at least 186 of them were transferred to the newly erected and unfinished camp in the nearby village of Monowice. This Auschwitz sub-camp would later emerge as a separate administrative camp, but for now, it housed fewer than 4000 prisoners, primarily Jews from the Reich, Polish political prisoners and German criminals. (Setkiewicz 2008: 118) The Norwegians became only a small proportion of the total number of prisoners in this camp within the next couple of months. The Auschwitz administration continued to pour in new and healthy prisoners to supply the build-up of the industrial workforce connected to the German industrial firm of IG Farbenindustrie.[6]

The Norwegians, as newcomers and Jews, had a higher chance of dying than those who had more experience in the camp. The prisoners were, as already mentioned, marked in accordance with the reason for incarceration, e.g. racial reasons. Jews were at the bottom of the hierarchy together with Soviet prisoners of war, followed by political prisoners, including Poles. What this meant in practice was that the colour insignia not only singled out groups for additional harassment, but it could also determine the employment of prisoners in the camp. As Auschwitz needed slave labour, and with the acceleration of the Holocaust, there was an impetus to exploit the Jewish labour force more systematically and lethally (Wachsmann 2015: 294-298). As a result of the constant arrival of prisoners of other categories, those who had survived the first period (1940-1942), primarily Poles, were able to take up better positions. This was primarily due to what was referred to as 'camp experience', which was also the reason why German Jews in Monowitz, deported from other camps, received better employment for some time. The most privileged positions were generally held by Germans, regardless of their category (Setkiewicz 2008: 134). In other words, labour employment in accordance with Nazi ideology remained intact, but was heavily dynamic and dependent on the internal needs of the camp. Therefore, Jewish labourers, especially newcomers continued to exist at the bottom of the camp hierarchy from the onset. From late 1942 onwards, this practice facilitated the mass-employment of Auschwitz prisoners in industry, as to become part of the workforce in Auschwitz required no qualifications.

The prisoners would have to learn the rules of the camp in order to stand a chance of survival, even in the short-term. Most perished before they managed this. In the context of the extreme shock that constituted admission to Auschwitz, the ability to overcome the initial impact of entry was of paramount importance to secure any prospects of survival. For Herman Sachnowitz, who survived the selection with his four brothers, the family context played a part in relieving the immediate shock of the camp. 'Vi diktet håp, og vi lot som vi trodde på det, enda vi alle visste det var narrespill vi drev med' (Sachnowitz 2005: 30) (We created hope and pretended to believe it, despite knowing it was a charade).[7] The Sachnowitz family was able to stick together throughout the one month of quarantine, despite the loss of one of the brothers early on during this period in 1943. Sachnowitz's narrative reveals that, in contrast to the solidarity of his family, several Norwegians had effectively abandoned all hope early on, which subsequently led to suicidal acts. To demonstrate this point, Sachnowitz mention a Norwegian who ran out of the marching column and was deliberately shot by the guards. This clearly underscored the important role of strong social bonds (such as family bonds) in providing hope and a reason to live.

Savosnick, who arrived in the camp without any close friends or family, was required to find another strategy during his first period in the camp: one that centred on his own individual interpretation of camp reality. Though Sachnowitz found strength and comfort in his brothers, Savosnick's narrative reveals a fundamentally different way of overcoming the initial trauma. Savosnick was preoccupied instead with contrasting himself with the other victims of the camp from the very outset. On observing the marching column of emaciated prisoners, he comments that they were just like him. They were as innocent as him and had gone through the same rituals of selection and dehumanisation; 'Tross det greier jeg ikke å identifisere meg med disse menneskene. Det er ikke i mine tanker at jeg selv skulle bli en av dem' (Savosnick 1986: 48) (Despite this I am unable to identify myself with these people. It did not cross my mind that I would end up like them). Savosnick's thoughts on this particular issue are indicative of the importance that he himself, in his memoir, attach to grasping camp reality as a way of confirming that not all hope was lost.

## Workers in Industry: December 1942-March 1943

Notwithstanding the importance of such individual coping strategies, scholar Frank Pingel observed that perhaps the most important factor that could ensure immediate survival was developing an understanding of how the camp functioned (1991: 176). Integral to this was finding a way of accepting the daily regimen of the camp without yielding to its purpose. In order to do so in a landscape dominated by death and dying, it was important to develop what researchers refer to as 'active denial' (Ibid). This was the process of acknowledging the reality of the camp in the context of one's immediate situation, whilst simultaneously suppressing the acknowledgement of the suffering of others; not practicing active denial would, more often than not, lead to the abandonment of any hope to live. The importance of such a strategy is illustrated by the advice given by an old prisoner to Robert Savosnick: 'Husk å arbeide med øynene og ikke med hendene' (Savosnick 1986: 54-55) (Work with your eyes and not your hands). This also revealed the problem of balancing acts of self-preservation, that of working as slowly as possible, to the danger of being caught. But as put by Savosnick; 'Uten et slikt forsvarsberedskap hjalp det lite med fysisk styrke' (Savosnick 1996: 55) (Physical strength was wasted without any type of defence mechanisms).

That such perspectives were valuable for prisoners is exemplified by the actions of Savosnick. Together with most of the other Norwegians, he found himself employed in the Buna Werke factory close to the Buna camp. Savosnick recalls that it dawned upon him that he would not survive working in the cement *kommando* and he therefore behaved pro-actively. He made the decision to not show up to the original *kommando* the next morning, but rather joined a group of prisoners waiting to be assigned work details (Savosnick 1986: 61). This action was prohibited. The importance of this decision for survival and the risks involved in carrying it out should not be downplayed, especially with regard to Savosnick's status as a newcomer, but also in the context of the fate of the other Norwegians. By March 1943, at least 75 had perished.[8] The survivors' impression in hindsight is that most of them were employed in heavy outdoor work *kommandos*. It was winter, and as newcomers they had little chance of being able to accumulate warmer clothing. Working in labour details also accelerated the process of malnourishment. The fact that the work was outdoors and easy to supervise meant that any attempts at saving energy would be futile. Sachnowitz writes that 'Gang på gang ble vi slått og sparket fordi vi ikke jobbet fort nok' (Sachnowitz 2005: 39) (Time after time we were beaten for not working fast enough). The inmates then had to carry their dying comrades back to the camp where death would likely follow, either by natural causes or by admittance into the hospital. It was this cycle of death against which the prisoners needed to mobilise themselves.

Savonsick's success at surviving was in many respects attributable to luck, but this factor brings us back to the importance of adapting to camp realities, whilst maintaining mechanisms of defence to avoid the '[…] unconditional surrender and subjugation to its dictates' (Pingel 1991: 177). As a rule therefore, the longer one survived the better one's chances were to depart from the camp alive. Although Sachnowitz was losing his brothers one by one, it is clear that the efforts to survive worked across two levels: that of ensuring his own survival as well as that of his brothers. Being surrounded by family generated hope throughout Auschwitz, but it also brought the devastation of witnessing the death of so many loved ones in such a short space of time. In mid 1943 there were only two Sachnowitz brothers left in Auschwitz, and the youngest one, Frank, was in such a state of severe emaciation that even moving his feet was problematic. Sachnowitz reflects on the importance of his brother; 'Han var Frankemann og Gud skal vite at *jeg* trengte *ham*. Han var meningen med livet mitt. Han var halmstrået jeg klynget meg til. Uten Frankemann ville alt vært over' (Sachnowitz 2005: 57) (He was my little Frank and God knows that *I* needed *him*. He was the meaning of my life. He was the straw to which I clung. Without Frank it would all be over – original emphasis). It is evident that saving his youngest brother Frank served as an incentive in decisive moments of action, such as when the two brothers found a hidden treasure in one of the barracks: a woman's sock filled with valuables. They collectively decided to engage in the camp's black market, in which prisoners and guards participated alike. The black market itself is a testament that social interactions in the camp did run contrary to the established hierarchies (Suderland 2013: 137). Those who had anything to trade, ranging from bread and cigarettes to anything considered of value to prisoners or guards, could therefore progress in the camp's social hierarchies, and improve their chances of survival. The two Sachnowitz brothers were able to trade food and even work details by bribing a *Kapo* (i.e. prisoners who worked as supervisors or who were assigned administrative tasks, and who often exercised great brutality). These situations arose partly because of the luck involved in finding the sock and its contents, but it was through the agency of the brothers that they managed to take full advantage of the situation. As Sachnowitz describes, they knew full well that if they were caught their lives would be at risk, as '[…] Mange var blitt hengt for mindre, ellers sendt ut på en dødskommando, der de sjelden fikk leve arbeidsdagen ut' (Sachnowitz 2005: 55) (People had been hanged for less or sent to a death *kommando*, where they would seldom see the end of a day's work).

## Surviving the Hospitals: 1942-1943

Such episodes clearly reveal the importance of active choices and risk-taking involved in survival strategies. However, individual agency alone could not be the determining factor of survival in the long run. Rather, as Sachnowitz and Savosnick were able to live for weeks and months, the camp itself underwent developments. By August 1943 almost 75,000 people were imprisoned in Auschwitz. Despite the constant influx of prisoners to this camp over the previous eighteen month, prisoners were dying too fast to constitute a lasting and productive labour force. The high mortality rate of concentration camp prisoners became such a pressing issue that by late 1942 and early 1943 actions were taken to combat this high mortality rate, which did not aim at halting the extermination process as such, but rather preserving the workforce temporarily (Wachsmann 2015: 425-427). This accounts for the fact that in Auschwitz the principle of 'selection' was abolished for all prisoners except for Jews from mid-1943 onwards. In earlier periods, 'selection' was one of the main causes of the devastating mortality rates, as prisoners deemed unlikely to recover from disease were immediately gassed or injected with phenol. Despite the continuation of this deadly practice on Jews, the changing attitude towards the labour force resulted in physical recovery being permitted. These improved chances of physical recovery were further increased by a change in the hospital staff. Polish political prisoners and Jews with appropriate qualification replaced the former German criminal inmates in 1943. Thus, staff at the hospital were now not only allowed but also willing and able to help prisoners to the best of their ability (Strzelecka 2000: 298). These are the two main points which made the difference between life and death in the hospital. In the case of the Norwegian prisoners, it appears that these changes were crucial for survival. As has already been established, almost half of the Norwegians inmates died early on, and external documents suggest that at least half of them were hospitalised prior to death.[9] Savosnick and Sachnowitz were both admitted to the hospital on numerous occasions, and assistance from fellow prisoners played an important role in their staying alive (e.g. admission dates were amended in the records in order to generate sufficient time for their rehabilitation). This further illustrates the fact that the timing of hospitalisation and the hospital's daily routines had an impact on an individual's chances of survival. In fact, Savosnick found himself as part of the hospital staff in the main camp in April 1943; and while this job proved to be short-term, it illustrates that new contexts for survival in the camp now existed.

As significant as these changes in the hospital were, the crucial factor in prisoner life remained the nature of the work that they performed. Most prisoners did not state their true profession upon arrival in Auschwitz out of fear, and most Jews were in any case largely employed as unskilled labour regardless of previous employment. One of the admission routines was to fill out a form with personal information. Savosnick did not state that he was a student of medicine at the University of Oslo, but in 1943, as he himself writes, the camp needed qualified personnel. Sachnowitz, however, had made it known to fellow prisoners that he was 'Musiker von Beruf' (musician by profession). After the disappearance and later death of Frank in May 1943, Sachnowitz found himself struggling to stay alive, as '[...] alle dager var like. Gledesløse, grå evigheter i et liv som ikke hadde annet å by på enn den samme smerten og det samme savnet hver dag' (Sachnowitz 2005: 71) (Every day was the same. Joyless, grey eternities in a life with nothing to offer but the same pain and longing every day). Luckily for Sachnowitz, the newly established orchestra in the Monowitz camp was recruiting, and even made an exception towards accepting Jews (Lachendro 2015: 116).

## Alte Häftlinge: 1943

As previously mentioned, there tended to be a correlation between social status, that of being a newcomer or *Alte Häftlinge* (prisoner with an old number), and the type of work that the prisoner performed. This leap in social status was not automatic or a given in any way. Both Sachnowitz and Savosnick make comments regarding what appeared to be their improved social position in the camp. As Savosnick arrived in the infirmary in the main camp, he writes that the group of nurses and doctors instantly felt uneasy by the sight of the '[...] nakne, utmagrede fanger, nærmest som skjeletter overtrukket med pergamentaktig tørr hud' (Savosnick 1986: 68) (Naked, emaciated prisoners, almost like skeletons covered in parchment-like dry skin). This description is not so much a means for Savosnick to look down on other prisoners, but rather to affirm his own position; he was not like them. His physical appearance was still somewhat intact, he could still survive. And this was of paramount importance, especially when he lost his relatively stable job in the infirmary, 'Jeg måtte igjen starte på det umenneskelige slitet. Være på vakt […] Aldri noen mulighet til å slappe av' (Savosnick 1986: 75) (And my brutal struggle started again. Always to be on guard. Never any opportunity to relax). He became employed in a so-called 'Death *kommando*' where his job consisted in writing down the numbers of deceased prisoners. Here he was able to steal various items from the dead including a pair of leather boots. These boots not only improved his overall ability to move more efficiently than with the wooden clogs, which the prisoners were forced to wear, but also enabled him to present a more reputable appearance amongst the SS and the guards. As a result, he one day became employed to brush the boots of the SS and to help a *Kapo*. Despite the fact that Savosnick attributes these episodes principally to luck, they would have been less likely to have arisen without his efforts to look as presentable as possible, and thus not be shunned by the guards (Langbein 2004: 70). The most presentable prisoners in the camp would have been the members of the orchestra, at least when they played concerts for the SS on Sundays, attired in white uniforms. Although the camp orchestra did not function as a work detail as such, its members were exempted from the standard work details for some months and its members were eligible for extra food. Sachnowitz was acutely aware that he found himself in a better position than earlier, as he observes in a passage where he discusses his philosophy of never succumbing to envy of those better off than him since that would mean staring death in the eye (Sachnowitz 2005: 82). Sachnowitz acknowledged that he had climbed the social ladder, and as a result, he could hold onto a realistic hope for survival. This social advancement was crucial as Sachnowitz was still plagued by diseases and hunger, despite employment in the newly established SS vegetable garden in the Monowitz camp, which constituted '[…] den beste [tiden] under hele min fangetid' (Sachnowitz 2005: 103) (the best time of all during my incarceration). In this *kommando*, he worked unsupervised and was surrounded by vegetables, which he was able to steal and share with other prisoners. All the skills that the two Norwegians had gained over the past years would be tested in the two final years of the war. In October 1943, Savosnick was sent to an impromptu camp in Warsaw to clean up after the failed ghetto uprising of that year. After a while he was promoted to the role of nurse in the improvised hospital and he survived the death march to the Dachau camp in Germany. Sachnowitz was evacuated from Auschwitz in mid January 1945 and was later liberated in the Bergen-Belsen camp.

This article has sought to examine Norwegian survivals in concentration camps through the exploration of two case studies using memoirs and archival sources. This analysis of camp survival is of course not in any way intended to subject the dead or the survivors to objective reasoning or judgement. Auschwitz remained a place in which death was seen as the ultimate aim, yet as the war rumbled on and the casualties of the conflict mounted, slave labour in camps like Auschwitz became more important. Those who had survived the first months of imprisonment had by this point gained knowledge and developed skills that would increase the chances of short-term survival. These skills also included mental and psychological coping strategies for the daily realities of the camp. For the Norwegian Jews, deportation to Auschwitz came as a complete surprise, and most died early on as a result of hard labour and fatal hospital practices. Changing circumstances within the camp as well as the decisions and manoeuvrings of internees within their limited circumstances were factors in the survival of many prisoners. Fortune would also play a role, but the internees had to take advantage of events as they unfolded and develop strategies to maximise the effect of any lucky circumstances.

## Endnotes

[1] 'This is not a party', original quote, Robert Savosnick (1986: 40). *Jeg Ville Ikke dø* (I

Didn't Want to Die). Oslo: Cappelen Forlag

[2] For a general introduction to the history of Auschwitz see Sybille Steinbacher (2013) *Auschwitz: A History.* New York: Harper Perennial.

[3] Author's approximate for Auschwitz, and includes three other transports from Norway. The overall figure for Jewish deportees and survivors deported from Norway is usually higher, but this includes those interned elsewhere. See; Bjarte Bruland (2012), *Øyenvitner, Rapport etter norske jøders hjemkomst fra konsentrasjonsleirene (Eyewitness accounts of the homecoming of Norwegian Jews from the concentration camps).* Oslo: Dinamo Forlag pp. 15-16

[4] For an introduction to the history of the Final solution, see Peter Longerich (2012) *Holocaust: The Nazi Persecution and Murder of the Jews.* Oxford: Oxford University Press; for a more recent perspective that includes Norway see Christian Gerlach (2016) *The Extermination of the European Jews.* Cambridge: Cambridge University press. For Norwegian perspectives, see Bjarte Bruland (2011). "'Norway's role in the Holocaust: The destruction of Norway's Jews'", in Jonathan C. Friedman, *The Routledge History of the Holocaust.* Routledge & Terje Emberland, T. and Matthew Koht (2012). *Himmlers Norge. Nordmenn i det Storgermanske prosjekt (Himmler's Norway: Norwegians in the Aryan project).* Oslo: Aschehoug. Especially pp. 355-365.

[5] Figures based on the author's research, in addition to the works by Danuta Czech (1990), *Auschwitz Chronicle: 1939-1945,* (New York), p. 276 and Bruland, *Øyenvitner,* p. 16. This figure precedes the March 1943 transports, but includes two minor transports of December 1942.

[6] A wealth of literature on this area exists. This article primarily draws upon Nikolaus Wachsmann's 2015 book *Kl: A History of the Nazi Concentration Camps.* New York: Farrar, Strauss and Giroux. Specific books on Auschwitz include Franciszek Piper and Wacław Długoborski (eds.), *Auschwitz 1940–1945: Central Issues in The History Of the Camp, Volume I - V.* Oświęcim: Auschwitz Birkenau State museum & Piotr Setkiewicz, P. (2008). *The Histories of IG Farben Werk Camps 1941-1945.* Oświęcim: Auschwitz Birkenau State Museum

[7] All translations are the author's own unless otherwise stated.

[8] Calculations based on sources connected to Norwegian fatalities available, to be found in the following archive sources at the Archiwum Państwowego Muzeum Auschwitz-Birkenau (APMAB): Register of Deaths and Mortuary Registers of Auschwitz 1: DAuI-5/2, Mortuary Register for Auschwitz 1; D-AuI-2/29, Register of Deaths

[9] Documents connected to Norwegians in hospital are available in the following sources: APMAB, D-AuI-2/30, Registers of Deaths; D-AuI-5/1, volume 1 Record Book of Block 20; D-AuI-5/2, volumes 1, 3, 54, 55 Mortuary Book; D-AuI-5/2,

volume 2, Surgical Ward Registers; D-AuI-5/7, volume 393, Record Book of Block 28; D-AuI-5/10, volumes 10, 12, Surgical Records; D-AuIII-5/1, volume 1, Transfer List; D-AuIII-5/1a, volume 2, Transfer List; D-AuIII-5/4, Buna Register of Deaths; D-AuIII-5/4, Transfer List; D-AuIII-5/7, Transfer List.

# References

## Primary Sources

Archiwum Państwowego Muzeum Auschwitz-Birkenau (Archives of the Auschwitz-Birkenau State Museum, or APMAB), Oświęcim:

D-AuI-2/29, Death Books

 D-AuI-2/30, Death BooksD-AuI-5/1, volume 1 Record Book of Block 20

D-AuI-5/2, volumes 1, 3, 54, 55 Mortuary Book

D-AuI-5/2, volume 2, Surgical Ward Registers

D-AuI-5/7, volume 393, Record Book of Block 28

D-AuI-5/10, volumes 10, 12, Surgical Records: X-ray

D-AuIII-5/1, volume 1, Transfer List from the hospital in Auschwitz III (HKB Buna)

D-AuIII-5/1a, volume 2, Transfer List from HKB Buna

D-AuIII-5/4, Buna Death Book

D-AuIII-5/4, Transfer List from HKB Buna

D-AuIII-5/7, Transfer List from HKB Buna

## Secondary Sources

Bruland, B. (2012). *Øyenvitner Rapport etter norske jøders hjemkomst fra konsentrasjonsleirene (Eyewitness accounts of the homecoming of Norwegian Jews from the concentration camps)*. Oslo: Dinamo Forlag'.

Bruland, B. (2011). 'Norway's role in the Holocaust: The destruction of Norway's Jews', in Friedman, J. C., *The Routledge History of the Holocaust.* New York: Routledge, pp. 232-247.

Czech, D. (1990). *The Auschwitz Chronicle: 1939-1945.* New York: Henry Holt and Company.

Dahl, H. F. (1992). *Vidkun Quisling: en fører for fall (Vidkun Quisling: A study in Treachery).* Volume Two. Oslo: Aschehoug & Co.

Emberland, T. and Koht, M. (2012). *Himmlers Norge. Nordmenn i det Storgermanske prosjekt (Himmler's Norway: Norwegians in the Aryan project).* Oslo: Aschehoug.

Gerlach, C. (2016) *The Extermination of the European Jews.* Cambridge: Cambridge University Press.

Kristian, O. (1995). *I Slik En Natt. Historien om Deportasjonen av Jøder fra Norge (What a night: a history of the deportation of Jews from Norway).* Oslo: Aschehoug.

Kushner, T. (2006). 'Holocaust Testimony, Ethics, and the Problem of Representation', *Poetics Today*, 27, pp. 279-280.

Lachendro, J. (2015). 'The Orchestras in KL Auschwitz', *Auschwitz Studies 57*, pp. 7-148.

Langbein, H. (2004). *People in Auschwitz.* North Carolina: The University of North Carolina Press.

Longerich, P. (2012). *Holocaust: The Nazi Persecution and Murder of the Jews.* Oxford: Oxford University.

Pingel, F. (1991). 'The Destruction of human identity in Concentration Camps: The contribution of the Social Sciences to an analysis of behavior under extreme conditions', *Holocaust and Genocide Studies,* 51 (2), pp. 167-184.

Pingel, F. (2010). 'Social life in an unsocial environment: the inmates' struggle for survival', in Chaplan, J. and Wachsmann, N. (eds.).

*Concentration Camps in Nazi Germany: the New Histories.* New York: Routledge, pp. 58-81.

Piper, F. (2002). *Auschwitz Prisoner Labor.* Oświęcim: Auschwitz Birkenau State Museum.

Piper, F. and Długoborski, W. (eds.) (2000). *Auschwitz 1940-1945: Central Issues in The History Of the Camp, Volume I-V.* Oświęcim: Auschwitz Birkenau State Museum.

Sachnowitz, H. (2005). *Det Angår Også Deg (It Concerns You Too).* Oslo: Holm & Tangen forlag.

Savosnick, R. (1986). *Jeg Ville Ikke dø (I Don't Want to Die).* Oslo: Cappelen Forlag.

Setkiewicz, P. (2008). *The Histories of IG Farben Werk Camps 1941-1945.* Oświęcim: Auschwitz Birkenau State Museum.

Steinbacher, S. (2013) *Auschwitz: A history.* New York: Harper Perennial.

Strzelecka, I. (2000). 'The Hospitals at Auschwitz Concentration Camp', in Piper F. and Długoborski, W. (eds), *Auschwitz 1940–1945: Central Issues in The History Of the Camp, Volume II.* Oświęcim: Auschwitz Birkenau State museum, pp. 291-332.

Suderland, M. (2013). *Inside Concentration Camps: Social Life at the Extremes.* New York: Polit Press.

Wachsmann, N. (2015). *KL: A History of the Nazi Concentration Camps.* New York: Farrar, Strauss and Giroux.

# At the Crossroads of Estonian and Finnish Identities

## Cristina Sandu

Sofi Oksanen was born in Finland in 1977. Her mother grew up in Estonia under Soviet occupation before moving to Finland in the 1970s after which she often returned to Estonia with her daughter to visit relatives. The division between East and West is a constant theme in Oksanen's fictional writing. In interviews she remembers, on the one hand, the Estonia of the 1970s and 1980s with its idealisation of the West, and, on the other hand, the negative stereotypes that dominated the Finnish perception of Estonians which subsumed Estonian under Russian culture (Benedek 2011). Her novel *Stalininin lehmät* (*Stalin's Cows,* 2003) tells the story of Anna who grows up in Finland in the last decades of the twentieth century, and whose mother is an Estonian immigrant. The novel establishes a parallel between Anna's life in Finland and the lives of Anna's mother and grandmother in occupied Estonia, in the midst of the executions, deportations and violent questionings that took place under Soviet occupation. Hence, *Stalin's Cows* places questions of belonging, cultural violence and racism at the centre of its story of immigration and border-crossing in the Finnish and Estonian contexts.

Oksanen's novel raises a topic scarcely discussed in Nordic literature: issues of migration and identity between former Soviet colonies. It therefore urges us to rethink postcolonial theory in order to apply it to literature in the context of Soviet postcolonialism, particularly since postcolonial readings of the literature of former Soviet countries remains thus far rather limited. But it also adds another dimension to the problem: it is not only about exploring the repercussions of Soviet (post-)colonialism, but also about exploring the effects of uneven conditions of Soviet colonial domination on the relations

275

between neighbouring countries. Indeed, Finland and Estonia have both experienced Soviet colonialism under varying conditions, but neither have ever colonised the other. Yet the varying conditions and experiences of Soviet colonialism have fundamentally shaped the relations and perceptions between these two neighbouring countries. The aim of this article is therefore to explore how these effects of Soviet postcolonialism have shaped the Finnish perception of Estonia and the Estonian perceptions of Finland, as well as how individuals moving between these cultural contexts negotiate these issues.

Previous research has approached Oksanen's work from the point of view of women's experiences of political violence (Mavrikakis 2013, Clarke 2015); trauma (Roos 2014); or from the perspective of the process of acculturation between Finnish and Estonian cultures (Dervin 2013). Yet Oksanen herself suggests a more postcolonial reading. In an interview with *The Guardian*, Oksanen defines herself as a 'postcolonial author.' She states:

> We know about British colonialism. Russian colonialism is not so well known . . . I think we should call it what it was – and is . . . Russia has never been "an overseas kind of empire" . . . rather a state that's sought to exploit and colonise its European neighbours. (Harding 2015)

Oksanen calls for an increased recognition of the history of domination of the USSR on its neighbouring countries as part of colonialism. She therefore calls for a more diversified understanding of (post-)colonialism which would not simply subscribe to established paradigms of colonialism as understood in terms of, for example, British colonialism: colonialism does not only have to do with overseas empires, but can also happen between neighbouring countries. Exploring other paradigms of postcolonialism would therefore shed new light on problems of postcolonial identity formation. Indeed in *Stalin's Cows*, Oksanen explores how colonial history has left its marks upon Estonia and Finland, and how it affects the identity-shaping of those living between these two countries. Both countries are former colonies of the USSR, but they have developed in very different ways: Estonia long remained a colony while Finland developed as an independent state.

For this analysis of *Stalin's Cows*, I will rely especially on the works of the leading postcolonial theorist Homi K. Bhabha, particularly his writings on home and belonging. I will begin by briefly discussing the notion of postcolonialism and its application to former Soviet countries. Second, I will analyse how Oksanen's characters in *Stalin's Cows* struggle to find a place of belonging between Estonian and Finnish societies. Lastly, I will discuss the cultural violence that Oksanen's characters face in Finland as Estonian women, using Bourdieu's notion of 'symbolic violence.'

## The Colonial History of Finland and Estonia

The term colonialism is usually applied when discussing geographic locations such as South Asia, Latin America, North Africa, and the Middle East, as exemplified in the writings of Edward Said, Frantz Fanon, and Gayatri Spivak. These authors understand colonialism in a similar fashion, i.e. as the explorations and conquests undertaken by a nation, aiming at promoting commerce and strengthening industrial wealth (Spivak 2006: 829).[1] There are obvious differences between the expansion of the Soviet Union and that of European nations: the Soviet Union did not correspond to the 'single-nation model' typically present in the history of European colonialism (ibid.). However, as Spivak argues, colonialism can have more than one model (2006: 828). In fact, recent debates in Slavonic Studies call for analyses of the former Soviet state from a postcolonial perspective, and researchers have explored how postcolonialism could be modified in order to be applied to the Soviet context (Condee 2006; Chernetsky 2006; Ram 2006).[2] Soviet culture has not often been analysed and understood in terms of colonialism and postcolonialism, and Finnish literature even less so, particularly in comparison with work done on European colonialism (for example analyses of Conrad and Naipaul). However, as this article will demonstrate, it would indeed be fruitful to apply the theoretical perspective of postcolonialism to the cultural relations between Finland, Estonia and their coloniser the USSR.

After the Second World War, the relationship between Finland and Estonia was defined by their political relation to the Soviet Union. Estonia, as still part of the Soviet Union, could not have an independent foreign policy, and hence the relations between Estonia and Finland as two autonomous states could not officially exist. Finland had retained its independence since 1917, whereas Estonia, after its independence in 1918, was again under Russian occupation from 1940 until 1991. Thus Finland could develop as an independent state in the twentieth century, whilst Estonia was under Soviet occupation. Finland's policy however was still subject to 'finlandization',[3] which meant that Finnish politicians had to privilege relations with the Soviet Union as a whole over individual Soviet states, and could not show any kind of sympathy towards the aspirations of the Estonian people as an independent country. Rather, Finnish politicians accepted the position of Estonia as an inseparable part of the Soviet Union. For this reason, Spivak's definitions of colonisation where 'an alien nation-state establishes itself as ruler, impressing its own laws and systems of education and rearranging the mode of production for its own economic benefit' (2006: 828) can be applied to cast light upon how the history of Soviet colonialism has shaped the relations between Finland and Estonia. Specifically, *Stalin's Cows* shows how the problematic relation between Estonia and Finland, continuing throughout the twentienth century, is underpinned by cultural stereotypes and racism. The racism is connected to Finland's need to separate itself from its former colony, the USSR, and by extension Estonia which still is part of it. In the novel, Anna's mother is an Estonian immigrant to Finland who feels that she has to hide her background in a country which seeks to separate itself from anything Soviet and, by extension, Estonian.

## The Unhomely Condition

Writers dealing with issues surrounding the concepts of nation, identity and postcolonialism, such as Homi Bhabha, identify the end of the twentieth century as a transition period, where identity and the idea of society become conceived in a new way. Instead of relying on static notions of class, gender, nationality and race, the formation of social identities are rather to be understood as complex processes articulated in the midst of cultural differences (Bhabha 1994: 2). Bhabha calls the space in which these new identities are produced 'in-between' zones: identity is not associated to one place clearly meaning 'home' (ibid.). Bhabha uses the term 'unhomely' to describe the estranging feeling connected to the relocation of home (1992: 141). 'Unhomely' is a paradigmatic postcolonial experience, connected to migration and cultural relocations. In addition, 'unhomely' can be a literary trope exploring or expressing cultural dislocations in the midst of 'historical conditions and social contradictions' (1992: 141-142).[4]

In *Stalin's Cows*, a dominant theme is that of a constant movement between Estonia and Finland (two countries which, despite their proximity, represent for Oksanen's characters two opposite examples of the East/West polarity), a position that renders any kind of clear and static notion of 'home' problematic. Even if they praise Finland as a prosperous Western country, Anna and her mother Katariina experience it through feelings of isolation, fear and shame, all because of the need that they feel to hide their Estonian roots. Estonia, in turn, is the place closest associated to home, as Anna always portrays it through positive images from her childhood. Anna and Katariina are therefore examples of characters living in what Bhabha calls an 'in-between' position, an unhomely condition where they move between the two countries without managing to feel at 'home' in either of them. Anna and Katariina's position of 'in-betweenness' is also marked by the fact that they need to adopt a certain role in Estonia: they have to keep up the roles of envied Westerners, and learn to use Finnish products in order to be accepted and to gain people's trust.

Despite hiding their Estonian identity in Finland, Anna and Katariina often return to Estonia (thanks to the ferry connection opened between the two countries in 1965). These visits enable Anna and Katariina to live in one place but constantly return to the other, called by Anna 'Annan maailma' (82) 'Anna's world'.[5] Their lives are marked by the constant movement between these two countries, which means that there is no stable notion of 'home.' In Estonia, Anna and Katariina have to pay attention to the role they adopt: they are Finns. For instance, Anna needs to wear 'imported' clothes in order to seem like a foreigner (38). This is especially important because of the way the West is idealised and associated with Finland in Estonia, whereas Estonia experiences itself as subordinate to westernised Finland. Katariina's friends and relatives in Estonia admire Finland, with regard to food, consumer products, even the silence of the streets (71). Anna's narration in particular emphasises her feelings of estrangement in both countries: she always has to reflect on the kind of image she gives in order to appear like a Finn both in Finland and in Estonia. However, Anna and her mother do not manage to find peace within either of these two countries. The representation of their lives is marked by a continuous longing to return to Estonia, as well as a 'restless movement' between the two countries that exemplifies Bhabha's writing on the experience of living in-between cultures (1994: 2). The shaping of one's identity in-between cultures seems to take place in one's struggle between two poles: rootedness and rootlessness. When in Finland, Anna feels out of place and misses Estonia, but when as an adult she is free to return to Estonia, she feels like a stranger in her mother's country – she realises that the Estonia of her memories does not exist anymore (Oksanen 2003: 64).

In 'The World and the Home', Bhabha writes about the postmodern sense of belonging. For him, the state of unhomeliness does not mean lack of home, but the confusion of the line separating the world and the home, i.e. a home which does not feel like one's own (1992: 141). Anna continues to miss home without it ever becoming clear where home is. Anna and Katariina live in what Bhabha calls a 'Third Space', a space beyond binary oppositions (1990: 211-212): they are not simply inside or outside the culture, nor are they only Finnish or wholly Estonians. Their lives are marked by a constant shifting between countries, and the different identities – Finn, Estonian – are not something pure or obvious, but are constructed throughout the narration.

## The Imposing of Finnish Identity

As Oksanen states, in Finland the Soviet occupation of Estonia was only addressed through euphemisms – whether in politics, the media or the arts – and Estonia did not even feature as a separate entity on the maps in Finland (Oksanen 2014). At the same time, the Finnish Security Intelligence Service (SUPO) kept track of Estonians who moved to Helsinki in order to monitor the activities of the Soviet Communist party. This included immigrants from Soviet countries, such as Katariina in *Stalin's Cows*, who lives with the constant fear of being spied on and having her phone tapped (111).

The fear of being identified as Estonian is present in the everyday lives of Oksanen's characters as they are constantly afraid of being assimilated to Russians. The tendency of assimilating Estonia to the Soviet Union is exemplified, for instance, by the ignorance that students and teachers in Anna's school show towards the particular history of different countries within the Soviet Union. It also appears in the discrepancy between the daily lives of Anna's Estonian family members (for whom the times of war and the annexation of Estonia are still very much part of reality) and the limited knowledge of Estonia and its history in Anna's school (Oksanen 2003: 117). While Anna is shocked by the ignorance she sees in her second homeland, Katariina is questioned by the SUPO, and even at the end of the twentieth century lives with the obsessive fear of being under surveillance. Moreover, she transmits this fear to Anna who, as a result, becomes obsessed with hiding her Estonian roots.

In this context, Finnishness becomes something that her mother tries to impose on Anna: 'Minusta piti tulla suomalainen. Piti puhua, kävellä kuin suomalainen, näyttää siltä kuin suomalainen, vaikka olin jatkuvasti poissa paikaltani, jotenkin pois sijoiltaan...' (45) (I was meant to become Finnish. I had to walk and talk like a Finn, look like a Finn, even though I was constantly out of place, somehow dislocated...). Anna feels forced to take up a Finnish identity, even though she experiences it as violence towards her Estonian self.

## Anna and an Outsider's Perspective

Roger Bromley's *Narratives for a New Belonging. Diasporic Cultural Fiction* (2000) helps to understand Anna and Katariina's position as simultaneously inside and outside Finnish society. Bromley discusses narratives which explore the boundaries around nations and cultures, and in which 'figures look in the society from the outside, while looking out from the inside' (2000: 4). Bromley calls these narratives, like *Borderlands* (2011) by John Shirley and *My Year of Meats* (1998) by Ruth L. Ozeki, 'fictional explorations of belonging and identity, marked by the shifting and cross-cutting cultural experience of relocation' (ibid.) This idea of shifting between cultures and the ability of observing them from an outsiders' perspective on the inside describes the case of Anna. She experiences both societies through an outsider's point of view – in Finland, that of an Estonian, and in Estonia, that of a Westerner. For instance, in her way of observing her Finnish relatives from her father's side, Anna seems to be strongly attached to the Estonian side of herself: in contrast with the Estonian countryside, everything in her Finnish grandparent's house seems too clean and quiet (287). Anna, always observing places and people with her outsider's critical eye, remains an outsider herself. She has no close relationships as they are always tainted by having to keep up a certain role and hiding a significant part of her identity.

## Symbolic Violence

An analysis of *Stalin's Cows* from a postcolonial perspective further illuminates the silent and covert ways in which colonialism can shape social relations. For instance, the prejudice against Estonians in Finland must be understood in a context of Soviet (post-)colonialism. As Minna Suihkonen argues, the attitude of Finns towards Estonians used to be problematic, especially in the 1970s and 1980s, as dominant feelings of hatred towards the former occupying Soviet Union were transferred onto Estonians who were seen as Russians (2006).[6] The prejudice and racism that the characters in *Stalin's Cows* face is well-captured in Pierre Bourdieu's notion of 'symbolic violence.' Bourdieu coined this term to describe the oppressive practices which are exercised by a dominant social group within society (Bourdieu 1977: 408). These practices are seen as legitimate and approved, and hence they are not questioned or conceived as oppressive (Bourdieu 1989: 22).[7] As María Isabel Menéndez-Menéndez suggests, the notion of symbolic violence helps to reveal those practices that contribute to the reproduction of violence against women (2014: 64).

In *Stalin's Cows*, the instances of symbolic violence are connected to the characters' Estonian identity as well as their gender. In addition to the above-mentioned stereotype that assimilated Estonians to Russians, Russian (and by extension Estonian) women used to be labelled as prostitutes (Benedek 2011: n.pag). This latter stereotype is nourished – as *Stalin's Cows* also suggests – by the fact that Tallinn, Estonia's capital, is known as a place where many Finns travel for sex tourism (Marttila 2006). *Stalin's Cows* thus explores how these stereotypes affect a half-Estonian woman trying to adapt to Finland. 'Kaikkia virolaisia kutsuttiin ryssiksi ja sitten jo kohta ymmärrettiin, että jokainen paitsi venäläinen niin myös virolainen nainen on huora' (68) (All Estonians were called 'Russkie', and soon it was understood that not only each Russian but also each Estonian woman is a whore as well). As long as Anna is a child, she is safe from these assumptions; however, as she grows older, her mother warns her not to be taken for a prostitute (51). Thus, Anna learns to associate her Estonian identity with prostitution, and she is constantly scared of being treated like one of 'niitä naisia' (68) 'those women'. The fear of appearing like an Estonian or Russian prostitute becomes a pervasive part of Anna's womanhood in-between Estonian and Finnish cultures. Moreover, Anna's problematic relation to her womanhood is further compounded by her father's secret relationships with Russian prostitutes (89).

## Control in *Stalin's Cows*

Anna reacts to this problematic development of her womanhood by attempting to control her body with eating disorders like anorexia and bulimia. Anna's only childhood friend, Irina, whose mother is

283

also Estonian, is labelled as 'ryssäpillu' (131) 'Russian pussy' at school because she speaks openly about her origins. Conscious of the negative attention Estonian women get in Finland, Anna experiences her body as shameful (88). Therefore, her eating disorder is a reaction to the shame that dominates her identity as an Estonian woman. Sarah Sceat writes that by controlling what passes inside and outside the body, what transgresses its boundaries, one can cherish the idea of a clean and proper body (2000: 69).[8] Through bulimia, Anna reaches a momentary feeling of being clean from shame. Anna states that she tries to 'syödä häpeän pois' (316) 'eat her shame away', and, by vomiting the food she eats, she manages to see what is left in her without the shame (88).

The boundaries of the body become important because, by controlling them, Anna feels she can also control the way she is perceived – not as an Estonian or a prostitute, but as a perfectly sized body:

> Annalle ei vihelletä sen takia, että hänen äitinsä puhuu korostuksella … Ei siksi, että hänen kuvitellaan olevan prostituoitu. Ei siksi, että hän on virolainen, venäläinen, suomalainen, väärässä maassa väärässä kielessä väärässä ruumiissa. Saatuaan ruumiinsa mitat kohdalleen Anna on solahtanut oikeaan paikkaansa, oikeaan ruumiiseensa, oikeaan kokoonsa ja tullut juuri sillä tavalla hyväksytyksi kuin on tarpeen. (232)

> (Men do not whistle at Anna because her mother speaks with an accent … not because she is Estonian, Russian, Finnish, in the wrong country in the wrong language in the wrong body. After having fixed the sizes of her body, Anna has found her right place, right body, right size and has become accepted exactly the way she should.)

Losing weight appears as the sole solution Anna finds to cope with the attention she feels her body gets from Finnish men.

Anna's eating disorder is also connected to another dominant part of her identity, her rootlessness or 'unhomely' condition. Food is associated with the feeling of being homely. Cooking and eating become so

Cristina Sandu

familiar to Anna that she describes the kitchen as the only cosy place in her childhood house (226). Furthermore, by bringing Estonian food products to Helsinki, food becomes a medium to shorten the distance between these two countries (383). Thus, food and eating are not only a way to shape her own body, but they also offer something stable in Anna's life in-between the two societies, marked by feelings of longing and displacement.

When it comes to Katariina, she does not give as much importance to her own body and the attention it gets, but she feels her identity is threatened in another way. When she moves to Finland and passes through the USSR consulate of Helsinki, her name is accidentally written down as 'Jekaterina' in her new passport, because it is the Russian version of 'Katariina' (222). This event echoes the fate of Katariina's relatives who lost their own names in Siberian labour camps (241). Furthermore, the incident with Katariina's name emphasises what an important part language plays in these instances of symbolic violence: the imposition of a new name makes one feel as if one's identity has been torn away – hence the comparison with prisoners in Siberia.

In conclusion, scholars have previously discussed the potential applicability of the notion of postcolonialism to the context of the Soviet Union (Chernetsky, Spivak, Condee). However, the study of Finnish and Estonian authors from a postcolonial perspective is still new, as it does not fit the usual conception of postcolonial literature. Oksanen's work is therefore significant: it raises awareness of the problems of racism, prejudice and problematic identity politics even in prosperous cultures.

Furthermore, Oksanen shows the effects of Soviet occupation upon the following generations: even if her character Anna grows up Finland during the last decades of the twentieth century, Anna still feels obligated to conceal any Estonian connections in order to be accepted in Finnish society. Anna, despite having a comfortable life in a prosperous Western country, grows up with a problematic position in-between the two cultures.

Anna and Katariina's position of 'in-betweenness' is further complicated

285

by the political context in Finland in the second half of the twentieth century, which rendered the relations between Finns and Estonians problematic as Finns equated Estonians with Russians. Hence, *Stalin's Cows* opens up a topic barely discussed in Finland: the prejudices and racism (or 'symbolic violence', as Bourdieu calls it) faced by Estonians.

Anna and Katariina react differently to their problematic position in-between Estonian and Finnish cultures. Katariina completely isolates herself in a small Finnish town. Furthermore, her unhappiness in Finland is compared to her relatives' suffering in Siberia. When it comes to Anna, she finds an escape in food and control over her own body, which gives her a feeling of safety from the negative attention men give to Estonian women, associated with the fast rise of prostitution in Russia and other East-block countries before and after the collapse of the Soviet Union (Roos 2014: 64). Anna's eating disorder becomes an increasingly strong part of her identity, something as dominating as her Estonian identity. Thus, the political power that traumatised her mother and grandmother during the times of Soviet occupation in Estonia (Soviet authorities used violent interrogations techniques such as rape) is turned into a different kind of power, the torturing of her own body through eating disorders.

## Endnotes

[1] Of course the term is applied as well to the Caribbean and North America. However, the majority of writings focus on these regions.

[2] The idea of Soviet colonialism was first introduced in 1992 by Marko Pavlyshyn in his 'Post-colonial Features in Contemporary Ukrainian Culture', but it was either ignored or ridiculed by those specialised in Russian culture (Chernetsky 2006:834).

[3] 'Finlandization' is defined as 'The process or result of becoming obliged for economic reasons to favour (or refrain from opposing) the interests of the former Soviet Union despite not being allied to it politically' (OED).

[4] Bhabha uses *Beloved* by Toni Morrison and *My Son's Story* by Nadine Gordimer as examples of 'unhomely' conditions.

⁵ All translations are the author's own unless otherwise stated.

⁶ This hatred has to do especially with the time after Finland's independence, when Russia continued supporting the Communist Party, as well as with the history of wars between the two nations (Winter War, Continuation War) (Vihavainen 2013).

⁷ See also: Bourdieu 1996.

⁸ Here Sceats uses Julia Kristeva's idea of abjection and bodily boundaries (*Powers of Horror: an Essay on Abjection* 1982).

## References

Benedek, M. (2011). "'I wanted to tear those stereotypes apart". An Interview with Sofi Oksanen'. *Hungarian Literature Online*. 7 May, Available at: http://www.hlo.hu/news/i_wanted_to_tear_those_stereotypes_apart (Accessed: 2 September 2011).

Bhabha, H. K. (1990). 'The Third Space. Interview with Homi Bhabha', in Rutherford J. (ed.), *Identity: Community, Culture, Difference*. London: Lawrence and Wishart, pp. 207-221.

Bhabha, H. K. (1992). 'The World and the Home', *Social Text* 31/32, pp. 141-153.

Bhabha, H. K. (1994). *The Location of Culture*. London: Routledge.

Bourdieu, P. (1977). 'Sur le pouvoir symbolique', *Annales. Économies, Sociétés, Civilisations*, 32(3), pp. 405-411.

Bourdieu, P. (1989). 'Social Space and Symbolic Power', *Sociological Theory*, 7(1), pp. 14-25.

Bromley, R. (2000). *Narratives for a New Belonging. Diasporic Cultural Fiction*. Edinburgh: Edinburgh University.

Chernetsky, V. (2006). 'On Some Post-Soviet Postcolonialism', *PMLA*, 121(3), pp. 833-836.

Clarke, D. (2015). 'The representation of victimhood in Sofi Oksanen's novel *Purge*', *Journal of European Studies*, 45(3), pp. 1-16.

Condee, N. (2006). 'The Anti-imperialist Empire and After: In Dialogue with Gayatri Spivak's "Are You Postcolonial?"' *PMLA*, 121(3), pp. 829-831.

Dervin, F. (2013). 'Rethinking the Acculturation and Assimilation of "Others" in a "Monocultural" Country: Forms of Intercultural Pygmalionism in Two Finnish Novels', *Journal of Intercultural Studies*, 34(4), pp. 356-370.

Harding, L. (2015). 'Sofi Oksanen: "We know about British colonialism. Russian colonialism is not well known". *The Guardian*. 18 April. Available at: http://www.theguardian.com/books/2015/apr/18/sofi-oksanen-interview-russia-finland-estonia-putin (Accessed: 2 September 2015).

Kristeva, J. (1982). *Powers of Horror: an Essay on Abjection*. Trans. L. S. Roudiez. New York: Columbia University.

Marttila, A.-M. (2006). 'Finnish Men Buying Sex in Finland and Estonia', *European Journal of Criminology*, 7(1), pp. 61-75.

Mavrikakis, C. (2013) 'Le corps de la filiation: répétitions et détournements de l'Histoire des femmes dans le roman *Purge* de Sofi Oksanen', *Tangence*, 103, pp. 57-78.

Menéndez-Menéndez, M. I. (2014). 'Cultural Industries and Symbolic Violence: Practices and Discourses that Perpetuate Inequality', *Procedia – Social and Behavioral Sciences*, 161, pp. 64-69.

Oksanen, S. (2003). *Stalininin lehmät*. Helsinki: Bazar.

Oksanen, S. (2014). 'Santa Claus Speaks Finnish.' *Sofioksanen*. Available at: http://www.sofioksanen.com/speech-frankfurt-2014/ (Accessed: 16 September 2015).

The Oxford English Dictionary 'Finlandization, n.' *OED*. Available from: http://www.oed.com/view/Entry/242930?redirectedFrom=finlandization (Accessed 28 October 2015).

Ram, H. (2006). 'Between 1917 and 1947: Postcoloniality and Russia-Eurasia', *PMLA*, 121(3), pp. 831-833.

Roos, L-L. (2014). *Post-Soviet Identity in Nordic Fiction: Trauma of Occupation and Sex Trafficking in Sofi Oksanen's Purge and Lukas Moodysson's Lilya 4-ever*. PhD. Thesis. University of Washington. Available at: http://publications.tlu.ee/index.php/bsmr/article/view/218 (Accessed: 4 September 2015).

Sceat, S. (2000). *Food, Consumption and the Body in Contemporary Women's Fiction*. Cambridge: Cambridge University.

Spivak, G. C. (2006). 'Are You Postcolonial? To the Teachers of Slavic and Eastern European Literatures.' *PMLA*, 121(3), pp. 828-829.

Suihkonen, M. (2006). 'Kirjailija Sofi Oksanen: Taiteella traumojen kimppuun', *Monitori-lehti*, 3. n.pag.

Vihavainen, T. (2013). *Ryssäviha. Venäjän-pelon historia*. Helsinki: Minerva.

Lightning Source UK Ltd.
Milton Keynes UK
UKOW06f1645041116
286880UK00002B/34/P